TWISTING MY MELON

TWISTING MY MELON

SHAUN RYDER

BANTAM PRESS

LONDON • TORONTO • SYDNEY • AUCKLAND • JOHANNESBURG

TRANSWORLD PUBLISHERS
61–63 Uxbridge Road, London W5 5SA
A Random House Group Company
www.transworldbooks.co.uk

First published in Great Britain
in 2011 by Bantam Press
an imprint of Transworld Publishers

This book is substantially a work of non-fiction based on the life, experiences and
recollections of the author. In some limited cases names of people, places, dates,
sequences or the detail of events have been changed solely to protect the privacy of
others. The author has stated to the publishers that, except in such minor respects
not affecting the substantial accuracy of the work, the contents of this book are true.

A CIP catalogue record for this book
is available from the British Library.

ISBNs 9780593068274 (cased)
9780593068281 (tpb)

Addresses for Random House Group Ltd companies outside the UK
can be found at: www.randomhouse.co.uk
The Random House Group Ltd Reg. No. 954009

The Random House Group Limited supports the Forest Stewardship Council
(FSC®), the leading international forest-certification organization.
Our books carrying the FSC label are printed on FSC®-certified paper.
FSC is the only forest-certification scheme endorsed by the
leading environmental organizations, including Greenpeace.
Our paper procurement policy can be found at
www.randomhouse.co.uk/environment

Typeset in 11/16pt Life by
Falcon Oast Graphic Art Ltd.
Printed and bound in Great Britain by
Clays Ltd, Bungay, Suffolk

2 4 6 8 10 9 7 5 3 1

MIX
Paper from
responsible sources
FSC
www.fsc.org   FSC® C016897

To my wife, Joanne

Acknowledgements

My thanks go to my wife, Joanne Ryder, and my children, for being there for me and being my backbone. I will always love you all.

Big thanks to my manager, Warren Askew, for seeing that I had a future beyond the old days, and special thanks to his wife, Hayley, and the kids for looking after me when I'm down south.

To my mam and dad and family

My mother-in-law, Grannybag Joan

Mama Big Jo

Amelia Ryder

Peter Diver

Leon

My personal trainer, Gavin Kelly

Muzzer

Platty

Matt, Pat, Karen and Sam

Maria Carroll

Uncle Tom and Aunty Mary, RIP

Too Nice Tom Bruggen

My current band: Mikey, Johnny, Dan, Jake Ryder, Julie and Tonn

Bryan Fugler and David Berens

Nikki Stevens

To all those who have taken time to help me remember the parts of my life that were a bit hazy.

And a big thank-you to my fans for their support over the years.

To Sarah Emsley, Polly Osborn, Richard Roper and Vivien Garrett at Transworld Publishers.

To Matthew Hamilton, my literary agent, at Aitken Alexander Associates.

And a massive thanks to Luke Bainbridge who listened to a lifetime of memories and helped me put pen to paper.

Picture Acknowledgements

All images courtesy of the author unless otherwise stated.
KC = Kevin Cummins; TS = Tom Sheehan; KA = Karin Albinsson.

Section one
Page 8: all images courtesy Stephen Parker.

Section two
Page 1: courtesy TS. Pages 2–3: *Melody Maker* photoshoot and SR
with Bez both courtesy TS; SR and Tony Wilson, and Horseman in
Iceland both courtesy KC. Pages 4–5: SR with Kit Kats courtesy KC;
SR and Bez at Glastonbury: Brian Rasic/Rex Features. Page 6: all
images courtesy KC. Page 7: all images courtesy TS except SR and
Paul courtesy KC. Page 8: all images courtesy KA.

Section three
Page 1: Happy Mondays group shot courtesy TS; SR and Russell
Watson courtesy Denis Jones/*Evening Standard*/Rex Features. Page
2: SR and Bez courtesy KA; SR with Joanne courtesy David
Fisher/Rex Features. Page 3: all images courtesy ITV/Rex Features.
Pages 4–5: all images courtesy ITV/Rex Features except SR and
Stacey Solomon at National Television Awards courtesy Yui Mok/PA
Archive/Press Association Images. Pages 6–7: all images courtesy KA
except SR and Joanne in January 2011 courtesy *Manchester Evening
News*. Page 8: all images courtesy KA.

CHAPTER ONE

'I'm a simple city boy, with simple country tastes'

People still come up to me and say, 'Do you feel lucky that you're still alive?'

No, I don't.

'But you must have been near death . . .'

Maybe I was, but I never saw it like that. I never thought I was close to death. I've been right down to rock bottom and I've been in some very dark places when I almost wished I was dead. I've been addicted to crack cocaine in Barbados and gone cold turkey in Burnley. But, if I do see myself as lucky, it's not because I'm still alive. It's because I'm lucky still to be in the game, and that I even managed to get in the game in the first place. I'm a kid from Salford who had severe learning diffi-culties and left school at fifteen with no qualifications and without even knowing the alphabet. I could have ended up in jail or dead, like a lot of kids from round our way. Compared to that, going on a celebrity TV show and jumping out of a helicopter, or eating a crocodile's dick, is nothing.

Not that jumping out of that fucking helicopter at the start of *I'm A Celebrity . . . Get Me Out of Here!* felt like nothing at the time. Mainly because I couldn't breathe. I've never been able to breathe through my nose. Nothing to do with drugs, although I've put enough of them up there. It's a hereditary condition. A lot of our family have sinus problems and my mam even had to have a bone taken out of her nose so she could breathe properly. Hanging out the side of a helicopter at twelve thousand feet, it's almost impossible to breathe through your mouth, so I was really struggling. Not only was I jumping into one of the oddest gigs of my career, I also thought I was going to pass out live on TV like a right goon. I've never been as relieved as the moment I got down on the ground and sparked up a fag.

A lot of people know me as Shaun Ryder, and a lot of people know me as Shaun William Ryder, but my full name is actually Shaun William George Ryder. George is my confirmation name. I always thought that was pretty funny, years later. Named after George the dragon-slayer, and then I ended up chasing the dragon for years.

I'm from Salford. People always assume I'm from Manchester, because Happy Mondays were so closely associated with the whole Madchester scene, but I'm not, I'm from Salford. Big difference. We're a different breed and even Mancunians are a bit wary of us. My family is a big, Irish, mostly Catholic family. All my mam's side come from Greengate, not far from where I live now.

Greengate is also the home of the Salford Sioux. At the end of the nineteenth century a gang of Native Americans came over as part of Buffalo Bill's Wild West Circus and they disappeared when they reached Salford. It turned out they were wanted by the US government to answer charges of war crimes after they beat General Custer, so they just vanished under the arches at Greengate and the locals hid them, because they saw them as great warriors, not war criminals. They ended up having loads of kids with the locals and a lot of them are buried at Pendleton Church. I often wonder if that might explain why people from Salford are a slightly different breed, why they have no fear – if it's because they have a bit of Native American blood in them.

There's a huge Irish community in Salford and Manchester, going back generations. My mam's dad's dad – my great-grandfather – was the first of her family to come over from Ireland. He was looking for work like most of those who arrived on the boat. My mam's family are the Carrolls – that's her maiden name – although their surname actually used to be O'Carroll. Her grandad decided to take the O' off when he arrived in England as he didn't want to be so obviously Irish. Anything with O' in it made you stand out immediately as a left-footer and at the time he was running about trying to find work, that could count against you. There were still signs saying 'No dogs, no blacks, no Irish', so you can understand the lingering paranoia.

On my dad's side, my nana, Emma, was also from Salford, and my grandad, Fred Ryder, was from Farnworth, up towards Bolton.

We moved about Salford quite a bit when I was a kid, but we mostly lived in Little Hulton. Over the years it's become fully sub-merged in Salford, but originally it was just this huge, sprawling overspill council estate. When they were first married my mam and dad lived at my nana's – my mam's mam, on Coniston Avenue, and I was born at home in the front room upstairs. My mam and dad decided to call me Shaun, but used the English spelling instead of 'Sean', because they too wanted to play down our Irish descent. I was their first kid. I don't remember that house, because when I was only a few months old my nana bought her first house and moved out of Coniston Avenue, and we moved to a flat over a pub on Darley Street in Farnworth.

We seemed to move a lot when we were little kids, or it seemed a lot to me anyway. Some people, like my missus, Joanne, live in one house for their entire childhood, until they leave home and get married, but we always seemed to be flitting about. It was partly because of my dad's jobs and partly because we were skint at times. Derek, my old fella, was a fitter originally, working on aeroplanes. Then he worked on the papers, not as a journalist but on the printing presses, and then we had a chippy for a year, before he ended up as a postman. Much later, when the Happy Mondays took off, he came on the road with us. Not many people had what you would call a career round our way back in the late 60s; most people would just find work where they could, so it wasn't that unusual that my dad didn't stick to one trade. Wages weren't great, so people would change jobs if they could earn a bit more doing something else.

My mam, Linda, was a nursery nurse, a real Salford woman, and a good cook, in a traditional steak-and-veg way. We grew up on egg and bacon, pie and chips, stews, hashes, tripe and tongue, that sort of thing. I was even slightly podgy at times as a kid because my mam was such a good cook.

After the flat above the pub we moved to Canterbury Close in Atherton, which is where my little brother was born. There's only eighteen months' age difference between me and Our Paul. Although my mam and dad come from big extended families, where there could be nine or ten kids in a household, they were both only children and neither of them wanted a big family themselves, so they decided early doors they would just stick with the two of us. We stayed in Atherton for a couple of years, and I do have some memories from there. I remember pushing Our Paul on his trike in the street when he was only about eighteen months old, and he fell off and banged his head quite badly, so we had to take him to hospital. We had to take him back there again after we were playing 'army' one day and I threw a wooden brick which hit him on the head. Reading this back, it sounds like we must always have been hurting each other, but these incidents only stick out because we were generally pretty happy and we played together a lot.

When I was three we moved in with my nana and grandad for a few months, in their bungalow in Swinton. That's where my memories really start. We ended up staying there quite a bit over the years, when we were in between houses. My nana, Annie Carroll, was a lovely, tough Salford woman. Her mam and dad had died when she was really young, so she had ended up raising her siblings. Her and my grandad, Big Billy, lived in their council house on Coniston Avenue, where quite a few of our family had homes, until they became some of the first people round our way to get a mortgage and bought a two-bedroom bungalow on Charlton Drive in Swinton. This was a big deal for them, coming from a family where no one had ever owned a house before. When we moved in with them, my nana and grandad had one bedroom, and my mam and dad, me and Our Paul had the other.

My grandad was a huge Irish fella with a big reputation and a deep, rough voice. There were loads of Carrolls in Salford, but everyone knew Bill, *everyone*, and everyone liked him. He was kind of cock of the estate. We didn't find him scary; to us he was just our grandad. Bill worked on the *Daily Express* printing presses on Great Ancoats Street in town, although he seemed to spend a lot of his time in the nearby Press Club, that had extended licensing hours for those who worked in the printing game. He'd go in there and get hammered and not get home until about five in the morning. It still exists, the Press Club. It's just off Deansgate now. You don't really have to be in the printing game to get in; it's also for people who work at the theatres and stuff like that, but you can just blag it in on the door. Or you used to be able to. We would go in there a bit ourselves later on, in the 90s, when there was fuck all else open at that time in the morning.

After a few months at my nana's, we moved to a house on Cemetery Road in Swinton. My dad was working at Coach Brothers' Inks then, another printer's, which was an okay job though it still didn't pay that great. But as my parents were both working full time, they managed to get a mortgage. Like my nana, that meant a lot to them, as they were the first of their generation to buy a house, but it left them skint. They had this saying when I was young: 'Some people have a nice car, and some people have a nice house', which they really believed. It didn't seem to occur to them, or to many people round our way, that you might be able to have both. Even as a kid it was obvious there wasn't much money to spare in our house, but I didn't think we were particularly hard up, especially compared to some of the people we knew. It's only when you're older and you look back that you can see how things really were.

My mam worked at the local primary school, so whenever the school had a jumble sale she would get first dibs and be able to have a root through all the clothes and pick out some of the best stuff before everyone else arrived. My mam is quite a proud woman, so she probably doesn't like the fact that we got some of our clothes from jumble sales, but because she got in there first we actually got some decent clobber.

With my mam being from a big Catholic family, we went to Catholic school and we went to church every week. My dad, on the other hand, came from a Protestant background and his dad, my grandad Fred, was the head of the local Orange Lodge, but there was never any friction in the family over religion. For our generation, it was just something that was there in the background; it didn't dictate life.

*

My mam worked at St Mark's Primary School, which was also my first school, so I was actually in her class when I was five. Well, there were two nursery nurses who took the class, my mam and another nurse. I remember that year really well, because that was the first time I ever got into trouble. In the teacher's desk there was a great big tin of sweets, nice sucky toffees and all sorts. I had this little trick going, where just before playtime I used to go in to the bog and push one of the windows up and leave it open. The classrooms would be locked at playtime, and I would go into the playground, go round the back when no one was watching, jump in through the window, and go and rob some toffees out of the teacher's tin. I was doing this almost every day for what seemed like ages. I would do it at dinnertime, playtime, whenever. Then one day they realized that toffees were going missing and asked the class, 'Who's been at the sweets?' Obviously no one owned up, so I left it a couple of days, then I was back at it again, but this time when I got in through the window and into the classroom, my mam and the other nursery nurse jumped out and caught me. They had been lying in wait. I was paraded in front of everyone as the guilty one. I knew I shouldn't have been doing it, and I felt bad for my mam because she'd had no idea it was me and I'm sure she was embarrassed and a bit ashamed, but I didn't think it was the end of the world – it was only a few toffees. I didn't do it in a bid to get attention or anything like that; I just wanted to get my hands on the sweets.

I had problems at school from early doors. At primary school, a lot of it stemmed from the fact that I was originally left-handed, which was considered a real no-no. Nowadays teachers wouldn't mind if a kid was left-handed, but back in the 60s it was still very much frowned upon. When we were learning to write, every time I picked up a pen with my left hand I got hit with a ruler across the back of the hand by the teacher. So I would start off writing with my left hand, from left to right, which felt natural, then I would get hit, so I'd have to switch the pen to my right hand and then for some reason I would start writing from right to left, so I was writing in fucking circles.

Being hit with that ruler, and being told that what felt natural and right to me was so wrong, had a big effect on me. It somehow affected the wiring in my brain, and after that I found it really difficult to learn anything. Looking back, I probably needed some specialist teaching to help me overcome my learning difficulties, but back in the late 60s there was still a stigma attached to anything like that. A few other children at our school did get specialist teaching, and went off to dedicated classes, but my mam didn't want me being ostracized and, because she worked at the school, she was able to have a quiet word and make sure I didn't get any specialist treatment. I suppose she thought she was doing the right thing back then.

Because of the way I was taught, I now write right-handed, but I'm left-handed for most other things. If I'm playing pool I use my left hand, if I'm throwing something I use my left hand, if I'm shooting a gun I use my left hand, and if I'm playing football I use my left foot, but if I'm writing, I'm right-handed. I think that's what originally triggered my 'fuck-off' response to school. I'd been told what felt natural was wrong, and then found it really difficult to learn, so I became frustrated. St Mark's wasn't a bad school, and some kids came out of it okay and did well for themselves, but I do think the education system failed me.

At home, my mam and dad were quite strict. My dad could rule with an iron fist, and my mam didn't take any crap either. My old fella would give me a bit of a hiding if I deserved it, but that was pretty normal in Salford in the late 60s. If you stepped out of line, or you were caught up to no good, you knew you'd have it coming to you. I got away with plenty of shit as well, though, as I learned quite quickly how to be a bit sneaky and avoid getting caught.

There was always music on in the house when we were growing up. My mam and dad loved all the 60s music – the Beatles, the Stones and the Kinks – but by the time the 60s really kicked off they were married with kids, so a lot of their record collection was the original rock 'n' roll gear, from Chuck Berry to Buddy Holly through to Fats Domino. They would play all that stuff at home, and so would we. Both me and Our Paul went through their record collection as kids, and the records got ruined thanks to us, but they let us play with them anyway because it kept us quiet. They had one of those box record players, the ones that you could stack about a dozen singles on and it would play them one by one. You could even stack LPs on it.

As well as his various jobs, in his spare time my dad was also trying to make it as a musician and a comedian. He used to play all the working men's clubs and pubs to earn a bit of extra dough on the side. I didn't go with him that much, but I did see him when he used to play some of the Irish pubs and the more folky gigs. About seven o'clock most nights he'd go off to various pubs or clubs to do his thing. He once entered a talent contest and came second to Lisa Stansfield, who is from Rochdale so must have been on the same circuit. Years later, when Happy Mondays were playing the Rock in Rio festival, Lisa was also on the bill. She was on the same plane as us back from Brazil, and my old fella was with us and she remembered him from that talent contest.

At the time I didn't really think it was cool that my dad was out playing music, but you don't when you're a kid, do you? Whatever your parents do can feel embarrassing. I mean, fucking hell, as a kid sometimes you don't even want to acknowledge that your mam and dad exist. You want them to be invisible – every kid does. But my dad worked the pubs and clubs, so people knew who he was, and my mam worked in the nursery, so everyone knew who she was. Especially as she would sit on the top deck of the bus on the way there, smoking cigars. Not just the little thin ones, but big King Eddies, puffing away.

By the time we were six or seven years old, we were roaming about the neighbourhood quite a bit – that's what you did when you were kids; you weren't kept in the house all the time. I wouldn't let my kids out on their own now, but it was different back then. I'm not saying it was safer, because Salford could be rough as fuck, but that didn't stop people letting their kids play out.

There are a few incidents that stand out in my mind from this time. One day I was messing around with some mates and we went down to this park near us in Pendlebury, which had a great big slide in it. When we got there, we spotted that someone had stuck razor blades all the way down the slide, with chewing gum. Luckily we saw it before any of us got on the slide, so we told everyone who needed to be told and luckily no kids got injured. What sort of sick fucker does that, sticks razor blades on a kids' slide?

We would get into little scrapes and fights all the time, almost on a daily basis, but that just seemed normal. Looking back, I suppose it was quite rough, but all I had known was Salford, so I didn't have anything to compare it to. One day when I was in Junior One I was walking home from school, through that same park in Pendlebury with the big slide, when I was jumped by three kids. Two of them held me while the other one just kept constantly kicking me in the fucking bollocks. Little bastards. I hadn't even done anything to deserve it, which is why it sticks out in my memory. I probably did deserve a kicking sometimes, but even when I did I could usually sweet talk my way out of it, which is why this occasion stands out so vividly.

We became quite creative as kids. We had to make our own fun. We would do stuff like constructing our own smoke bombs by getting a ping-pong ball, breaking it up into little pieces and then wrapping it inside tinfoil. We would then light a match and stick it inside the foil until it started burning, and put the smoke bomb in someone's desk or drop it through a letterbox.

Another of our favourite things was simply going out and getting a chase off someone. We'd do all sorts of stuff to wind people up and get a reaction. Ridiculous things. We'd try and smash a football through someone's front-room window, or drop our trousers at the greengrocer. There were certain people who you knew you could always get a chase out of, particularly some of the shopkeepers. We loved the buzz you would get off getting chased. Sometimes we would run back to Nana's and wait for the inevitable knock on the door, but my nana was great, as she'd cover for us and swear blind that we'd never left the house.

Throughout my whole childhood, I was always out and about doing something, and I developed an entrepreneurial spirit at a really young age, partly because there wasn't much money at home. I knew that if I wanted something then I was going to have to find a way to get it myself. The first real example I remember is when I was about seven years old. I borrowed some plastic bags from my mam and walked for what seemed like miles, to where I knew there was a field full of horses. I walked round the field collecting all the horse shit, then carried it back to our house and split it all up into these smaller plastic bags that my mam's balls of wool had come in.

After I'd bagged it all up, I went round all the houses on the estate, selling the manure to the housewives to use on their roses as fertilizer. I made a few bob out of that – not bad for a seven-year-old.

I shared a room with Our Paul in our house at Cemetery Road, and my dad made us bunk beds, by hand, when I was seven and Our Paul was five. I was on the top bunk and he was on the bottom. The bunks were painted red, and underneath the mattress the bed-base was that green-diamond metal fencing, the stuff that people have round their allotments or sometimes round school playing fields. Every time I moved in bed it made this loud, creaky metal noise, 'creak, creak'.

We never went abroad on holiday when we were kids, but no one on our estate did, really. The first time my dad ever left the country was when he came to New York when the Mondays first played there. When we were kids we went on holiday to places like Blackpool, Southport, Bournemouth or Cornwall. That was normal for working-class folk. My nana and grandad were some of the first to go abroad from round our way. They went to Spain in the late 60s, and then they used to go to Jersey quite a bit, which seemed quite flash at the time.

The first kids I remember knocking about with were my cousins the Carrolls, and then other kids round our way, like the Doyles, the Callahans, the Murphys, the Coxes, the Joneses, the Lenahans and the Healeys. There were actually two sets of Carrolls, because both my nana and her sister married blokes from Salford whose surname was Carroll. The two fellas weren't related – well, not until they married my nana and her sister; they were after that, obviously – but to us they were all part of one family. There was just this huge mass of Carrolls. So although Our Paul was my only sibling, we were very much part of this massive extended family and we had loads of cousins about our age, which meant there was always a big gang of us at birthdays and other occasions.

I would go round to my Aunty Mary's quite a lot. She had nine kids in a four-bedroom house. Our Matt and Pat were the ones that I would hang about with the most, because they were a similar age to me. I would often crash over at Aunty Mary's. If you were round there and it was getting late, you would just sleep in one of their beds. There were about three or four of them in a room anyway, so one more didn't make a difference. It was like the Waltons, but in a small council house in Salford. I also spent a lot of time at my nana's, as she lived quite close to my school and I got on so well with her.

Round our estate everyone knew our set of Carrolls, especially because my grandad was well known and well liked. He used to take us to the rugby, to watch Salford Reds at the Willows or to Swinton Rugby Club, and later we would go on our own. Our Paul actually went on to play for Salford rugby youth team. When it came to football, all our family were Manchester United fans. Everyone from Salford supports United. If you see a City fan in Salford, they must be lost. I used to go to the match now and again, but I wasn't fanatical about it. I was one of those kids who was more likely to be found fannying around outside Old Trafford while the game was on, getting into mischief, or looking for something to rob, rather than inside watching the match. My cousin Matt and a few others in our family were mad on watching footy, but I could take it or leave it. I enjoyed playing it but I never really understood the amount of time that some people invested in it. Even at a young age, I'd rather be acting the Charlie big bollocks and going round trying to cop for girls.

We first discovered booze through Bill, as stashes of all sorts of stuff would turn up at their house all the time. Crates of

Newcy Brown off the backs of wagons or whatever. That wasn't unusual in Salford. When there isn't much money about, people are less likely to ask questions about where something has come from. Bill always had loads of booze in his shed and our mission, when we got to nine or ten years old, was to try and nick it and drink it. This went on until we were about thirteen or fourteen. We were allowed a drink in my nana's house from about the age of ten and I remember being shown how to pour a glass of beer around then.

My mam and dad didn't really drink when we were growing up, although they do have a drink now. My dad was usually off playing the pubs and clubs, so he would always be driving, but Bill was a big drinker and most of the Carrolls liked a drink. There was one other uncle who had a bit of a drink problem and would sometimes sell furniture from the house so he could go to the pub. We were taught about alcohol from an early age and I've never been an alkie. I'm forty-nine years old now and I've hammered drugs and I've had periods when I've drunk a lot, but I've never had an alcohol dependency. Obviously, like everyone, I used to like to go for a few pints and get pissed, especially as a young lad, but I've never really been addicted to alcohol. I don't even drink at home nowadays, and if I did go to the pub for an interview or something I'd be half cut after four or five pints. I drink a lot of energy drinks like Red Bull or Relentless now, and could quite happily sit there all night in the pub with a Red Bull while everyone else is sinking the pints. Although, admittedly, I'll probably stick a bit of vodka in if everyone else is boozing.

Because I live back in Salford now, I bump into kids from school now and again, and those who look a bit fucked have inevitably been abusing the booze. The ones that are my age but look about three hundred years old – usually they appear that way because of alcohol, not drugs. You can't repair the damage that alcohol does to you. The weird thing about bumping into someone from school now is that I often haven't seen them since they were about fourteen, so they've obviously changed a lot, but because they've seen me on TV or in the press for the last twenty-five years, they don't think I've changed a bit.

Over the years, Salford and Manchester have had a big problem with smack. It was about 1980, when the smokable heroin hit, that it started to get bad, but I vividly remember being at primary school in Swinton in 1969 and the police coming in to school to talk to us about heroin. They told us about the dangers of it, and about needles and all that. I was seven years old and I can actually remember thinking, 'I'm *never* going to get involved with that stuff, no way am I getting involved with that . . . that sounds *terrible.*'

When I was nine, my grandad Fred Ryder died from bowel cancer, which was horrible, as you could almost see it eat away at him. That prompted another move, back up to Farnworth. My dad had a compassionate and overwhelming urge to move nearer to his mam, because she was now on her own, so he packed in his job on the newspapers and we took over a chippy on Harper Green Road. It was a real old-school chippy, which looked pretty similar to the one the Khan family run in the film *East Is East*, which I thought was a pretty realistic depiction of what it was like growing up in Salford in the 70s. Certainly more realistic than most I've seen on screen, although the reality was a bit rougher. There wasn't much racism though. I was about ten before I even realized that people at school were different races – it just wasn't an issue.

We used to have chips for tea almost every night while we were living here, which I didn't complain about, and I can still remember the smell of the freshly baked pies being delivered at six o'clock in the morning. It was actually a good chippy, and my mam and dad were a bit more forward-thinking than most, because they served curry sauce, which not many places did back then, not round our way. I didn't have to help out in the chippy, but I would sometimes rob them a bag of potatoes from round the back of the greengrocer's or somewhere. They didn't ask me to do it, I just did. They had the chippy for a year, which coincided with the power cuts of the early 70s, so often there would be a couple of times a week when they couldn't open because there was no electricity. They found it hard work, and towards the end my dad got a job at the post office, and did both jobs. Eventually they decided to sack off the chippy, my dad went full time at the post office and we went back to Nana's for a few months, before moving to Avon Close on Madam's Wood Estate in Little Hulton, where we stayed for a few years.

Behind our house on Madam's Wood there was a sewage works, which was so close you could often smell it while you were eating your dinner. You could even taste it sometimes; it must have been in the air. You'd be trying to eat your Sunday roast and it would taste like it had grit in it. The only things that grew on the sewage works were tomato plants, because the human body can't digest tomato seeds, and that put me off tomatoes for years. We would mess around up there when we were bored, just doing stupid things like throwing bricks and other stuff into the sewage works, then later, when we got an air rifle, we would shoot the rats that were scuttling about.

There was also a train track behind our house and we would throw stones at the trains and put shopping trolleys, tree trunks and all sorts, even shit from the sewage works, on the lines. I honestly don't know how we never injured anyone or even killed anyone, considering all the daft stuff we did as kids. But we just didn't think. Then they would send out special trains with railway police on them, trying to get all us little urchins who were hanging round the train tracks and the sewage works, but we had loads of places to hide around there.

I also used to love what we called 'sneaking' – tiptoeing into shops and sneaking behind the counters, robbing stuff, without getting caught. It was only small stuff at first, and when I started I did it as much for the buzz of not getting caught as anything else.

Although my mam and dad were both still working, they weren't on great wages and were still stretching themselves to pay the mortgage. When I was fourteen, we moved to Kent Close, facing the sewage works and me and Our Paul got our own bedrooms and my dad sawed the bunk beds that he'd made out of wire fencing in two to make single beds, but they still creaked. I could never have a wank as a kid, because the bed made such a fucking noise. Our Paul whinged and whinged about his, and eventually broke it on purpose, so my mam and dad bought him a new single bed, but they couldn't afford to get me one as well. I was now fourteen and I was still in this creaky bed that I'd been in since I was seven, and it was *impossible*. So when Granny Ryder got a new settee, I was given her old battered one to use as a bed. It was really knackered and had bloody springs sticking out of it.

That's all I had in my bedroom when I was fourteen – Granny Ryder's tired old settee for a bed, and a chest of drawers. Our Paul had cabinets with a fitted Binatone stereo system – a record player, a tuner, an amp and everything – which my mam and dad had bought him. Even though I was the eldest, he got everything, partly because he was the baby, and probably partly because I was a bit of a tearaway. It didn't really bother me at the time, because I knew they couldn't always afford to buy for two, and I just thought, 'He's my younger brother, fine, let him have it.' You don't necessarily think anything like that is unusual when you're a kid; whatever situation you're in seems normal. The way I saw it, there was only enough for one, so the kid brother gets it and the older brother is left to fend for himself a bit. That was probably one of the reasons I started robbing. I would just go out and get my own gear.

The other thing that I felt counted against me in other people's eyes was that I wasn't very good with my hands. I've never been the sort of person who's good with mechanical things. Even now, I'm useless at working out what's wrong with a car engine. I struggle to change a lightbulb. But I always had that entrepreneurial spirit and I could always find or make money, even then.

To some extent, I was seen as the stupid one. Our Paul was the bright one who was going to go to college. I was never going to amount to dick: 'Just leave Shaun, he's never going to do owt.' But that wasn't something that ate away at me, and it's really important to me that people understand that. I didn't hold anything against Our Paul. We were really close when we were young, and throughout most of our time in the Happy Mondays. I don't have a chip on my shoulder. Through rehab and cold turkey I've had to do so much self-analysing and reflecting that I'm pretty sure of who I am and how I got here. If anything is eating away at you inside, it's going to come out eventually, but I really don't have this massive hang-up that I wasn't appreciated or anything like that. I just thought, fine, I'll sort myself out. That was the real lasting effect it had on me. It made me independent.

This might seem like a slightly odd comparison, but a few years later I watched this film called *Quest for Fire*. It's about a group of Neanderthals who have one fire that they have to keep going at all times, because they don't know how to start another fire from scratch. They end up on this marsh after a battle with another tribe, and their fire dies, so they send three of the tribe off on a quest to find another. These Neanderthal geezers go off roaming the land, having all these adventures, and find fire and bring it back to the marsh. The other motherfuckers are still there grunting, 'Fire! Grunt grunt fire!' and they haven't built a house or shelter or anything. Weirdly, this reminds me a bit of my situation growing up. I sometimes felt like I was the geezer who was sent off to get fire while the rest of them were waiting back on the marsh.

By the early 70s I was beginning to get more into music. There was always music on in our house and when I was round at my Aunty Mary's I was exposed to all different music and influences because there were nine kids who were all into slightly different scenes. Our Pete was the oldest and he had a huge collection of thousands of albums that were leaning against every wall in the front room, about a yard deep. He was into stuff like the Flying Burrito Brothers, the Byrds, Captain Beefheart and Link Wray. Our Joe was an early skinhead, and into soul stuff like James Brown, Billy Preston and a bit of ska. Our Mag was into soul and the Tams. She was a long-hair skin girl at one point, which is a girl skinhead who doesn't have a fully shaved head, and then she got into stuff like early Elton John, Gram Parsons and Townes Van Zandt. Our Gel was into her reggae, U-Roy, Bunny Wailer and Gregory Isaacs (who I got into a bit of trouble with, years later, when we played on the same bill and were misbehaving together backstage). Our Pat had a load of soul records that he used to buy on import from Robinsons Records in Salford or Yanks Records in town, as did Our Matt, and all of them were into Northern Soul. They were all a few years older than me, so I was exposed to all these great, diverse music styles and scenes at an early age.

My cousins were also the first ones of our family to go to

university. Our Bernadette, Carmel and Joe all went, and Our Matt and Pat went to Salford Technical College to do art and ended up, years later, doing all the artwork for Happy Mondays and Black Grape.

Top of the Pops was a big thing back in the late 60s and early 70s. I can remember seeing the Small Faces on there when I was only six or seven, and thinking, 'Oh, they look smart, they look cool', and asking my mam if I could get my hair cut like Steve Marriott. My other strong memory of *Top of the Pops* was watching David Bowie as Ziggy Stardust in 1972, singing 'Star Man' with his electric-blue guitar. I can remember that really clearly, because Bowie looked cool as fuck.

Seeing David Essex in *That'll Be the Day*, when I was eleven in 1973, also had a massive influence on me, as did *Stardust* when that came out the year after. Watching those films made me want to be a rock 'n' roll star. I had no fucking idea how I might go about it, and I couldn't play an instrument or read music, so it was a complete pipedream, but it was one of the few things I could see myself doing. It was the lifestyle, as much as the music. I thought, 'I fancy a bit of that.' I can't really remember wanting to be anything else. Although I'm sure I'm not unique in that. I'm sure every kid in the cinema was thinking the same as me. It was just like the tagline in *Stardust* says: 'Show me a boy who never wanted to be a rock star and I'll show you a liar.'

CHAPTER TWO

'How old are you? Are you old enough?
Should you be in here watching that?'

When I left school I could read okay, but I couldn't spell properly and I didn't know the alphabet. I ended up teaching myself years later through rhyme, you know like kids do? 'A, B, C, D, E, F, G . . .' I didn't actually get round to it until I was about twenty-seven years old and we started to make some serious money with Happy Mondays. I remember Nathan McGough, our manager, telling us one day that our company was going to be worth a million, and for some reason I thought to myself, 'Fucking hell! I better learn my alphabet then.'

My problems at school weren't simply down to me being a bit thick, despite the difficulties I did have with learning, because when I arrived at Ambrose High School at the age of eleven I was put in Set Two for English and maths. There were four sets, and Set One was for the brainiest kids, then Set Two was for kids who were pretty clever, but easily distracted. I clearly had some potential, but at the end of the first year when we had to do various tests on spelling and maths I didn't do as well as I could have and I suddenly dropped down to Set Four. This wasn't just because of the test results, it was also because

I was a bit disruptive in class; it was a combination of the two.

When you're stuck in the bottom set and it's clear that half the people are there because they're not bright enough to be anywhere else and the other half are there because they're too much trouble for the teachers to handle, you very quickly get to the stage where you go to school in the morning not really expecting to learn anything. I wasn't stupid, I just didn't pay attention, and after I was put in the bottom set I just couldn't be arsed. So that was it. Once you're in those sets, nobody cares if you're there or not. Especially if they know you would only fuck about if you did turn up. By the end of the first year of high school I had given up on it almost entirely. There was always somewhere else to go and something better to do.

I was a bit of a joker at school. I thought I was cool, although I was probably a bit of a knob. But more than anything I was becoming a bit of a bad lad. I got caned almost every day. I would walk in some days and the first thing I would hear was, 'Ryder, go and get the cane.' I became so disillusioned with school that it got to the stage where it was a good day if I was told to go out to the playground and pick up litter. When I had to do that, a pal of mine who was also disruptive would have to spend all day painting the bogs. Being sent to pick up litter in the playground was great for me, as it meant I could smoke all day while I was doing it, and run off out the school gates and sneak down to the precinct when no one was looking. That was better than being in class.

By this point my main mission was making some money and buying nice clothes. I was far more interested in having cash in my pocket and looking good than learning anything. Because we went to a Catholic school, we had to wear a bloody blazer and a jumper, which I wasn't into, especially as you couldn't really customize them and make them your own. I'd always liked clothes and I can remember mithering my mam for a pair of bell-bottom trousers at the end of the 60s when I was only about seven. They had become really important to me by the time I reached high school. In the mid-70s it was all about Doc Martens, parallel trousers, two-tone trousers, patch pockets, platforms and Royal shoes which were popular with Northern Soul fans. Looking good was important, so any money I laid my hands on, I spent on either some new clobber or on booze.

Ever since I first nicked the toffees at primary school, going on the rob had seemed natural to me, but by the time I was at high school nicking stuff became almost my main mission. There wasn't much money at home and, as I'd become frustrated and disillusioned with school, there wasn't a great deal else to do. It became a bit addictive as well. I'd steal anything – toffees, money, booze, clothes, bikes. I wasn't unique in that. Most of my pals that I knocked about with were doing it as well. We would sell a lot of what we nicked, especially the booze, which we'd sell to ice-cream men, who would flog it from their vans. Back in 1973 we were lucky enough to have the Bulmers and Schweppes depots round our way, so we would rob both of them. The Bulmers depot had barbed wire and that black tar anti-climbing paint on the wall, but we would get over it quite easily. At Schweppes you used to have to get into the yard first, then kick a couple of doors in and then you'd be in the store where there were crates of booze – whisky, vodka, all sorts.

We also used to hit pubs and off-licences near us. One pub – which is actually not far from where I live now, so I'd better not name it – used to keep all its stock in a garage attached to the pub, so we'd break in there. We weren't professional, we were just kids, so we just used to kick doors in or smash windows, or go through skylights to get in where we needed to. I didn't have a particular partner in crime; there'd usually be a few of us, including some of my cousins. We might not have been professional, we were just kids, but we were good little sneaks, so we hardly ever got caught.

In 1973, a huge superstore called Scan opened near us, in Walkden. It was the first place of its kind in the area; we had never seen anything like it. Even now, it would be considered a big superstore. It was bigger than most of the places you get at those out-of-town retail parks. It was fucking huge. They sold everything from sports gear to guitars to records to food, but basically they had it set up like a fucking greengrocer's – a couple of those useless security mirrors and then twenty old biddies on the tills. There were no security guards or anything. In Salford! It was a joke. It was an open invitation to nick stuff. We used to go shopping with my mam and dad sometimes, and we would purposefully put our fishtail parkas on, which had holes in the linings. We would then walk out with all sorts in the linings – records, airgun rifles, darts, you name it. It got ridiculous in the end. They had these old country and western amps in there and you could even get away with literally carrying them out. So we did. We ended up using some of that stuff when we were first trying to get a band together a few years later.

One of the few places we never robbed, funnily enough, was the clothing firm Henri Lloyd, which was based just next to our estate in Little Hulton. Henri Lloyd is now quite popular with young lads in Salford, but back in the mid-70s we didn't even know it was a clothing label, we just thought it was an office of some type. If we'd known it was full of clobber we would have been in there, I can assure you.

I had plenty of different places where I used to stash stuff I'd nicked. There was a hidden gap underneath the chest of drawers in my bedroom, which was quite handy, but I had to be careful about stashing stuff at home because my mam would catch on. She's not stupid and she became a bit of a rooter after a while. If she thought I was up to something, she'd have a look around while I was out of the house. So I started to stash stuff in the fields behind our house and on the railway banking, and even on the roof of my nana's bungalow. It had a pitched roof, and if you pulled away a few tiles there was a hole underneath where I could hide stuff like money and digital watches. I don't think my nana knew I used to do that, but she may well have done. She turned a blind eye to a lot of things.

I would make sure I left stuff that I couldn't explain away, like a nicked bike for instance, at other people's houses. I would even keep clothes, like trench coats or more expensive shoes, at someone else's so I could leave our house in one set of clothes, nip down to a pal's and get changed.

Given that I was often up to no good, it was a bit ironic that when I got nicked for the first time I hadn't really done anything wrong. I was riding my bike down the road by Fountain Square, near Swinton precinct, and a copper beckoned me over with his finger. I rode over the road, up on the pavement and over to him.

'Name?' he said.

'Why? I've not done owt.'

'Riding your bike on the pavement.'

'But I wasn't riding on the pavement.'

'You're on the pavement now.'

I thought, 'You cunt.' He obviously just needed to make up his arrest numbers or something, so he nicked me for riding on the pavement. I had to go down to court with my dad a couple of weeks later, and I got a small fine and a criminal record. My dad wasn't that angry with me because it was so obvious that the whole thing was an absolute farce. This wasn't the last time I got in trouble, though, and I ended up down the cop shop a couple of times over the next few years, or they would come round the house if I got caught setting fire to something or accused of robbing, but usually I would just get let off with a talking to or a warning.

Me and Our Paul once robbed a couple of hundred quid off my grandad, Bill. We knew where he stashed his money in his wardrobe and we found £200 in there, so we just had it away. I don't know how we thought we would get away with it. That was a lot of money back then, in the mid-70s, but I spent my half quite quickly on booze and clothes. We got rumbled for it, and I got a good hiding for that from my dad, but I took the blame and kept Our Paul out of it. I was supposed to pay Bill back, and I did try, but £200 was a lot of money. About a year later, Our Paul turned round to me and said, 'Oi, knobhead, look at that,' and chucked a post office account book at me. He'd only gone and opened an account with his half of the money and he still had £75 left, the cheeky bastard. Not only had I taken the hiding for him for it, but he was always pestering me for dough – 'Our Kid, lend us a fiver will you?' – and all the time he had £75 in the post office.

Our Paul was up to almost as much mischief as me. He did a lot of the same stuff that I did, but he never got caught, and I never grassed on him. I would take the blame, so they thought he was the good one. At that stage he was the one that was going to go to college and make something of himself. I was seen as a bit of a lost cause. I'm sure I was a nightmare for my mam and dad. From when I was thirteen, my mam used to panic whenever I walked through the door because she didn't know what trouble I was bringing with me. I could see the dread on her face every time the phone went, as she would always be expecting the worst. Looking back, I can see that when I did get a hiding off my dad he was doing it to try and protect my mam as much as teach me a lesson.

I used to go to the pictures a lot when I should have been in school. I liked Clint Eastwood films like *Dirty Harry* or *Magnum Force*, or Bruce Lee in *Enter the Dragon*. There were some great films made in the early 70s. There was one particular cinema, the Princess in Monton in Eccles, which is part of Salford. That place was a belter. They'd let us in to see *anything*, even though we were only ten years old. And we didn't even sneak in to the Princess – we would pay.

I had plenty of money then. I think part of my recklessness with money in later life came from having pockets full of dough as a kid, because it meant I didn't really learn the value of money. I could always get money if I needed it. It was a bit of a shock later when I ended up having to get a job at the age of fifteen and I was on £17 a week. When I was thirteen I would spend that in a day, easy; I'd spend that in an *hour*. I'd go in a shop and buy a bike, ride it around all day and then just leave it somewhere if I couldn't get away with taking it home. I was probably making £100 a week at that stage. I was a thirteen-year-old kid and I would be jumping in a black cab with my girlfriend and going into town to the Golden Egg, a café on Deansgate that would serve us alcohol. We'd be sitting there having a mixed grill and a lager when we were supposed to be at school.

On the rare occasions I did go into school, I started rhyming in the playground. My little crew, who went around together setting fire to stuff and robbing, would also all stand around and make rhymes up. We would just come up with silly little riddles and poems about 'Miss Annie had a smelly fanny' and stuff like that. Really childish nonsense, just to amuse ourselves.

If the teacher back then had said to our class that one of us would become famous one day, none of the other kids would have ever thought it would be me. I wouldn't have thought it would be me. I suppose the first person from our school to become famous was the kid who strangled this woman with her own tights, round the back of some pub, just after he'd left school. If we'd known that one of us would become famous, we probably would have presumed it would be for something like that – for killing someone or getting caught doing an armed robbery or something. We certainly wouldn't have thought it would be for music or anything in the entertainment world.

There was actually one other kid from our high school who did become famous. On my first day at Ambrose we got chased by the older lads, who wanted to flush our heads down the bogs. One of them managed to get hold of me, and his name was Nigel Pivaro. He later became Terry Duckworth, Jack and Vera's tearaway son in *Coronation Street*. He was a couple of years older than me, but we ended up becoming pals and we even knocked about with him later when we were in the Mondays.

I started wagging school when I was about eleven. Initially I tried to cover myself, but by the time I got to thirteen I just didn't bother hiding it. I didn't give a fuck. I can remember quite clearly in the third year of high school thinking to myself, 'I haven't learned a fucking thing since I've been here.' My mam and dad went to parents' evenings at school anyway, so always found out what was going on, and things would often get back to my mam because she worked in the nursery.

Even though I liked messing around with words and coming up with rhymes, I was never really into reading. The only books I read were the *Skinhead* and *Suedehead* books by Richard Allen. Well, I say 'read', but I never really read them properly. I would look at the covers, then just skip to the bits where there was swearing and shagging. I read a few music autobiographies as well, but that was it. Even now I only really read music books.

I got my first bits of work in the summer when I was thirteen, working on building sites. There was an older lad who had a group of lads working for him and he recruited me as part of his gang. You were supposed to strip the wallpaper and take the window frames out, but rather than stripping the paper I just started knocking the walls down, because it was easier. So I was sacked.

It was around that summer that we were first able to get served in pubs. There's a road called Bolton Road in Salford, which runs from Irlams o' th' Height pretty much right up to Bolton. On the part which ran from th' Height all the way through Swinton and Pendlebury there was a pub, without a word of a lie, about every ten yards. Pubs galore, and most of them were infested with underage drinkers. It was notorious in the 60s and 70s. They were always getting busted, and people were always getting nicked. It's nothing like it used to be now. The landlords all knew we were under age, but there were certain pubs that would let us drink. I started off, originally, on pints of bitter, usually Stones Bitter or Boddingtons.

We also started going to the Wishing Well in Swinton, which was quite rough and pretty infamous round our way. You were supposed to be eighteen, but they just let everyone in. At that time, if a place played Northern Soul it could attract a lot of drugs, fighting and trouble, so some places, like the Wishing Well, would err towards playing more straight Motown and pop. Most kids round our way were drinking by the age of thirteen. One day our games teacher, Brin Cooper, told us that he didn't drink or smoke, and the whole class was just amazed. Everyone went, 'You don't drink, sir?'

'You don't smoke, sir?'

'What *do* you do then, sir?'

'What else is there to do, sir?'

Because everyone in that class, at the age of thirteen, either drank or smoked, and most of them did both. Even the goody-goodies.

I had first started smoking occasionally when I was about ten, but I was smoking properly by thirteen. My mam and dad both smoked and they did try telling us that we shouldn't, but they were just saying it for the sake of saying it, I think. My dad's and my nana's generations had all worked since the age of thirteen, so by the time you got to that age you were almost treated like an adult. I still couldn't light up in my mam and dad's house, but I could at my nana's. Any kid could buy cigs back then, and you could also just buy 'singles' – single cigarettes – if you only had a few pence. I also used to rob cigarettes. I would sneak into newsagents' stock rooms or wherever. I was an opportunist. I spent the whole day on the lookout for things to sneak.

I first smoked a joint when I was about fourteen, but I didn't start smoking pot properly until I was about seventeen. I'd have the odd blast if someone had a spliff, but it wasn't that easy to get hold of it when we were growing up; it was easier to get hold of other drugs like speed. I saw my first syringe around the same time, when I was at a fairground in Pendlebury with a girl and we were on this ride called the Over-Rider. As we were going up and round, we spotted the police pull up at the fairground in cars and vans, and the girl just pulled out her works and stuck them down her knickers. That was the first time I'd seen a syringe, although I was probably more interested in seeing what was down her knickers, to be honest. I can't even remember her name, and I didn't really know her that well, so didn't know she was injecting. It wasn't heroin, it was speed.

There were a lot of amphetamines around Salford in the mid-70s. Our Matt got some speed about the same time and showed me, but my first reaction was, 'No way, not a chance.' He was only having a dabble, but I wasn't interested at first. There were a few speed pills knocking around school a year or two later – Dexys or blues or bombers – and I did try them, but I never really got into it. I was always lively enough as I was. Even later, when I was a bit of a garbagehead and would take pretty much anything, I was never into speed. So it was mainly cigarettes and alcohol when I was still at school.

I also lost my virginity when I was thirteen, to a girl I knew from Salford, in an underground car park in central Manchester. I was wearing parallels at the time, which meant I could easily get my pants off without taking my shoes off. I didn't want to be messing around trying to get my eight-hole Doc Martens off in some underground car park, so I just whipped my pants off and kept my Docs and my socks on. She didn't seem to mind. I wasn't the first of my pals to lose their virginity; I was probably about the average age. Most of us had girlfriends from the age of seven or eight. You might have not done much, but there was still the 'doctors and nurses' sort of games going on, you know what I mean? So losing your virginity at thirteen was no big deal. Although it always seemed like someone else was getting it more than you, to be honest.

It sounds really bad now, and I'm not proud of it, but during our teenage years we also robbed a couple of houses. Not properly, but if we saw a window open in a house, we would be up the drainpipe and in through the window. There were a couple of my pals who used to do that with me, but I won't name them as I'm sure they're not proud of it either. I still run into them from time to time, because they both live in Salford.

When I was thirteen or fourteen there were a few occasions like that when my dad really reached the end of his tether with me and threw me out of the house for a few days. When that happened I would usually go down to my nana's and stay there, although sometimes my dad would ring Nana and say, 'If he comes down there, don't let him in.' On those occasions I would usually crash at a mate's, but there were a couple of times when I ended up sleeping rough in a cardboard box. I found this spot behind the laundrette where there was a kind of extractor fan which pumped out hot air, so if I put the box near there I could keep warm.

I was shit scared of my old bloke until I was about fifteen, because I knew he would leather me, and that would make me think twice about doing things. To be honest, I got into so much trouble then that if it hadn't been for me being afraid of my old fella, and that slightly curbing my behaviour, I would have been absolutely out of control. It's a good job I was scared of him.

When I was fourteen I got a job travelling around the country ripping out cinema seats. My mam and dad didn't bother about me going to school much by this stage and one of the reasons was that I had started working. It was pretty clear from day one that I wasn't going to be academic, so as long as I was working they didn't mind.

The first major trouble I got into was when I was fifteen. I was with my mate when he took his dad's mate's Ford Granada. I was still at school, just about. Well, I wasn't *at* school, but I was supposed to be. I wasn't actually one of those kids who was bang into joyriding. I was always more about doing things that made money. But we did take this Ford Granada, and he crashed it into this old couple's garden wall and got nicked for it. I wasn't driving, but I was in the car, and thankfully my name was kept out of it all.

I was actually waiting for my starting date for my first proper full-time job, at the post office, and if I had been charged with anything I would have lost the job. I had managed to get the job because my dad worked there, and if you had family in the post office you got put to the top of the waiting list. I didn't want to work really; I didn't want to be doing any job, especially one like that, but I had no choice. I needed the money. I started out as a messenger boy, which meant you could be put on different shifts. You could be on earlies or lates, or you could be on overtime and be there from six in the morning until seven at night, or even later.

It was on my way to work early one morning, not long after I started, that I first saw a UFO. I was on an eight o'clock start, and I was just about to get the bus, so it was probably just after 7am when it happened, because it was still pitch black. It wasn't just me who saw it – there was a little kid in a blazer there, on his way to grammar school and getting the same bus as me. It wasn't that close to us, but we got a good look. It seemed about the size of a beach ball, but as it was quite far away in the sky it must actually have been quite big. It moved across the sky at incredible speed – it must have been going about 5,000 miles an hour. It zigzagged all over the place, all over the sky, and then it just shot off. I wasn't scared at all, for some reason, not one bit, and the little kid didn't seem to be freaked out either. The two of us just stood there watching it, without saying anything to each other.

It's well documented that a lot of paranormal activity took place at this time, over towards Bolton, up on the moors, but we could see it from where we were in Salford – this thing flying about at ridiculous speeds, just bombing about. I've seen a few things like that over the years. I saw a lot of strange things going on in the skies around Salford in the late 70s, and a lot of other people did as well. All sorts of mad things. If you go back and look at the papers from about 1978 to about 1981, the *Salford Reporter* and *Manchester Evening News*, and even the *Daily Mirror* and the *Sun*, it was widely reported. If you watch the Discovery channel and see people talking about stuff like this, a lot of it seems to have happened over northern England around that time. I think anyone who doesn't believe that there is life out there will end up looking as ignorant as those people who used to think that the earth was flat and if you went too far out to sea in your boat you would fall off the end of the world. Ridiculous.

When I started work full time, there were post offices all over Manchester city centre, on Oxford Road, Portland Street, York Street, and the main one on Newton Street, and we'd work in all of them. One of the things that I really enjoyed about it was that it was the first time I had really met lads from other parts of Manchester, lads from Ancoats, Blackley, Hulme, Moss Side, Wythenshawe. Before that I didn't know that many people outside Salford. I didn't appreciate having to work, but we did have a great laugh, and we were always up to something.

The famous story from my early post office years is about when I poisoned the pigeons, but it didn't happen quite like it's been reported over the years. It wasn't me and Our Paul, for a start, like they showed in *24 Hour Party People*. Not that anyone should believe what happens in that film. The Shaun Ryder in that film is a caricature. It amazes me how many people just swallow everything whole. Although, in a way, part of Shaun Ryder was always a caricature. You're not going to make it in the music business just by singing songs; you need to be a bit of an extreme character. Especially nowadays. People need something to latch on to, something that makes you stick in their mind. If you look at someone like Lily Allen, she'll admit that the Lily Allen the public sees is an exaggerated version of her true self, and likewise the Shaun Ryder the public saw was always part caricature. I was always aware of that, and it didn't bother me one bit. It makes it easier in a way, because it means you don't have to bare your soul, or any of that bollocks. When the Mondays were first coming up, there was none of this reality TV nonsense. The less you showed of yourself and the more you presented a façade, the better. I knew it would never work if we tried to be the deep and meaningful moody types, because there was no air of mystique about us. People didn't understand us, and thought we were from another world, but that's because who we were and where we came from was alien and a bit shocking to them, so I just played up to that. That's what you do. You play the game. Then you bring in a pal who's a real nutcase, like Bez. Bez is actually pretty talentless at anything apart from being Bez, but he was *really fucking good* at that. He was better at being Bez than anyone. He's certainly not thick and he loves his music, and knows a groove, but he hasn't got a musical bone in his body. He can't play an instrument and he can't write lyrics, but he can certainly be rock 'n' roll. Me and Bez were always rock 'n' roll. Always. It just came naturally. We were rock 'n' roll long before we were in a band. Long before we had any money.

The pigeon incident was actually me and another post boy I was mates with from Blackley. One lunchtime we were sat in St Peter's Square by Central Library, eating Kentucky Fried Chicken, and the fucking pigeons wouldn't leave us alone. They were all over us, hassling us and trying to grab the chicken out of my hand. I was shooing them away, shouting, 'You dirty fucking vermin! You horrible cannibal bastards!' But they kept on hassling us and it really wound me up. After lunch, we found a box of rat poison behind a door in one of the post office buildings and I said to the other lad, 'Do you think this rat poison will kill pigeons?' We just stuck a load of it in some bread and went round town throwing it to the pigeons. I didn't actually see pigeons falling to the ground but they must have done because there were eyewitness reports in the newspaper about pigeons dropping out of the sky, dive-bombing trains and splattering on Market Street. One of the headlines in one of the papers was 'Sick Maniacs Poison Thousands of Pigeons'. They never found out it was us. It only came out much later, when I started talking about it. I have slightly mixed feelings about that incident now. I'm still not happy with pigeons. I just don't like them. We're not talking about racing pigeons here, we're talking about vermin. So I don't necessarily have any massive regrets about doing that, but on the other hand I'm a very different person now. I've changed a lot over the last ten years. I wouldn't hurt a fly now. If I found an insect in the house, I would actually try and remove it and put it out the back door rather than kill it.

Those early years working at the post office were a brilliant time for me. The postie's uniform made you look older, so I'd have no problem getting served anywhere in town. The pubs were ace then, really smoky, bustling places, rammed full of blokes, posties and villains. At lot of them would have strippers and comedians like Bernard Manning on at lunchtime. They were pretty rough, but I loved it. We used to go in the John Bull, which was up on Brown Street, and we would also go to Fagins and Rafters on Oxford Street, which were nightclubs that opened during the day. We'd stay in there all day. The pubs were supposed to shut in the afternoon back then, from 3–5pm, but there were always places where you could get a bevy all afternoon if you wanted to. It was like a northern episode of *The Sweeney*.

I also started going out in town at night when I was about fifteen, to places like Pips. I was just too young for the punk thing. I never went to the Ranch Bar, and I missed the Sex Pistols at Lesser Free Trade Hall in 1976, although I did see the Ramones there a couple of years later. I didn't officially leave home until I got married at nineteen, but from around the age of fifteen I stayed away quite a bit, at mates' houses or birds' houses or whatever.

Although during the day we could get served in the pubs with our postie uniforms on, when we started going to places like Pips we had to get some false ID. On a night out it would usually be me, Our Paul and a pal of mine from school called Mark Pierce – Piercey. Our Paul might have been eighteen months younger than me, but he actually looked older than I did at that stage, so he'd be all right for getting in, even though he was still at school. He was bigger than me as well, by then. By the time I was about sixteen, Our Paul could deck me if he wanted to.

I lost touch with Piercey for years, then in 1991, after the Mondays had made it, I was back visiting my mam and ran into him and another kid I knew from school, called Pez, in the pub and they were slightly arsey with me. They were a bit drunk, but they were a bit off with me. I think they presumed I'd changed, and I was now this Charlie big potatas pop star, even though I wasn't acting like that. But since I've moved back, twenty years later, Piercey and anyone else I run into is fine. We're all grown up these days . . . He's a builder now. He's the only kid from my school that I still really know and we get on well. He was brought up in Pendlebury but now lives just over the East Lancs Road from me. Where I live there's a bit of a running joke about the two sides of the East Lancs. I live on the Worsley side, which is supposed to be the posh side, and he lives on the other side, which is the Swinton side, but there's not much difference. A lot of the houses over his side are privately owned now as well.

Pips was great; it was one of our favourite hang-outs in town. It had eleven bars spread across nine different rooms, playing nine different types of music, including a Roxy and Bowie room, a disco room, a pop room, and so on. We used to hang out in the Roxy and Bowie room, which was the coolest. And we might show our faces in the pop room, depending on where the birds were. A lot of the Roxy and Bowie fans would get all dressed up to go down to Pips, but we didn't; we were more on the Perry Boy vibe. The Perry Boys were the original scallies, influenced by football terrace culture, who later became Pure Boys. By 1978 we would have side partings and a Fred Perry top, or if you were really lucky a Lacoste top. That was our look at the time.

By this stage we were really into clothes and had started shopping at the indoor market in town. There was a shop called Oasis (nothing to do with the Oasis high street chain), which the song on the first Mondays album is named after. A friend of ours called Si Davis worked there and the guy who owned it used to buy clobber off the kids who brought it back from sneak trips abroad in the late 70s. He'd have loads of one-offs in there, trainers that you couldn't get anywhere in this country. Everyone wanted stuff that no one else had, so there were kids who would go abroad specifically on shoplifting trips and then sell the clobber on to places like Oasis. Stuff that was so rare it was like rocking-horse shit. I remember one shop in Manchester having two Fila shirts, which was a massive deal at the time.

When it came to going out, I kind of did things in reverse. When I was really young and had just started going out, I would go to more grown-up places, like Oscars and Rotters, not the punky places. I was old before my time really, from the age of thirteen to about seventeen. When I was fifteen I was going in working men's places, drinking beer, seeing comedians, watching strippers and doing little marijuana deals. It was a couple of years later when I got into bands, whereas most people would do it the other way round – spend a few years into bands and then progress to the older men's type of gaffs.

I ended up at the post office for about five years, and there's no way I would have lasted that long if it wasn't for the unofficial 'perks'. When I started I was taking home about £17 a week, and I had to give my mam £5 for board, so after I'd bought my weekly bus pass there was fuck all left. Thankfully, being a messenger boy in the post office came with a lot of unofficial opportunities. In those days the banks used to send out bank cards along with the pin numbers, rather than sending them out separately like they do now. They were quite easy to spot, so I could pocket a new card and have an afternoon round the shops, buying some new clobber and even something for my mam. I could get away with murder. Because I had a uniform on, I could basically walk into any part of any post office building and no one would question me. So I'd pretend to sort a few parcels and then do one with a few that looked interesting. It was that easy.

Later it got to the stage when I would load a van full of parcels that were supposed to be for the shops in the Arndale Centre and take them down to a guy I'd met called Everton, who, like everyone else, did a bit of this and that to make money. He was a ticket tout but could get rid of anything I would take down to him. He'd just give me a couple of hundred quid and the stuff would end up on Moss Side market. Everton later came and worked as security with Happy Mondays.

Our Paul started at the post office eighteen months after me. That was towards the end of the 70s, when me, him, Our Matt and Pat started knocking about together more, and going to gigs quite a bit. We went to see the Buzzcocks at Belle Vue stadium when I was sixteen, in 1978, and that was the first time I saw Tony Wilson. I pointed him out and said, 'There's that bloke off the telly!' and threw my plastic pint pot of beer at him, but missed. That was my way of showing my appreciation, because I thought Tony was great. He hadn't started Factory Records yet, but we had grown up watching him on *Granada Reports*, and the music programme he had called *So It Goes*, was great. He had the best bands in the country on there, in my opinion, and a lot of them, like the Buzzcocks and later Joy Division, were from Manchester, which made the music business seem less distant. One of the great things about Manchester is it's a big enough city to have a strong music scene, but small enough for you to feel a part of it, because you would see people like Tony Wilson and Pete Shelley from the Buzzcocks at gigs or around town.

We went to see the Ramones at the Free Trade Hall in Manchester when I was seventeen, which was great. Afterwards we got on the bus home to Salford and were on the top deck at the back. You could smoke on buses then. On the bus I met a girl called Denise Lomax, so I started chatting her up, and we arranged a date and I got her number. She was a really cool girl and we started seeing each other. She was two years older than me, at nineteen, and really into her music. It was actually Denise who first introduced me to Joy Division, when she lent me her copy of *Unknown Pleasures*.

At that stage I loved David Bowie and Tamla Motown and all sorts of music. *The Man Who Fell to Earth*, in 1976, had been another big influence on me, more in fashion than music. David Bowie with his duffel coat on and that wedged centre parting, like a mushroom centre parting, had a great effect on what became terrace fashion. But the two biggest influences, ones that made me want to form a band and be in the music business, were David Essex and Joy Division.

I never saw Joy Division live, but my Denise did. The fact that they were a local band made a huge difference to me. They also had side partings and dressed almost like we did;

they had a slight Perry Boy thing going on. They looked cool.

I remember Ian Curtis dying. I was working at the post office and one of the older posties said, 'I see your mate's dead . . .' I thought he was talking about a fellow postie who was a mate of mine and a bit mental, but he actually meant Ian.

As I've already said *That'll Be the Day* and *Stardust* were important influences on me because they were about the whole lifestyle and fashion and everything that came with music. They made me think, 'I'm having some of that.' But it was Joy Division that made the whole thing seem like a more realistic prospect. They had a big effect on me. By the end of the 70s I knew I wanted to be in a band, and it didn't seem quite such a ridiculous proposition any more.

CHAPTER THREE

'If you've got to be told by someone,
then it's got to be me'

Before we started Happy Mondays, it sometimes seemed that
all we ever did was talk about being in a band. It was mainly
me and Our Matt, and two other kids from Little Hulton –
Martin Langford, who we called Langy, and John Jordan, who
we called Jordy. Langy was a mate of Our Matt's who joined the
post office after me. In fact, he still works for the post office
now. I saw him just recently at my Uncle Tom's funeral and
reminded him, 'Fucking hell, Langy, you were in the band
before we were a band, when we were just pretending we were
a band, before we had any instruments!' He was never very
musical, though. He was a music-lover, but he wasn't a
musician, so I don't think he worries that he missed his
vocation in life.

We got our first gig before we had any instruments or had
even played a note. Our Matt, the daft bastard, managed to
blag us a gig supporting the punk rock band Salford Jets. We
used to go and watch the Jets all the time, from about 1977
onwards, at the pubs on the top road near our house. They
played all those places, right up to 1979, when they played the

Bulls Head in Walkden. We used to talk to the singer, Mike Sweeney, after the gigs and one night Our Matt said, 'Come on, Mike, give us a gig. We're called No Exit,' and Mike said, 'All right, get your gear and come down on Saturday.'

After we left we were like, 'Matt, you fucking knob, what are you doing? We haven't got any instruments, and none of us can play anything even if we did. We've got no songs, apart from these stupid little rhymes we've made up, and yet you've got us a gig!' So it never happened in the end.

Years later, when the Mondays had made it, Mike Sweeney said to me, 'Yeah, I remember when we gave you a support slot and you played with us,' and I had to correct him and say, 'Mike, *we didn't!*'

After that, we decided we would actually try and start a band, because it looked like we would be able to get a gig. I pushed the others into it, really. Someone gave Our Matt an old battered acoustic guitar that only had two strings on it, and I fancied being a drummer so I got myself a drum kit from a music shop in town. I can remember one afternoon trying to bang something out with Our Matt in the front room of Lanky's house. Lanky got hold of an old guitar as well, and I can't even remember what Jordy had.

I quite quickly sacked off my drum kit, because I couldn't get into it. I sold it to a kid called Tony Martin, who is actually still gigging around Manchester in some sort of Blues Brothers trib-ute act, although he's not still using my old kit, obviously, as it would be over thirty years old now. After that we picked up a little drum machine, one of the first ones that came out, and used that instead. I think my dad's still got it somewhere.

We recorded a very, very early demo at my nana's house, with just three of us – me, my dad's mate Barry and Our Matt on guitar – and a drum machine. I had tried to write some songs, but I was basically just copying Ian Curtis. Barry was playing some basic barre chords, and Our Matt was strumming alongside him, while I was singing 'Voices in my heeaaad . . .' over the top of it.

Then Our Paul got a bass, and he learned to play much quicker and better than Our Matt, Lanky or Jordy. He couldn't read music, but pretty quickly he got to the stage where he could play something when he heard it. So Our Paul was definitely in; he was part of the band. At that time we had nowhere to rehearse, so we would go down and try and jam in the front room at Lanky's house. This was around late summer of 1980 and we didn't even have a name or anything.

There was a bloke at the post office called Alan Day, who was sort of my boss. He was my AI, which stands for Assistant Inspector, and he told me that his son played guitar. I'd probably caused Alan a bit of mither with my various scams, like the Yellow Pages incident. When the new editions of the Yellow Pages needed delivering, you could book yourself in to do a few rounds and you got something like 10p for each one you delivered, so I booked myself in to deliver five thousand of the fucking things. At the time, the council estates didn't get much post, so they would have more houses on each walk (which is what we called a postman's round). On one walk in Little Hulton there were seven hundred houses, but they only got mail once or twice a week, whereas a walk on a private estate would only deliver to 250 houses, but each house would get mail every day. So I booked myself in to deliver Yellow Pages on quite a few walks around Little Hulton and claimed the money, which was about £500 – a lot of money back then – but never actually delivered them. I just dumped them. They were turning up on wasteland, in ponds, on railway bankings. I was terrible.

Mark Day was also a postie, and by coincidence he worked with my old fella who suggested we hook up together. Me and

Our Paul went round to his house one day and had a bit of a jam in his loft. Mark was all right, if a bit dull, but more importantly he could already play guitar and he could read music as well, which none of the rest of us could. In fact, none of the other Mondays ever learned to read music. Mark lived in his mam and dad's little terraced house in Wardley. The living room was only a bit bigger than a pool table, but they had a piano in it, which looked ridiculous. Because the piano didn't really fit in the tiny room, they'd mounted the fucking thing on the wall. So when you came in through the door, you had to edge round this piano that was sticking out of the wall. I wouldn't mind, but I never even saw anyone playing it. Maybe it was just a fashion accessory – let's mount this fucking piano on the wall and take up half the room. A very odd set-up.

We came up with the name Happy Mondays during those very early rehearsals in Mark's loft. Our Paul claims it was his idea, but that's not quite how I remember it. I remember it as more of a joint effort. I think it was Mark who actually suggested the Mondays bit. It's a terrible name for a band, really, but we all quite liked it for that reason. It's a bit cheesy, a bit gay and it was kind of the opposite of what we were like, so we thought it might work because of that. We always thought it was a shit name, but that was kind of the point. We didn't want a scally type of name; we wanted a name that jarred with us.

We started to practise in Mark Day's loft through the end of 1980 and into early 1981, when we could get past the piano on the wall, and also we'd get together the odd time at my nana's. Our Matt had a second-hand electric guitar by then, so he jammed with us now and then.

Eventually we settled on me singing. All of us had a go, but I was better at it than the others, and when we started trying to write our own songs I was also better at rhyming and coming up with the words. I never demanded to be the singer; we just sort of naturally reached the conclusion in those early rehearsals that I should do it – it just felt right. We played a few cover versions at first, including a couple of Joy Division numbers, as we had to know we could actually play together before we could figure out what we sounded like and try and write our own songs.

By 1981 I was properly seeing Denise. She was a pretty cool girl, Denise, and, as I said, it was her that first got me into Joy Division and bands like that. She knew we were trying to get a band together and her little sister Bev told her that someone in her class at school played drums. This kid was called Gary Whelan and she introduced me to him, but I actually knew who Gaz was already anyway. I'd seen him about because he lived near my nana and he was good at football. We had never really spoken to him because he was about three years younger than me and a year younger than Our Paul. I was eighteen then and Gaz was only fifteen and still at school. But when Bev introduced us he seemed all right, so I was like, 'Okay, he's got a drum kit and he can play the drums and he's got a side parting, Farah trousers and a Pringle jumper . . . he'll do.'

That seemed like a line-up to us – vocals, guitar, bass and drums – and it began to feel like a group. But then I got approached in the street by this kid, Paul Davis. I can still remember Paul Davis as a little kid. He was a freak of a boy, with this huge big head and a dead little body. I didn't know his name then, but I'd seen him cycling around years earlier, when he must have been about five years old. One day, a few weeks after Gaz had joined the band, Paul Davis marched up to me in the street and blurted out, in his high-pitched little voice, 'Do you know Gaz Whelan?!' and I said, 'Yeah.'

'Is he in your band!?'

'Yeah.'

'He's a dick! Get 'im out! I wanna be in your band. *Get 'im out, he's a dick! Lemme be in it!*'

I'm thinking, 'Rrrrright. Okay. You're fucking mad, you.' So I said, 'What's your name again? Paul Davis?' Then next time I saw Gaz I said, 'Do you know Paul Davis?' and he said, 'Yeah, course I do, he's my best fucking mate!'

We had just started renting a little school hall at a primary school in Swinton for our rehearsals. All Saints Primary, I think it was called. It's not there any more – it's been knocked down. I think even then people were referring to it as *my* band, even though I never did. It was just kind of obvious that I was the leader of the gang.

Paul Davis turned up at rehearsals giving it, 'I wanna be in your band!'

He came with a bass, so I said, 'We've *got* a bass.'

And he went, 'Yeah, but I wanna play bass.'

So I explained again: 'Look, *Our Paul* plays fucking bass.' Jesus Christ. He was a real fucking oddball, even then. He wouldn't take no for an answer.

He turned up at our rehearsals again the next week. 'I really wannabe in your band. Look, I've brought me bass, I'll plug in, I've got this now and I've got that!'

I'm like, 'Listen, you dick! *We've. Got. A. Fucking. Bass. Player*. Can you even play bass?'

'No, but I'll learn!'

'But Our Paul can *already* play bass!' Fuck me. The kid was mental, y'know what I mean? Just wouldn't take no for an answer.

So we said, 'Right, okay, get a keyboard,' because that was one instrument we didn't have. So then PD was in.

Unfortunately, PD could not play keyboards. I'm not convinced he can even now. In the Mondays, particularly towards the end, big chunks were programmed, so basically he was just triggering samples and patterns. The parts that had been programmed were put into his keyboards by someone else, but he acted as if he was playing all of it.

After the Mondays split, Andy Rourke from the Smiths said to PD, 'Right, I'm getting a new band together. Paul, you can play keyboards.'

A couple of weeks later I got a phone call from Andy saying, 'Fucking hell, that lad can't play a note. How the fuck did he wing it through your band?'

So, that was the original Happy Mondays line-up before Bez joined. Shaun Ryder, Paul Ryder, Mark Day, Paul Davis and Gaz Whelan. X, Horse, Cowhead, Knobhead and No Arse.

We always called each other by our nicknames; we hardly ever used our real names. I was originally called Horse because my surname's Ryder. Horse rider. Then they started calling me X, because I was doing little drug deals here and there and it did my head in when we were in the pub or on the street and someone would blurt out, 'Shaun, have you got any weed? Have you got any whizz?' and I would have to take them aside and go, 'Will you stop shouting my fucking name out! I'll sort you out, don't worry.' So PD said, 'Oh, you think you're some sort of secret agent do you? OK we'll call you "X".' So I became X, and Our Paul then became Horse, and my old fella was Horseman.

PD was just called Knobhead because that's what he was, an absolute plum. But a nice plum, in the early days. Harmless. An idiot nutcase. A funny kid. It was only after the band took off and people started taking what he said seriously that he became annoying. He'd hit the whizz and the cocaine, which didn't do him any favours, and he became even more of a nutcase.

Mark Day was Cowhead because he looked like a cow, and he sounded like a cow with his big dopey voice, or Moose. Gaz

Whelan was either No Arse, because he had no arse, Ronnie, after Ronnie Whelan, or Pepe Le Pew, because he'd always fart when he walked into a room. He'd cock his leg and leave his scent everywhere.

My dad helped us out quite a bit in the early days. Just before we started he had stopped going out and playing gigs himself, so I suppose he transferred his enthusiasm and energy to us. From then on he was living his fantasy through us. He was just as enthusiastic about the band as we were, if not more so. He wanted to drive the van, set the equipment up, tune the guitars and do everything. It would have been a lot harder in the early years without his help. He even 'acquired' some of our equipment. It wasn't unknown for him to walk into some working men's club or venue, unscrew the speakers and walk out with them. Or part of an amplifier, or a mic stand. We got our equipment from wherever we could in the early days.

Horseman would come down and set everything up for us at rehearsals. I didn't want to sound ungrateful, but what we really wanted him to do was set everything up for us, make sure it was working and then leave. You don't want your dad around when it's your little gang trying to make music, do you? 'Will you just leave us to it, Dad?' It was nothing personal – no one would ideally want their dad around in that situation. But he would be like, 'It's my bloody equipment, so I'm staying!' He even got the name Happy Mondays put on a sticker across the windscreen of his old Renault 5. You know when couples would have 'Daz and Sharon', or whatever? Horseman had 'Happy Mondays'.

He really helped us out in the early years, but it affected our relationship for a long time. As I say, when we first started out he would do everything, hump gear and do the soundcheck and the monitors, but when you reach a certain level with a band you can't have one person doing everything, and he never got that. You need specialists. My old fella was still doing the sound on stage, mixing the monitors, when we played Wembley Arena for the first time, years later. I couldn't hear myself properly and I was trying to tell him, and he just went, 'It sounds fine to me,' and I'm going, 'I can't fucking hear myself!' We got into a row during the gig and he ended up coming across the stage and punching me, in front of ten thousand people.

Because my dad had been a singer, but never really made it past the local pubs and club scene, there was a little bit of rivalry between us, simmering underneath. He was also still quite young when the Mondays kicked off, as he was only a teenager when he had me. It's not healthy to be in competition with your dad, or your son, and it affected our relationship for a long time. We've got on much better over the last ten years or so, but it was only when I reached about forty that we stopped trying to be in competition.

When we first started writing our own songs, they were just full of in-jokes, because we didn't really think about anyone else hearing them. We were just writing songs for us, so they were full of our little catchphrases, observations, nicknames and references to films we liked. We did take the band quite seriously from the off, though. No one else would be allowed into rehearsals, it was just us. In a way it was the first thing in my life I had taken seriously, or at least the first thing I had put as much effort into as I did into stealing and making money. I suppose subconsciously we were beginning to think it might be a way out for us. None of us had a trade, or any great prospects.

Not that Mark Day ever saw rock 'n' roll as a great prospect. Mark is a very good guitarist, but he was never cut out to be in rock 'n' roll – he's just too square. Even back then, when he was nineteen and we'd only just started the band, he'd complain, in his dopey cow voice, that 'Rock 'n' roll's not a proper job. You don't get a pension with it.' That's the *whole point*, mate. That's why you get into rock 'n' roll. Because you don't want a proper job. You don't get into rock 'n' roll if you're worried about your final salary pension. For fuck's sake. Mark didn't even give up his job as a postie until we had been on *Top of the Pops* a couple of times. The first time we did *Top of the Pops*, with the Stone Roses in 1989, Mark had to get back up to Manchester afterwards so he could do his fucking post round the next morning.

Just after we started getting the band together, I was in the Wishing Well one night and it kicked off, as usual. Our lot were there from Salford, and there was a bunch of lads from Swinton there who wanted a ruck. Gaz was with the Swinton lot and one of them said to him, 'You know him, don't you? Ryder from Little Hulton?' and Gaz said, 'Nah, I don't know him, I've never met him in my life.' We'd been fucking rehearsing for three or four weeks already. Proper Judas. In fact, I could say Gaz has betrayed me three times. Once in the Wishing Well, once when the Mondays split up, and once more recently when he left the band again.

Our first gig was at Wardley Community Centre in Swinton, near my nana's house. I actually remember it pretty well. I was nervous so I got a bit pissed and stoned to take the edge off it. Well, I actually got *very* pissed and stoned. PD didn't play that first gig with us as he wasn't quite ready. He was coming to rehearsals but hadn't quite got it together to go on stage. I remember it felt pretty rammed, but it was only a small room, so there were probably about twenty-five people there. After we finished our set, these girls came up chatting to us. Our first gig and girls wanted to speak to us because we were in a band. But PD, the knobhead, came up and just blurted out, 'We don't want to talk to you!', screaming, 'Hey, fuck off,' so the girls did one. I turned to him and said, 'What did you say that for, you dick?' That's what he was like. Nice one, PD.

Denise and I got married on 22 May 1982. She was twenty-one and I was nineteen. If someone got married at nineteen nowadays, you'd think they were mad, but it wasn't a big deal back then. That's just what everybody did. I wasn't pressurized into it or anything. You'd think my dad would have pulled me aside and said, 'What you doing lad? Aren't you a bit young?' Certainly if one of my kids turned round to me at nineteen and said they were getting married, I'd just laugh and say, 'You're just a child, you're a baby! What are you doing?!' But it was a different world back then. Especially round our way. My mam and dad were married and had me by the time they were nineteen, and they're still together today and have had a long and successful marriage. Ian Curtis was married at nineteen as well. Although that didn't last, for obvious reasons. Bernard (Barney) Sumner got married pretty young when he was in Joy Division. None of my pals even said anything to me at the time, either, because most of their parents had married young, and a few other people our age were starting to get married. We thought we were really grown up at nineteen then, but we were just kids really. There's no way I was ready for marriage. But when you left school, round our way, most people didn't think, 'Right, I'm going to go out and have a career and do this and do that with my life.' They just left school, found a job and got married. That was it. I wasn't making any grand gesture about settling down or anything. I certainly wasn't thinking, 'That's it. That's me now. I'm going to stop going out and settle down.' Not for a minute.

On the wedding day itself I was totally embarrassed about what I was doing. We got married at St Edmunds in Little Hulton, but I wasn't there on time. My mam had to come and drag me out of the pub for the service. I was having a pint when I should have been waiting at the altar. I was actually also tripping, all my pals were. I don't think Denise knew I had taken acid on the day, but she knew I was on something – she wasn't stupid. I think she just thought that I was stoned. The Mondays were all at the wedding, apart from Bez, who I'd yet to meet. Gaz and PD were only sixteen and I'm not sure if they'd even left school.

After the service, when our wedding car drove down the main road, it must have looked like there was just a bride in it. Just Denise sat there in her wedding dress on her own, because I was hiding. I was crouched down with my head below the window so no one could see me, because I was so embarrassed. Nothing to do with poor Denise – I was just embarrassed about the whole wedding thing. I can't even remember if we had a honeymoon.

When we got married we moved into a house in Tyldesley, one of those Legoland-type semi-detached Barratt homes, which was a couple of years old and cost us £15,000. I think Denise realized quite quickly that being married to me wasn't what she wanted. She was two years older than me, and every-one knows girls are more mature than boys at that age anyway. She also came from a big army family. Her dad and her mam were both in the army and her dad was some big sergeant who had been based all over, so she had been to boarding school. As soon as we got married she grew up and joined the real world, and went and joined the TA. I think she began to think, 'Hang on a minute, I'm married to a kid here who's just into his music. Now I'm a bit older what I actually want is an army type of bloke, and an army type of life.'

But nothing really changed for me when we got married. I was still going out boozing and to nightclubs and trying to get the band sorted. Denise was into music, so she had liked the idea of me being in a band at first, but she just thought it was a temporary thing. When we got married and got a house, I was supposed to forget all that and 'grow up'. The band was now just childish and a bit wank to her. She thought we were a load of shite. I was also smoking a hell of a lot of weed, which she didn't like.

Denise and I were both children when we met, but when we married she became an adult and I almost regressed. I was getting more into the band, and I got the sack from the post office not long after that. It had been coming for a while. They knew I was robbing stuff and pulling all sorts of scams, so they sent the Investigations Branch after me. The IB were ex-police detectives who were employed by the post office. I'd been there for a few years by now, and I'd seen plenty of people join the post office just so they could rob stuff. But most of the mugs were so thick they just nicked stuff on their own patch and got caught within a couple of weeks and carted off. Robbing from the Royal Mail was an automatic prison sentence back then. You had to sign the Official Secrets Act when you joined and if you got caught there was no fannying about like there is now, when you can get a twelve-month conditional sentence and go and do some community service. Ninety-nine times out of a hundred you got sent down. Since I first started as a messenger boy, I'd picked up on every trick that the IB had to catch people out, and how they worked.

If you got to eighteen and you weren't driving, you became a real postman. You didn't necessarily have a round; you could be on indoor sorting. I did a bit of time in Newton Street, bit of time on Kings Road in Old Trafford, and then I ended up in Walkden, which was where I got the sack. I had a round then, and one day I clocked the IB following me. They knew I was pulling scams and were determined to catch me. So when I got to the end of a cul de sac I knocked on the door of a house where I knew the owners, explained I was being followed, and they let me jib through the house and out the back, while the IB were still waiting for me outside.

I used to take acid before I went out on my round sometimes, and another postie had already grassed me up for that. I had a lot of enemies at the post office by this stage, people who were pissed off that I was getting away with murder. The final straw was one day when I was tripping my box off on my round again. There was a little horrible mongrel dog at a pub on my walk, and every time you tried to deliver the mail to the pub it would attack you and try and bite you, 'Yap! Yap! Yap!' This particular morning I was on acid, this little pissing dog tried to bite me again and I just flipped and thought, 'You know what? I've had enough of you, *you little fucker!*' and picked it up and bit the thing. I bit the fucking dog and it yelped, then I threw it over the fence. Someone saw it and reported me, so I was up for that and for taking drugs. They suspended me on full pay for a few weeks – it might even have been a couple of months – while I was waiting for some hearing, but I knew what was coming, and sure enough they sacked me.

After I got the sack from the post office, I decided to hustle about on the dole and spend more time on the band. Denise wasn't too happy with that, obviously. She was working behind the counter in the post office in Swinton and she'd come home to find me and the band and a few other pals listening to music, smoking weed and dropping acid. I was the first one of our lot to get a house, so everyone would pop round to get stoned. Denise would come home and see us all off our heads, drinking cans of beer, and go mental. She really was like a fucking raging bull, so I started calling her Bull.

Bull hated me smoking weed, and hated it even more when I used to do little deals to make a bit of extra cash. I started to go to Moss Side now and again to buy a few ounces of weed, which I'd split and then knock out in fiver bags. Once I had a mound of it on my glass coffee table when all of a sudden there's a knock at the door and I look out the window and there's two coppers standing there. Not bobbies on the beat, or from a Panda car – these were high-ranking bobbies. *Fuck*. My arse absolutely went because I thought it was coming on top. If you don't know what 'coming on top' means, it's kind of a generic saying for when you're in the middle of a situation that is in danger of getting out of hand; either you're about to get rumbled for something or it's about to kick off. Either way, if things are coming on top you have to deal with it.

I closed the living room door to try and stop the smell getting out, and answered the front door to see what they wanted. It turned out all they were doing was going from door to door advising people on security because there had been a few robberies in the area, so I just listened politely to them and then they fucked off.

I never told Bull half of what was going on in that house. Half the deposit and the mortgage payments on our house had originally come from scams at the post office. As far as she was concerned they were savings, but I never told her dick.

After Ian Curtis had died, Joy Division had become New Order, adding Stephen Morris's girlfriend Gillian Gilbert on keyboards. Joy Division had never made it to America, but New Order were really influenced by their early trips to New York and its dance scene, and their time there working with people like the producer Arthur Baker. Together with Factory Records, New Order decided to open a nightclub in Manchester based on New York clubs such as Danceteria and Paradise Garage. They called it The Haçienda, which they took from a situationist quote, and it opened on 21 May 1982, the night before my wedding.

New Order were the main band on Factory at the time and a lot of the money that was spent opening the club and keeping it going in the early years came from their pocket, as Hooky never lets anyone forget. The Haçienda couldn't have been more different to the other clubs in Manchester, like Rotters and Oscars, which were all proper old-school nightclubs. Oscars even had tablecloths on the tables. The Haçi just felt super cool in comparison. I'd never been to New York, so it felt more German or European to me at first. It was a huge futuristic warehouse space, and even though it could be quite empty and draughty some nights, you knew it was an important place; it felt like a place where things could happen.

Our Paul went to the opening night, and probably went more than me at first – he was really into going and watching bands there. I would go with him and saw some great early gigs, like the Smiths, Orange Juice and Nico, but I was also doing other things, and I was still married.

When I did start to go regularly, I would see musicians from Factory like Barney or Hooky from New Order in there, but I never mithered them. I thought New Order were great, but I was never one of those who went up talking to people I didn't really know, and I certainly wasn't going to ask anyone for an autograph. Even when we eventually joined Factory and I became a bit friendly with Barney, I would never ask him questions or advice about being in a band.

Our next gig was a battle of the bands in Blackpool. My dad had found out about it through someone at the post office. It was in this weird venue with a kind of tinsel gold backdrop – a proper cabaret type of club, real *Phoenix Nights* tackle. We had put a few of our own songs in the set by then. They had terrible titles like 'Comfort and Joy' and 'Red', and they never saw the light of day, but they were a start. Someone actually emailed my manager, Warren, recently, saying, 'I bought this demo tape off Paul Davis who said it was an early Happy Mondays demo. These are the songs on it. Is it real?' and just by looking at the song titles I could tell it was. PD had obviously kept the early demos and photographs, then sold them to some obsessive Mondays fan.

We actually managed to record a couple of demos in the days when we were rehearsing at All Saints primary school, because my dad had bought a four-track from Johnny Roadhouse in town, one of those four-tracks that comes in a suitcase. He helped us record those demos. 'Comfort and Joy' and 'Red' were on the first one, then the later one had songs like 'The Egg' and 'Delightful'. By this stage, we were taking the band pretty seriously, practising quite religiously twice a week and beginning to think we might be able to make something of it. I think even my dad thought we were good, or at least thought we had *something*.

It was when I was married to Bull that I took heroin properly for the first time. I'd had my first taste of it in blowbacks, just round at people's houses at a party or whatever. The other person would smoke it, sucking it in through a tube, and then blow it back into your mouth through the tube. It's not as strong a buzz. It's like a second-hand heroin buzz.

The first time I smoked it myself properly was one night when Bull had gone to bingo with her mam. Me and a mate decided to get some gear that night, and we didn't have that much dough, so we only got a fiver's worth each. We were both up for it, neither of us pushed the other one into it. Smack then, in late 1982, was actually easier to get than weed or hash at some points, because it had come flooding in. Sometimes it seemed like everyone had heroin but hardly anyone had hash.

When you first do heroin, you either love it or hate it. Even if it makes you sick, which happens to a lot of people the first time they take it, the chances are you will probably have it again, because you enjoy it after your stomach calms down. But when I smoked it that night, I straight away had this instant sort of Ready Brek glow, this invincible 'I don't give a fuck' feeling.

My mate smoked his and just completely passed out and puked while he was unconscious. Which wasn't ideal, because watching him gurgle on his vomit was ruining my nice buzz.

I then clocked the time and realized I had to go and pick up Bull from fucking bingo, which was a right ball-ache. In the end I had to get hold of my mate, who was still passed out, drag him out to my car and stick him in the back seat while I went and picked up Bull. Her mam wasn't with her, thank God. I was driving a 120Y Datsun at the time, which looked a bit like Starsky and Hutch's car, except it was a Datsun and a sort of mustardy colour. So not quite as cool as Starsky and Hutch.

I don't think Bull knew I'd done heroin that night. She clocked I was wasted, that was fucking obvious because I was still pinned the next day, but I think she just thought I'd been smoking a load of weed or hash. I was still definitely wary of getting involved with the gear. I knew it was serious tackle, because it had been set in my head as a little kid when we were told by the police when they came to our school how addictive and dangerous it was. I was like 'Woooaahh, I've got to be *really* careful what I'm playing with here.' Especially as I'd already seen mates sucked in. There were quite a few of my pals who were at it, big time. My best mate at the time had gone from smoking to digging in a matter of weeks and you could see the effect on him. He didn't smile or dance any more. It was horrible to watch.

That's what we called injecting – 'digging' – and people who were injecting were called 'diggers'. I was never under the illusion that heroin wasn't quite as bad if you smoked it – I've never deluded myself like that. I'm just not a needle fan. I don't think it's macho or sexy to stick needles in your arm, so I was never going to be a digger. But once you could smoke it, then it seemed much more doable. It seemed an easier decision: 'OK, I'll have a go.' It was months before I tried heroin again, and even then I only had it a couple of times before I left it out altogether for a couple of years.

Obviously by the time the Mondays split most of the band had one vice or another. Eventually we were all either doing cocaine, taking heroin or smoking crack. Everyone, apart from Gaz Whelan. But at the same time they were *all* saying to me, 'This band's getting ruined because *you're* taking heroin and *you're* smoking crack and *you're* doing this.' All of them pointing the finger at me. But we'll get to that later.

After the battle of the bands we played another couple of gigs that my dad sorted out in youth and working men's clubs around Salford and Bolton. But we didn't want to be playing those types of places for ever, as no one was going to spot us playing a youth club in Bolton. I knew we needed to be going the other direction, into town. We got our first gig in Manchester at the Gallery, which was at the corner of Peter Street and Deansgate. The Gallery could be a bit moody, but all those gaffs that were late-night joints back then were like that – places such as the Cyprus Tavern, opposite Legends on Princess Street. We used to go to the Gallery on Saturday nights, when they played a lot of black music.

Our Matt did a poster advertising the gig; it was the first artwork he ever did for the Mondays. He used a photograph of a United fan from the 50s, a kid with a side parting and an old-school short back and sides, who looked like a very early Perry Boy. Me and Our Paul, PD and Gaz fly-posted them all over town.

It was a midweek night and there were about forty people there, mostly our mates. Lloyd Cole and the Commotions were supposed to be playing that night, but they'd just had a hit, so they cancelled. That gig at the Gallery was the first time we got listed in the *Manchester Evening News*, which made it seem a bit more real. Not that the paper ever helped us at all when we were starting out. It made me laugh years later when the *Evening News* journalist Mick Middles wrote a book about me and the Mondays, as he was one of those who always ignored us. Even when ecstasy took off and they had this bloody cultural revolution on their doorstep, it took the national press to write about it first before the *Evening News* realized what was going on.

The only journalist in Manchester who was interested was Andy Spinoza from *City Life* magazine and he was a fucking Cockney! He approached us after our first album came out, in the Haçienda I think, but he was the only local journalist who had a clue. Later on, when the rest of them cottoned on, the *Manchester Evening News* would moan if we didn't talk to them or if we gave an interview to someone else. 'Why are you speaking to them? Why aren't you speaking to us? We're your local paper.' I tell you why not. It's because you fucking ignored us for years, and now you're only interested in us because everyone else is.

By the time we played the Gallery we were aiming to get a deal. We used to send off loads of demos. We wanted to sign to Factory, because we were big fans of Joy Division and New Order, but we would have signed to anyone who would have had us. Apparently Our Paul put a demo tape through Hooky's door. I'm not sure I remember that, but after he passed his driving test Our Paul was a driver on the mini-vans, delivering telegrams, so he would go all over Manchester. If he did find out where Hooky lived, he probably would have put a tape through their door.

Around 1983 we started hanging around Phil Saxe's stall on the underground market in Manchester, which was on Brown Street, just off Market Street. It's all gone now, but it was basically just by where the Tesco's is on Market Street. Phil had a really cool stall. He had loads of decent gear, so we would hang about there because we were into our clobber. We were the first lot to start wearing flares, and we would get them off Phil. We used to ask him to get them in for us – 17-inch, 18-inch, 19-inch.

We were hanging out at the Haçienda more by this time, but it was just full of students. This was still way before ecstasy hit. The only people I would say who were in there wearing flares were our lot and Steve Cressa (who later became the Stone Roses' 'vibemeister' for a bit – their version of Bez), this other kid who had done an armed robbery, and Eric Barker. Eric was a great kid from Ancoats, who was a bit of a man about town and had a second-hand clothes shop in Afflecks Palace back then, but went on to put on loads of parties round town later, when the E kicked in. His little brother Andy used to DJ with his pal Darren Partington as the Spinmasters, and they later went on to be in 808 State.

As we hung out around Phil Saxe's stall, I got chatting to him more and more, and I discovered that he was a pretty cool guy. He was a north Manchester Jewish market stallholder, but he was also one of the original DJs at the Twisted Wheel, and had been one of the original mods and soul boys. It turned out that he knew people in the music scene, including Mike Pickering, who was in charge of A&R at Factory and was an old family friend. When I realized Phil was connected and had an in at Factory, it was a pretty obvious decision to ask him to manage us. I gave him one of our demo tapes and he came down to see us rehearse. I don't think my dad was best pleased at first, because he wanted to manage us, but I knew we needed more of a professional, someone from the outside, and although Phil hadn't managed a band before, he had connections. He seemed like someone who could make things happen and hopefully introduce us to Factory. There was still a place for my old fella, though, absolutely, and over time he kind of became Phil's right-hand man.

We then got this rehearsal space on Adelphi Street in Salford, in an old mill, which has been knocked down now. We didn't realize when we first started rehearsing there, but there was a hidden back room where they used to have bare-knuckle fighting. One day I was going to pay the geezer who ran it, to give him his rent, and I went behind the bar and discovered a door in the wall. It was a weird, small door, which was raised off the ground – you know like you would get on a ferry? I opened it and inside it was like something you see in a film – a dingy room full of smoke, and two blokes bare-knuckle fighting, going right at it, and all these geezers stood round betting on it.

Me and Bull ended up splitting up towards the end of 1984. We had been married for going on two years, but she'd grown up and we'd grown apart. It was obvious to both of us we were going our separate ways. It wasn't too painful a wrench for either of us, because it was so apparent that we now wanted completely different things, and different lives. We were only kids when we got married and we didn't really know who we were, what we were doing or what we wanted. You don't at that age, do you? The last I heard, which was at least fifteen years ago now, she was living in Wales and married to an air-force pilot. Which is probably what she wanted, really.

After we split up I started taking some trips to Amsterdam.

Since the late 70s lads I knew had been going to the Dam, so I would jib across there on the ferry for a few days whenever I got a little bit of dough. On one occasion I came back on the Magic Bus from the Dam to Manchester and I got pulled at Dover. I only had a few porno mags on me and some weed, but the bastards charged me with importation of pornography and marijuana, charges which would cause me complications a few years later with visas, especially with America.

After I split with Bull, I got myself a flat in Boothstown in Salford, which is just past Worsley, off the East Lancs. I'd just come out of my marriage and had my own gaff, so I had a couple of wild months there and that flat saw all sorts of activity. I was still really skint, but I found ways to get by, making a few quid here and there, doing small deals. We were still rehearsing hard with the band, at the rehearsal space next to the bare-knuckle fighters, and trying to get more gigs and get noticed.

That's when I first met Mark Berry – Bez. I'd heard about him before and people kept telling me I should meet him, then one day a kid I knew called Minny, who did a bit of wheeling and dealing, was dropping something off at the flat and Bez was with him in the car. I knew him by reputation, as he had just done a short term in Strangeways Youth for stealing. I didn't want him coming in the flat because I didn't want any more dodgy characters hanging around as I was selling a bit of gear. But we exchanged a brief hello that day. Then, shortly after, we met properly, really got on, and pretty quickly started hanging out and spending a lot of time together. Bez is Bez, you know. He's a maniac. He's a force of nature and creates chaos everywhere he goes. But there's a very likeable side to him, and he's great company, especially if you're going out getting wasted.

Bez started crashing round at my flat and so did Our Paul. Sometimes the only thing we could afford to get a buzz off was a tube of gas. Then someone told us about these sleeping pills and downers that you could get on prescription from the doctor, so we did quite a few of those, because they were free. It was pretty easy to get them from the doctor. Listen, if you were on the dole, living in a shit-hole of a dirty flat in Salford in the early 80s and went to your doctor and told him you were depressed, he wasn't going to question it, was he? Anyone could get depressed in that situation. I don't really look back on that really skint period through rose-tinted glasses. Some of the prescription drugs were quite trippy, and one of them literally sent you to sleep for a couple of days. We would sometimes take those if it was a couple of days before our dole was due, just so we could wake up a couple of days later when we would have some money.

When we did go out, me and Bez would often walk in to the Haçienda from Boothstown, which is about eight miles. We would set off in the afternoon and stop off at the pubs on the way. We had a scam going, which I'm not proud of. We would get chatting to birds at a pub table. Bez would chat them up, while I slipped my shoes off and got their purses out of their handbags with my toes. I would take the money out of their purses and then sneak them back into their handbags. I would try and make sure they had enough money left to get a taxi home, but it's still not something I'm proud of.

Around this time I started seeing a girl called Susan Bradbury, Suzy. I had first met Suzy when she was going out with one of my mates, Si Davis, who worked in Oasis. They would come down to the early youth club gigs and to watch us practise, and then when they split up I ended up with her. Suzy was great – she was really cool. She was blonde and she looked Swedish, or like a Dutch porn star. She worked as a secretary at some place on an industrial estate, and after we started seeing each other she moved into my flat in Boothstown. Bez and Our Paul had been crashing there a lot, but they had to get out then, although Bez was still round there quite a bit. He had a flat in Eccles that his grandparents were paying for, to help him back on his feet after he'd got out of Strangeways. Because I had Suzy living with me, I used to say, 'Come on, Bez, you've got to get off.' But to get home he had to walk down a really long road, which was pretty deserted, and if we'd been tripping and watching vampire films or something he wouldn't want to go home, because he'd be shitting it walking down that road, thinking that vampires were coming to get him. We were doing a lot of acid then. A lot of microdots. I remember watching *Watership Down* one day on acid, and both of us ended up crying.

Eventually, Mike Pickering at Factory heard our first demo through Phil Saxe. He says now that I sound quite different on it, a bit like Feargal Sharkey. That's probably because I was still trying to impersonate Ian Curtis a bit. We'd only done about five or six gigs at that stage, but through Mike we were invited to play a battle of the bands at the Haçienda. That was the very first time Bez ever got on stage with Happy Mondays. I remember saying to him, 'Just get up on stage and do what you're doing.' He would be in front of the stage or the side of the stage anyway, so I just told him to get up there with us. I knew we needed something else in the band. We were sounding better and starting to write some half-decent songs, but I knew there was something missing. This kid was a character. Bez was into his drugs and his music, and I needed a sidekick on stage. I've never run about on stage – I've always been pretty static, and the rest of the band were hardly very rock 'n' roll in their performance.

Bez didn't invent his way of dancing when he got up on stage with the Mondays that night. That's just how Bez dances.

That's how he's always danced. That's how he walks. He would dance like that all the time, even if he was in a gaff that was just playing cheesy chart music. He would dance like that when he was straight, if he was ever straight. Gaz Whelan got it – he understood. I think the rest of the lads just thought it looked ridiculous. But after that night Bez was in the band.

Mike Pickering was really into the Mondays. He got us more than other people on Factory at first. And he understood Bez. The other Factory directors, Wilson, Alan Erasmus and Rob Gretton (New Order's manager and Pickering's best mate), had pretty much given him licence to sign any band he really believed in, so he was pretty key to us joining Factory. Wilson also wanted us on the label, but at first that was more about him being into the fact that we were a gang of working-class lads from Salford than about the actual music. There was no big signing session when we joined, because there was nothing to sign – Factory didn't do contracts. It wasn't like joining a major label. But it was a massive deal to us, even though, in a way, nothing much changed and it only seemed real when we released a record.

Early on we played a gig in Leeds, supporting New Order, and it kicked off. Loads of Leeds fans turned up at the gig and started giving it out. I'm on stage singing, and these Leeds lot are all right in front of me, and they're all pointing at my trainers and laughing. I was wearing a pair of white Adidas with blue stripes; I can't remember what they're called. They'd only cost me £12, but they sell them now as Adidas Originals at £70 or something. But basically I had all these Leeds lot laughing at me, but they were all wearing Doc shoes and stuff like that, so I just thought, 'And you're laughing at me, you cunts?' One of them jumped on stage and Bez just laid into him.

We did end up making friends with some of the Leeds lot later, and some of them ended up in a band called the Bridewell Taxis after seeing us. (Bridewell Taxis was the nickname for the police vans that would nick people in Leeds.) They were just football heads who then decided to get into being in a band, and they supported us when we played Leeds Warehouse in 1989.

We didn't get an advance or anything when we joined Factory, but we really tried to keep our noses clean and stay out of trouble. Which wasn't easy, because we were so skint and there was a temptation to try and make some money on the side. You never want to get caught when you're up to something, but once we were with Factory we really did think we had a chance and we thought it would be over if we got nicked, so we were on best behaviour. People would ask me to look after stuff for them. They would give us a bit of money to look after a nine bar of weed for a bit, or give us a few grams of heroin and say, 'Try and sell that if you can.' They knew damn well I'd end up taking some of it and then owe them money and have to sell some heroin for them to pay them back. I'd stick the heroin out of sight in the loft, but then I'd have a few drinks and end up tapping into it anyway.

After we joined Factory, Tony Wilson would phone up my flat and ask us to come into town to drop him off some coke or some weed. He wasn't a big cokehead, Tony, but he did like a smoke. He generally kept his distance from us at first, though. I think the Stockholm Monsters had frightened him to death a bit, so he kept away from us. The Stockholm Monsters were a bit like us, really – just a bunch of lads. The bass player was a grafter from Blackley and a mate of Antony Murray, or Muzzer, who later became our tour manager and a best mate of mine.

Pretty soon after we joined Factory we were given a couple of dates supporting New Order. I think Mike Pickering organized that with Rob Gretton, their manager and Factory director, because they were best mates and sharing a flat at the time in Rusholme Gardens.

When we first went out with New Order I loved being on a big stage with a decent PA. We supported them on two dates – at Maxwell Hall in Salford, which is part of Salford University, and at Macclesfield Leisure Centre. We'd only done about six or seven gigs and we were supporting fucking New Order. It didn't feel like we weren't ready. We were living our dream, so we just went out there and did our best. We always got a decent reception wherever we played with New Order, because a lot of the people who came were fans of Factory in general, so they were intrigued and wanted to check us out because we were the new band on the label. New Order had just finished *Low-Life*, which is maybe not their best album, although it did open with 'Love Vigilantes', which is a great song.

It didn't bother me, making that step up to bigger venues with New Order; in fact I much preferred playing on a proper stage, with a larger gap between you and the audience. Once you start doing venues of that size, everything becomes a bit removed. I prefer playing bigger venues really, because when you're on stage it doesn't seem real. Playing small, intimate venues is more real to me and much more like proper, hard rock 'n' roll work – venues like Corbieres, a small cellar bar in Manchester, or Hull Adelphi, which was basically two terraced houses knocked through, and you were actually playing in the front room. In tiny venues like that there's no stage and the audience is literally a foot away, staring at you. That's hard work. That's where you learn your craft, doing those tiny venues, that's what beats you into shape as a band. I find playing the Manchester Evening News Arena or the O2 or somewhere much easier. When you're thirty feet up in the air on stage it seems more showbiz, so you don't feel a dick being rock 'n' roll. I don't care if there are 15,000 or 17,000 people out there. That doesn't bother me; it's not an issue. It's more scary when you've got 150 or 170 people in a small room, right up to you, in your face, when you're trying to be rock 'n' roll. I can see why punters like those intimate gigs, obviously, and if I could go and see the Rolling Stones play a tiny venue like that it would be fucking brilliant. I understand that. But actually playing small gigs like that myself I find terrifying.

After the New Order support gigs we went in to record our debut single, 'Delightful', for Factory. We recorded it at Strawberry Studios with Mike Pickering producing. I like Mike and I think he really did get the Mondays, but for me that recording session just didn't work. Looking back, I don't think we were nearly ready to record. It wasn't Mike's fault. We didn't know how the recording process worked and we didn't understand what a producer did, really; I just thought a producer recorded you. If you'd shown me a mixing desk back then, I'd have thought it was something you cut sheet metal on.

I was a bit disappointed with 'Delightful' because I was hoping it would turn out a bit spacier, and a bit dancier. I was after more of a looser new wave dance sound, like Mike's band Quando Quango. It turned out too fast. We sound like we're nervous or have taken too much speed. It was probably partly my fault. I didn't think we were ready so I just didn't want to be there. I can be quite difficult in a situation like that, a bit like I was on *Yes Please!*, the final album before the Mondays split up, years later.

The other two tracks on the EP, which we called *Forty Five EP*, were 'Oasis' and 'This Feeling'. 'Oasis' was named after the clothing store in Manchester where our friend Si Davis worked, and I ripped a few lines from Tom Jones's 'It's Not

Unusual' as well, although when we re-recorded it for our debut album later, we left those out. 'This Feeling' was a slower, more jangly number, which sounded a bit like Orange Juice, a band that we liked.

After getting their graphic design degrees from Salford Tech, Our Matt and Pat had moved to London for a bit, but they'd moved back to Manchester the previous year to start their own company, called Central Station Design, with Pat's girlfriend Karen Jackson. We got them to design the cover artwork for the EP, which was quite minimal, with green hills, blue sky and a couple of birds flying. They went on to design all the Mondays and Black Grape artwork over the years, but it would usually be much brighter and bolder than this first cover.

By this point we had started rehearsing in the Boardwalk, on Little Peter Street, not far from the Haçienda. It hadn't quite opened as a venue by that stage, but there were several rehearsal rooms there, and lots of Manchester bands have been through over the years. Oasis rehearsed there for a couple of years, before they were signed. When we moved in we took over the room that Simply Red had just moved out of. They were kicked out for various things, like putting plastic cups in the pockets of the pool table to stop the balls going down so they could get free games. This was just before they had their hit with 'Money's Too Tight (To Mention)'. Quite soon after they left the Boardwalk that single went massive.

Next door to us were the Jazz Defektors and when we recorded ourselves in there you could sometimes pick up their sort of acid jazz in the background, which I quite liked. James were upstairs and they were slightly separate from the other bands because they had 'Hymn from a Village' out and they were doing quite well. We were quite into James at the time. I thought they looked all right, with the side parting and stuff;

they had a slight Perry Boy thing going on – not Tim Booth the singer, but the rest of the lads. A Certain Ratio (ACR) were across the road, and we got on with them quite well. But generally, we didn't really knock about or socialize with too many other bands, as a lot of them were just studenty types in long macs and we just didn't mix with those type of people.

In September we played the Cumberland Suite in Belle Vue stadium with a few of the Manchester bands we did get on with, including ACR, Inca Babies, Kalima and the Jazz Defektors. That was the same venue that I'd seen the Buzzcocks at a few years previously, when I threw a pint pot at Wilson.

Another Manchester band we really did get on with was the Weeds, which was Andrew Berry's band. Andy – who was an old schoolmate of Johnny Marr of the Smiths – and Nick from the Weeds were hairdressers from the salon in the basement of the Haçienda called Swing. I think Andy did all the Smiths' haircuts in the early days. They completely changed my opinion of hairdressers, because they were just normal lads, and before that we had a really clichéd view of male hairdressers. We played Corbieres with the Weeds, which was a top gig.

At the end of 1985 we supported New Order again at the Haçienda and it was a great gig for us. I always found Bernard Sumner the most sociable one of New Order when we got to know them a bit, but I was never one who would bang on about New Order and Joy Division to him, so maybe he appreciated that. Hooky never liked us at first, as people; he hated us. We were just a bunch of scruffy, thieving cunts as far as he was concerned, and he thought that if he let us near their dressing room someone's handbag would get robbed. Never mind that he's from Salford, and his mam and dad still lived in Little Hulton. Or maybe that was why he didn't trust us: he'd grown up with kids like us, so he knew what we were like. Like I said before, we never got a negative reaction from the crowd when we supported New Order. The only negative reaction I got was from Hooky. At the Haçienda gig they had a rider and we didn't, and I was hungry. I thought, 'I'll be polite here,' and asked if I could get a drink and a sandwich from their rider and Hooky said, 'No . . . no you can't.' I thought, 'If you weren't in New Order I'd poke your eye out, you cheeky cunt.' I know Hooky well now and he'd be the first to admit he didn't like us initially. After we released our second album, *Bummed*, and it did well and we started to take off, he accepted us as musicians, but before that to him we were just a bunch of pain in the arse, scruffy, robbing bastards.

At the start of January 1986, I remember going down to the Haçienda for Bernard Sumner's thirtieth, which was a good night. I was only twenty-three, so thirty seemed a long, long way off to me. Thirty seemed really ancient. I remember saying to him that night, 'Fucking hell, thirty! That's *proper old*, you know what I mean?' Bernard just turned to me and said, 'You'll never reach fucking thirty!'

Terry Hall, from the Specials and Fun Boy Three, was also at that Haçienda New Order gig. Terry is a massive Manchester United fan. He was spending a lot of time in Manchester then and had a new band called the Colourfield. He must have thought we were okay, because he ended up inviting us to go on tour with them as support. We set off in the February. This was really good for us, as it was the first time we had been on a proper tour and it was good to see how professional the Colourfield were. I got on well with Terry Hall, and we were all massive fans of the Specials and Fun Boy Three. It was a bit of an eye-opener to me, personally, to see how Terry commanded the stage and the audience. He is actually a pretty shy guy when you meet him, but when he gets up on stage he's great. He doesn't put on a show, there's no posturing, but he really knows how to work a crowd. It showed me a different approach to being a front man – I could see that you didn't have to be prancing about and making a dick of yourself.

After the Colourfield tour we went in to record our second single, 'Freaky Dancin''. We initially tried recording with Vini Reilly, from the Durutti Column, but that only lasted about two hours before he decided he couldn't handle us. I like Vini, and he's a great guitarist, but he's a bit of a weird one and everyone knows he's a bit fragile. He once told everyone that I'd spiked him at the Haçienda, and the next morning I got phone calls from Wilson and other people at Factory, having a go at me, saying stuff like, 'Why did you do that to poor Vini? You know what he's like,' when I hadn't even fucking done anything. It was all in his mind.

Bernard Sumner ended up producing 'Freaky Dancin'' in the end, and he did a really decent job of it. Obviously we were big fans of Joy Division and New Order, but I also really liked Marcel King's 'Reach for Love', which Bernard had produced with Donald Johnson. It came out on Factory in 1984, but didn't really do anything, which was a real shame. Marcel had been in Sweet Sensation when he was young, who were kind of Manchester's answer to that Philly sound, and had a No. 1 with 'Sad Sweet Dreamer', but he ended up homeless, sleeping rough in his car in Moss Side. He died in 1995 of a brain haemorrhage, and then his son Zeus was shot dead in a gang feud. I thought 'Reach for Love' was a bit of a lost classic, and years later I ripped a bit of it for 'Get Higher' on the second Black Grape album, in the hope that people would go back and discover the original.

With 'Freaky Dancin'', Bernard managed to capture the dance element of the Mondays that Mike Pickering had some-how missed. I thought it came out much better than 'Delightful', but again, I don't think that was Mike Pick's fault; we were probably a better and tighter band by then, and had more of an idea about the recording process. Bernard captured that looser, dancier feel that we had when we played live, and when he caught me on tape going 'Ready? Right, we're ready . . .' he even kept that on the intro. People obviously presume that 'Freaky Dancin'' is about Bez, especially after he called his book *Freaky Dancin'*, but if anything it's about being on acid. The opening lyrics, 'You don't like that face because the bones stick out', are about looking in the mirror when you're tripping and thinking your face looks all misshapen with bones sticking out.

The B-side is 'The Egg', which had been on our quite early demos, including the one I think Mike Pickering first heard. The famous story of that recording was Bernard chucking away his Chinese takeaway and me and Bez fishing it out of the bin and eating it. Which, unlike a lot of Mondays myths, is actually true. There was nothing wrong with Bernard's Chinese, and we were skint and starving at the time.

That summer saw the Festival of the Tenth Summer. This was a big deal for Factory, because it was the tenth anniversary of the Sex Pistols playing the Lesser Free Trade Hall in 1976, which Wilson and the rest saw as the Big Bang for Manchester music or something, because Wilson, Joy Division, Morrissey, Mark E. Smith and even Mick Hucknall had all been there and had all gone off and formed bands afterwards. We played at Rafters with Easterhouse and the Weeds as part of the festival, which I just remember as being a real sweaty gig. The big gig of the festival was at the G-Mex Centre, with New Order and the Smiths. We didn't get tickets for the G-Mex, but I don't even think we asked for them. We were still the new boys at Factory then. We only really became fully accepted at Factory when the E thing took off.

*

We got an opposite reaction in London in the early days. In Manchester we weren't like any other band, but they occasionally saw people like us on the street and would cross the road to avoid us. In London they had never seen anything like us. When we first went down to meet Dave Harper, who was the first guy doing our press, we all drove down in the back of a transit and he'd never seen anything like it. He even got a photographer to take a picture of us in the back of the van, and then instead of putting out a press release he just recorded us arguing in his office and sent a transcript of that out to journalists.

Jeff Barrett, who later started Heavenly Records, worked at Creation Records at the time, doing their press, but was also putting on his own gigs in London and he booked us for quite a few of our early gigs down there. We called him Foxhead or Lionhead, because he looked like a big friendly lion with his mane of red hair and his freckles – a bit like the lion from *Wizard of Oz*. Lionhead was sound and really got the Mondays straight away; he totally understood where we were coming from, and in his eyes we were the most important new band around. I know that because he used to tell us.

The first gig he got us in London was supporting the Weather Prophets in Hammersmith. When I look back at a band like the Weather Prophets, it reminds me what we had in the Mondays, what we had built up over the years, and what the rest of the band threw away so lightly when the Mondays ended. The Weather Prophets didn't make it, but they were a great band. They wrote far better songs than I could at the time. They were another of those bands that Our Paul would go on about: 'We should be more like the Weather Prophets. You should write songs more like that.' They could really play, but when I compared them to us I could also see early doors that success wasn't just about the music. I could see we had something that they didn't, even though they were better musicians. I understood that from the start. If it was just about the music, we would have never made it.

We didn't have a big entourage at that time. There was probably us and about three or maybe four of our pals. Later on, when the E came in, there would be a lot of lads at our gigs, but they weren't necessarily people who travelled with us. They would just turn up wherever we were playing. Our pals would get about all over the place. A lot of them were robbers, sneak thieves, grafters or ticket touts. They would be in town anyway, working, and would just tip up at the gig.

Thanks largely to Lionhead, we were almost getting bigger crowds in London than in Manchester at that stage. He put us on a couple of times upstairs at a pub called the Black Horse in Camden. It wasn't even a gig venue; it had no stage, it was just a pub room with a carpet, and we had to play in front of a fireplace and a glass cage with a stuffed heron in it. Those gigs were all hard work. I had no choice but to connect with the audience. But we were off our nuts and got into it.

During those early Mondays gigs the band could always start a song together. 'One, two, three, four . . .' and off they went. But they could never stop – they could never get the timing right to end a song together. So a song that was only supposed to be three minutes long could go on for fifteen minutes. They'd all be looking at each other, looking for a sign from someone else, looking for someone to take the lead. Then Gaz would put another drum roll in, thinking if he did that the band would stop, but two of the others might think that roll meant carry on a bit more, so then they're back into another verse, even though there isn't another verse. I'd get really angry and turn round and start shouting at them over the music, but they would all have dead serious faces on, concentrating, especially if they were on speed. So I'd have to adlib another verse from somewhere, or end up throwing in some lyrics from a song that was out at the time, like 'She's Crafty' by the Beastie Boys.

Some of our songs were even born out of those gigs when I was forced to freestyle vocals. Sometimes my brain was at its best and most inventive when I was off my nut and just adlibbing, and we would record most of those gigs on the mixing desk. If Gaz and Our Paul were still carrying on, Mark would start playing some new guitar line over the top and if it sounded good I'd give him the nod to carry on and then I would start freestyling along with it. If I still thought something sounded good, then we would listen back to the recording of the gig afterwards, and perhaps try and work out what we'd played and work on it in rehearsals.

In August 1986 we supported Julian Cope at the Boardwalk. What an arsehole. He behaved like such a prick that we promised ourselves that when we became a headline act we would always make sure our support bands got a decent sound-check and we would never treat them like Julian Cope treated us that night. He said, 'Who do they think they are, the fuck-ing Undertones?' because we all had anoraks and cagoules on. The cheeky bastard. He fannied about with this stupid micro-phone stand he had that he could climb on and spin round like a performing monkey for about five hours, which meant we got less than five minutes to soundcheck. We were stood there glar-ing at him, thinking, 'Come on, you prick, fucking move, or we'll move you!' He was really lucky we didn't batter him.

We did get our first national press that autumn, when Dave Haslam did a piece on us with the Railway Children and the Weeds. Colin Sinclair managed the Railway Children and I think because we'd started having a bit of success or attention as a group of Manc-y lads, he decided he wanted a Happy Mondays-type band. I didn't really know them, but they didn't seem to be anything like us. As soon as Colin Sinclair got hold of them, he got them little two-seater MG sports cars because his dad had an MG dealership or something. They had joined Factory, but that didn't get them any money, although they maybe had also signed a publishing deal. I know for a fact when we played Finsbury Park the following year the Railway Children were pushed up the bill, past us, and we were pushed down. At that stage, a lot of people, including Wilson, thought they were going to be bigger than us, but I never thought that. When it came down to playing their instruments and crafting songs, actual songwriting, they were probably better at that than us at that stage. But even though what they were doing sounded better on record, or at least it was more together, it wasn't my cup of tea. When it came to watching a live band, even though they could play better, we were far more happening. It just didn't happen for them.

One of the good things about being an underdog is that you can never come out looking shit, can you? Happy Mondays were the underdogs right from the start. We were like the runts of the litter, the scruffy bad lads, and I've been the underdog ever since. I much prefer it that way. I liked being the underdog.

At the end of October, we were playing a gig at Blackburn King Georges Hall with ACR and the Railway Children which turned into a riot. A load of Blackburn youth turned up, and when we were playing one of them jumped on the stage and started giving Nazi salutes, so Bez smacked him one in the mouth. Next thing, loads of them jumped on stage, so all the band jumped in, hitting them with guitars and anything we could get our hands on. That was it then. The whole hall went up, and everyone was at it. I think most of the windows got smashed. We managed to get off stage in the end, but the place got trashed. The police arrived. Bez got nicked on stage and was took off, and I think they even had riot shields. That was quite a night. We would never go out to cause trouble like that, but wherever we were, if some idiot started something, then we wouldn't back down.

Even though we had gigged quite a bit by that stage, I still had a bit of stage fright. Until a couple of years ago I had never done a show without being on some sort of drug, or completely pissed. Not that you could always tell. Sometimes I would be completely hammered but able to keep it together so that other people thought I was straight as fuck. Later on, I dealt with the nerve thing through gear. The success was exactly what we wanted, and you think you know what you're getting into and that's what you want, but dealing with it is another matter. I just went into my shell with gear to deal with it, and all nerves disappeared then.

It sounds a weird thing for a lead singer to say, but I never really liked being the centre of attention. Part of the reason for getting Bez in, I suppose, was deflecting a bit of attention from me. It doesn't really bother me much nowadays, it's fine, but I've only recently become more comfortable with it, in the last couple of years, or even the last year. I don't know why it doesn't bother me now – I just woke up one day and it was fine. You can't always explain these things.

It wasn't until I reached my forties that I became more comfortable with being me, with being Shaun Ryder. I like doing what I do, and I don't mind doing interviews and stuff, but I don't like the attention being on me. So in some ways, I'm in the wrong fucking game.

CHAPTER FOUR

'Everybody on this stagecoach likes robbin' and bashin' . . . big blags abroad and smoking large amounts of hash'

When Factory decided it was time for us to record our debut album in 1986, it was Tony Wilson who first suggested the idea of using John Cale as the producer. Tony had always loved the production that John had done on Patti Smith's debut album, *Horses*, a decade earlier. John had also played at the Festival of the Tenth Summer that Factory had organized in Manchester earlier in the year, so there was a connection between him and the label. Tony also liked the idea of a member of the Velvet Underground producing Happy Mondays, for obvious reasons. He thought that would make a good story or publicity angle. As a band, we were all really into the idea, because we were big fans of the Velvets. I think Bernard Sumner was mooted as a possible producer as well, after we had worked with him on 'Freaky Dancin'', but I don't know how serious an idea that was, because Bernard didn't want to become a full-time producer.

What we didn't realize before we went into the studio with John was that he had just got himself totally clean and off the drugs. I don't think he was even smoking weed at the time; he just used to eat tangerines all day. So it was quite a straight recording session – it wasn't as if we were partying together. I don't think we really got to know each other during the recording, because he didn't show any emotion. We would argue amongst ourselves, but we were dead polite to him and he never raised his voice with us. I could never really be sure if he thought we were quite interesting, or if he just tolerated us.

Factory had booked us in for a fortnight at the Fire House studio in London to record the album, and we already had all the songs written by the time we went down there. I had spent more time writing and arranging the songs than I had when we went in to record 'Delightful' and 'Freaky Dancin'', and was more confident about their structure. As a band we also had a little bit more of an idea about the recording process this time, although we were still relative strangers to a recording studio. It was our debut album, so it was our first proper length of time in a studio; we'd previously only been in for a couple of days at a time.

We were still pretty skint when we went down to London to record, because we had been trying to stay out of trouble, keep our noses clean and really concentrate on the band and finish writing the songs for the album. Only Mark Day, who was still a postie, had a job; the rest of us were all on the dole. Factory had packed us off to London and said, 'There's eighty pounds each. That will last you two weeks.' I think my £80 lasted me an hour. Literally. It just went. It's £80, isn't it? Even then that wasn't a lot of dough. Factory had put us up in Belsize Park, in one of those big houses around there that are split into bedsits. The whole band – me, Our Kid, Bez, Mark Day, Paul Davis and Gaz Whelan – were all staying in one room which had six beds squeezed into it, and it wasn't a big room. On the floor above us were six builders and up above them were six electricians.

We all had to share the same khazis and showers. Two khazis and two showers between eighteen of us. We were just on nodding terms with the builders and electricians; we never really got talking to them, so they didn't know we were musicians. They probably thought we were just workers or grafters like them. It was hardly the most rock 'n' roll accommodation. God knows who found that place. Phil Saxe probably.

Because we were struggling for money, everyone in the band would be borrowing off each other, and a few times we ran out completely and had either to get someone to come down from Manchester with some money or get a friend to send some cash. We were starving at some points, we were so skint. Mark Day was the worst in that situation, because he was so tight – he was notorious for it. He wouldn't lend you a quid or even fifty pence. When we had money in our pockets, we would buy him a pint, or say, 'What you eating Mark? D'you want fish 'n' chips?' But if he had money and he had to get you a pint he would say, 'You owe me one pound twenty.' 'Shout us a fish 'n' chips, Mark?' 'That's two pound eighty.' He was one of them, a tight bastard. We would be starving and penniless and ask Mark if he had money, but he'd say, 'No, I'm skint too.' Then he would sneak off later and we would find him, after he'd swore blind that he was skint, sat in a café tucking into a full meal. He'd try and justify it by saying, 'You lot just spend all your money as soon as you get it!' and I'd say, 'Yeah, mate, but you know what, you help us smoke and snort our money, don't you? You don't say fucking no when we offer you a line or a pint or pay for your food!'

We had loads of arguments and fights with each other during the recording. I had a punch-up or two with Gaz, and my finger is still bent from when I hit him during one of our scraps. I punched him on the side of the head and broke my finger and never bothered getting it fixed. The amount of times I've had fights over the years and I've broken a toe kicking someone or something and haven't noticed until the effects of the drugs have worn off. Me and Our Kid would fight a lot. We would fight when we were kids, but healthily. It's your brother – you're going to fight, aren't you?

I don't think we took any smack to London, because we were skint, but I was definitely dabbling a bit at that stage. Bez was another one of those who dipped in and out of it for years. He was what I would call a garbagehead then. He was addicted to drugs, but not one particular drug, just drugs in general. He would have a little dabble in heroin, but never get addicted, then go on to whizz, then go on to coke, then go on to the E, then go on to whatever, then go on to that, then go on to that . . . he never stuck with one particular drug, he just kept moving from one to another. Bez will quite proudly say, 'I'm not addicted,' but I would argue he is. He's just not addicted to one particular substance.

When we started recording, it didn't seem to matter that John Cale was classically trained and we weren't, or at least we didn't notice it being an issue. The band were getting more and more proficient, and anything that he asked us to play, we managed to play. We had all the songs written, and what John did do was drill the band and get us really tight, then he basically recorded us like we were live. If anything, I think he made the band too tight. We were definitely better and more proficient after working with him, but the detrimental effect of that was that the recording lost a little of that signature space in the songs that was really important to the Mondays sound.

The title of the opening track, 'Kuff Dam', was taken from a porno called *Mad Fuck*, but I just misspelt it backwards. It was a ballsy, bolshy opening track: 'If you've got to be told by some-one then it's got to be me'. There were some lyrics on there that

I wouldn't dare use now, like 'Jesus was a **** and never helped you with a thing that you do, or you done', but I just didn't care then. My mam was religious but wouldn't say anything to me about something like that; she'd just shrug and let it wash over her.

'Tart Tart', which became the single, was the first track we recorded that I felt truly captured the essence and potential of the Mondays sound. To me, in a way, everything we had recorded before was really just us finding our feet as a band, feeling our way, getting used to the recording process and working out how we could best capture our own sound. It was named after a bird we knew from Chorlton called Dinah, who we affectionately nicknamed Tart Tart. She was older than us, well into her thirties when we met her, while we were only in our early twenties. She had been on the scene in the very late 60s and was still around and dealing speed on the music scene over fifteen years later. She would always be there when we played the Boardwalk in the early days. She took a bit of a shine to me and Bez and was very good to us, letting us crash at her place if we needed to and laying speed on tick for us. One day a guy we knew called Martin, a roadie who lived in Chorlton who also used to score whizz off her and knew her quite well, popped round to her flat and there was no answer. Because he was quite close to her, he suspected something was up, so he broke in and found her body. Poor Tart Tart had just had a brain haemorrhage and died. So I named the song after her, but it isn't all about her, although she is there in the lyrics – 'TT, she laid it on, and a few days later she's gone, going back to the womb, to get drowned, drowned, drowned, drowned, drowned.'

Most of my songs aren't specifically about one person or one thing. I would come up with snippets of stories, or what you would call vignettes, about different situations I'd witnessed, or people I knew, or tales I'd been told, and then I would string them together to make a song. 'Tart Tart' is a typical example of that. 'When he came out of the locker, he said I'm looking for something better, so he made a shock announcement' was about a pal of ours. 'Martin sleeps on a desk, he wears a sleeping bag as his vest' is a reference to the Factory producer Martin Hannett. We hadn't actually worked with him at this stage, but I'd heard stories about him. 'He says don't know if I should, cos I worry too much about the test on the blood' was a little nod to a pal of ours who had been diagnosed HIV+ through intravenous drug use. I think he was the first person we knew who was diagnosed with it. So I would bring together that mish-mash of ideas or little situations to create a song. That's the way I almost always work when I'm writing lyrics. It's not quite as abstract as 'I Am the Walrus', but it does mean people often put their own interpretations to the lyrics.

If I was interviewed back then, depending on what mood I was in, I might say a song was about something more specific, about this or that, when it wasn't really. Sometimes the songs were a little more abstract or surreal, just words that sounded good and created a good visual image in my brain when I was stringing them together. Half the time I was more concerned with how the words sounded than with what they actually meant.

''Enery' is a little more specific, as it's pretty much about sexually transmitted diseases – 'Pass your germ, pass your bug'. At the time I wrote that, Bez and Our Paul were crashing at my flat and there were a lot of sexually transmitted diseases passed on, so it would have been at the forefront of my mind. There were a number of girls we hung about with at this time. They weren't necessarily groupies, they were just part of your extended social group, and at that age almost everyone ends up shagging each other. The worst STD I picked up was a few months after we recorded the album, when I got this huge genital wart that was almost the size of a throat lozenge and I ended up having to go to the clap clinic in town to have it seen to.

There was one song that I didn't have lyrics or a title for when we went in to record. A lot of the time when the band were jamming at rehearsals I just used to make up words to go along with the tune, and then later I'd work them out in my head and eventually write them down and arrange them, and possibly find similar words or phrases that fitted the song better to make sense of it. When we were in the studio I was reading a book about horoscopes by Russell Grant which someone had lent me, and when we were recording this one particular song I didn't have lyrics for, I just picked up the book and started singing what was written on the back cover: 'Hold on to your hats, this is the book that you've been waiting for, the book that tells you everything you need to know to help you understand, not only the one you love, but yourself too . . .' I just read it word for word off the back cover, and managed to make it fit with the tune. I thought about changing some of the words, but it actually fitted so well, I thought, 'Fuck, why do I need to write words? We'll just have that and call it "Russell".' Which is what we did. I don't think Russell Grant knows he was the inspiration for an early Mondays song. Ironically, I think that was the only time I didn't get any abuse from Our Paul, who would sometimes have a bit of a downer on my lyrics when we finished a song.

I never used to read anyone else's lyrics for inspiration. I would listen out for lyrics in songs, but, you know how it is, no matter how much you think you've heard the words correctly, when you see them written down you realize you've been singing the wrong fucking words for twenty-five years. I do have a bit of attention deficit disorder as well, so I have to try really hard to concentrate and focus if I'm listening to lyrics. Otherwise I'll find myself drifting off and following the bass line instead.

'Olive Oil' is named after Gaz Whelan's girlfriend at the time. Again, it's not about her; it's just named after her. Just before we wrote it, we had all been away to Rhyl for a few days, taking acid, and while we were there Olive Oil just came straight out with it and asked, 'Will you write a song about me?' I don't really write songs like that, so I said, 'No, but I'll name one after you if you want.'

That was a mad few days in Rhyl. There was a whole bunch of us who drove down, boys and girls, and stayed in a caravan for a few days. In those early days of the band we did all knock about together – or at least me, Our Kid, Gaz Whelan, Paul Davis and Bez did. Not Mark Day so much. But the other five of us were all really good pals and hung about together as well as being in the band. In Rhyl there was me, Our Kid, Paul Davis, Gaz Whelan and Tall Minny (I knew two Minnys – so one was Short Minny and one was Tall Minny), plus the birds. Bez wasn't with us for some reason. We all stayed in one caravan, and we took a load of acid down with us. I'm pretty sure everyone was tripping, although maybe not every single one of the girls was.

I can remember, really clearly, tripping on acid when we were driving down to Rhyl, and I could see myself on the bonnet of the car. We took turns in driving, so I was either in the driving seat or the passenger seat, and I kept seeing myself stuck to the windscreen, with my face up against the glass, peering back into the car. I knew it was a trip, so I didn't freak out, but it was quite fucking weird seeing myself out there looking back at me.

I never did really freak out on acid. Some people are better at handling it than others. There was a space and time, around then, when me and Bez spent every day on acid for a good year.

Every day. It got to the stage where we were eating black microdots, which are quite strong acid, and they didn't even phase us any more. That was probably our drug of choice at the time, before the E arrived. We had been dropping acid since about 1980, but during that period, around 1986, we must have taken it daily.

I never had a really bad trip. I think you can bring bad trips on yourself, depending on how you react to the acid. I've got a pretty strong mind, so even when it was incredibly powerful acid and my whole world was completely taken over, when the real world disappeared and I was absolutely submerged in a complete cartoon existence, I was always able to say to myself, 'This is a trip.' I always, *always* had a strong enough mind to know what was happening. Even when the whole planet was one big cartoon and I looked up at the clouds and they had turned into great big Greek gods, who were climbing down out of the sky and talking to me – even then, I always had a strong enough mind, as did Bez, to say, 'No, this is just a trip, don't freak out.'

Me and Bez would trip together all the time, talking each other through it and walking all day and all night. We would walk everywhere. We would walk round town; we would go and sit in fields with horses and cows and sheep. We would even purposefully drop trips at eleven o'clock at night so that we could go out and explore throughout the dark night and still be out at the crack of the dawn. You would develop this night-time vision with weird trails and then BANG! it's daylight, and you're soaked in glorious technicolour. As dawn approached, we would be waiting for the sunrise, waiting for those colours to just overwhelm us.

We carried on doing that up until just before our second album, *Bummed*, really, until the E came in and took over. We weren't acid purists, though; we were garbageheads, as I said.

We'd do anything. If someone came along with some speed or heroin or whatever, we'd do it.

So 'Olive Oil' certainly wasn't about Gaz's girlfriend; it wasn't about anything in particular, although there are elements of the band in there – 'Everybody on this stagecoach likes robbin' and bashin' . . . big blags abroad and smoking large amounts of hash, that's sweet . . . the bigger the dream, the better the time.' In those early days, I was often just observing things that were going on around me and stringing bits together to make a song, which is why there are lots of in-jokes and references to people we knew. If something struck me, or if I was somewhere or with someone and something happened which I thought would translate well into lyrics, I would try and remember it through word association if I could. But if not, I would scribble it down on whatever was at hand – scraps of paper, beer mats or cigarette packets. Then when we were rehearsing and writing new songs at the Boardwalk, I would get all those scraps of paper and start piecing them together, and maybe try different snippets with different songs. Then when a song had started to form, I would write out the lyrics on a blank sheet of paper, and arrange those various scribbles and snippets into something more structured.

The original album had a track called 'Desmond' on it, which we had to take off after the initial pressings because someone at Factory got nervous that it was too close to 'Ob-La-Di Ob-La-Da' by the Beatles. I had ripped it a bit, nicked a bit of the melody, and the lyrics started 'Desmond did a tour in the market place', but apart from that it wasn't *that* similar. That's what I would call 'ripping' a record – that slight magpie approach which I had on some songs, where I might nick a bit of a vocal melody from one song, or reference a lyric from another. But they were never direct lifts or straight plagiarism; we always made the songs our own. I'm not sure if anyone even seriously complained about 'Desmond' to Factory; they were just being overly cautious. If it was a smash-hit single that topped the charts, then I'm sure someone would have taken issue with it, but it was just a vocal melody, almost in homage, on a record that was only going to sell a handful of copies in the bigger scheme of things. But certain people, usually lawyers, are overly cautious and paranoid. The same thing happened again with 'Lazyitis' on the second album, although we kept that on the record, but we credited Lennon/McCartney because the vocal melody and lyrics are ripped from 'Ticket to Ride'.

So after the initial pressings of the album, we replaced 'Desmond' with '24 Hour Party People'. That was another bit of a step up for us, songwriting-wise. Along with 'Tart Tart', it's one of the first signature songs to really capture the essence of Mondays. In particular, '24 Hour Party People' captured that dance side of the band that a lot of people had missed before then. We recorded it quite quickly at Suite Sixteen studios in Rochdale, with Dave Young, who had engineered the album sessions. I was happy with the lyrics, but I was never completely happy with the production. There were some really good elements to it, but there were some bits that I just couldn't stomach. We didn't quite nail it.

The full title of the album was *Squirrel and G-Man Twenty Four Hour Party People Plastic Face Carnt Smile (White Out)*, which I pieced together from a few different sources. 'Squirrel and G-Man' are PD's parents. His mum was called Squirrel, because she looked like a squirrel, and she chewed and ate like a squirrel, and his dad was G-Man because he was a high-ranking police officer. 'Twenty Four Hour Party People' was me and Bez and a few others. A lad we knew called Short Minny used to call us the Twenty Four Hour Party People, which is self-explanatory really. Then one day he came down to see us and we'd all done too much Charlie or whizz, and he said, 'Fucking hell, what's wrong with you lot? Plastic face, can't smile, white out!' I just pieced the whole thing together.

I was as happy as I could be with the album when we finished it, although I am always pretty hard on myself when it comes to songwriting, and I pick holes in any recording once it's finished. *Squirrel and G-Man* was definitely a big step up from our previous recordings, though. I think I only ever listened to it once. I was given a finished copy, I played it through, and I don't think I've ever listened to it again. I've never been one to sit at home and listen to our old albums. Back then I would always rather move on and think about the next thing. I was sent copies of *Bummed* and *Pills 'n' Thrills* when they were both reissued and repackaged in 2006. I don't think I had heard *Bummed* since it was released nearly twenty years previously. But I sat down and listened to it and thought, 'Fucking hell, this is all right, this album!'

'Tart Tart' was our first single, and we made our first promo video to go with it. It was directed by a Mancunian duo of film-makers, Keith Jobling and Phil Shotton, who called themselves the Bailey Brothers, and they went on to direct almost all of the Happy Mondays' videos. I really got on with them. I thought they were great, and I still see them from time to time. Keith now designs websites, and did a Mondays site for us a couple of years ago, after we re-formed. Phil is still involved in film and was working on something recently with Saltz, who used to be in the Jazz Defektors.

We shot the video at Strawberry Studios in Stockport. I had never really mimed before and I didn't want to mime in the video because I felt ridiculous. A lot of artists wouldn't mime back then, because they felt that real bands should sing live. Like miming was cheating. Bands like the Clash would refuse to do *Top of the Pops* because they would have to mime, so I got swept along in that kind of mood.

Anyway, I was uncomfortable miming because I felt I looked ridiculous, so I decided I would purposely mime out of time, which I thought would look cool. So that's what I did on the shoot and I was thinking to myself, 'Yeah, fuck that, I'm not miming. This will look *great*.' But when the video was finished and edited and I saw the final version, I thought, 'Fucking hell, that just looks shit. It's just unprofessional and crap.' It doesn't look like I'm doing it on purpose; it looks like I can't mime in time. I just look a bit of a goon. But I only made that mistake once. After seeing it I realized that I was wrong and by the time we had to film the video for '24 Hour Party People', which was the next single, I was into the idea.

'Tart Tart' was the first time we ever got on *The Chart Show*, which was a big thing for us. *The Chart Show* was on ITV on Saturday mornings and it was the only show on television at the time that showed the indie charts. That was our first experience of being on one of those shows. Nowadays there are hundreds of these chart-type shows and any two-bit band that's starting up can get their video on. But back then there was only *The Chart Show*, and to get on there on a Saturday morning as an indie band was brilliant. I remember being sat at home watching the indie chart run-down and there we were, Happy Mondays, which was great. That really did seem a big step for us.

The reviews we got for the album were all pretty positive. I don't think the Mondays ever got bad album reviews, or hardly ever, until the last album, *Yes Please!* When *Squirrel and G-Man* came out we also got our first front cover, from *Melody Maker*. That was a really big deal. It was only me and Bez on the cover, wearing anoraks with our hoods up, biting empty Budweiser cans. I remember going down to my local paper shop to buy *Melody Maker* that week and they didn't recognize me from the cover when I bought it, because you can't tell who it is, really, because we've got our hoods up. That was the photographer Tom Sheehan's idea. Halfway through the shoot he just said, 'Put your hoods up' and that's the shot they ended up using on the cover. It was the first hoodie cover as well, I suppose, because no one else was wearing their hoods up at the time. Factory actually framed the shot and had it hanging in the office for quite a while.

Of course, the rest of the band were pissed off that it was only me and Bez on the cover. But that wasn't our idea or decision; it was either *Melody Maker*'s or the photographer's. It certainly didn't come from the band or management. I always had a 'one for all and all for one' mentality when it came to the band, and so did Bez, so we didn't notice it at the time, but the rest of them would have loved to have been on that cover. The jealousy wasn't right in our faces, so we didn't clock it at the time, but looking back I think that's where it all started. That was the first time me and Bez were singled out from the rest of the group and treated differently. By the time we did become aware that there was resentment and jealousy, a few years later, it had already built up and built up and built up over the years. Don't forget that none of the rest of the band had been that keen on Bez joining in the first place – that was my idea.

A few months after the album was released we went to New York with Factory. It was our first time there, and first time in America, but we had no desire to go sightseeing or do any of the usual tourist things. The first thing me and Bez wanted to do when we landed was to get our hands on some crack. We wanted to sample it, we wanted to know how to make it, we wantedto know all about it.

We were met by a woman who was working for Factory in

New York, who we'd met before when she came over to Manchester, and I asked her to take me and Bez to an area where she knew we could score, but she wouldn't drive us all the way up there because it was too dangerous. She stopped her car a few blocks short and said, 'I'm not going any further up there in my car.'

Me and Bez carried on up, on foot, and met this black geezer on the street, who had this green army coat on, like an anorak without a hood. When you're looking for drugs, you generally know the score; you can weigh up the situation and tell who's dealing and what's what. You only have to look at the right person a certain way and you'll clock each other, and you've done the deal without even saying any words, just by eyeballs and movements. We got chatting to him and he told us he'd been in Vietnam, and he knew what we were after so he said, 'Come to my crib, man.' So we went to his crib, which was in the basement of a nearby building. He built the pipe for us and I went first. Bez was going, 'What's it like? What's it like? What's it like?' and I just went, 'Fuuucckin hell . . . fuuuuuccckkkininnnnnnn hhhhheelllllll . . . I'm going through fucking space,' and Bez was like, 'Lemme have a go! LEMME HAVE A GO!'

That's what that first hit felt like. It felt like going through space and the universe at a million miles an hour, 'Boooom!' It lived up to expectation and the hype. We'd read all the scare stories in the press: 'This new drug has hit in America, one hit and you're hooked', and the first hit was no disappointment. It did exactly what it said on the packet.

We then bought some rocks from this geezer. I think we paid $5 or $10 a stone, and we got about four each. But by the time we got back to the hotel we had smoked all of it. So we decided we had to go back and see the geezer to get some more. Unfortunately, we took a wrong turning and ended up in another part of the ghetto. It was now beginning to get dark, as it was about nine o'clock at night.

We met a different geezer, and we got the same look, the same vibe, and he comes over as Mr Friendly. He had the crack on him and gave it to us in these vials, and we just did the deal there on the street. After we left him, we stopped so I could skin up and were quickly surrounded by a bunch of street kids, about half a dozen of them, who were a bit younger than us, probably in their late teens. I was skinning up and Bez was talking to them, but when he's off his tits he sometimes sprays when he's talking. All of a sudden, this one guy, a scrawny, wild-eyed black kid, who was off his tits, shouts at me, 'You motherfucker, you spat at me, you asshole!' It obviously wasn't me, but I thought, 'I can't go it wasn't me, mate, it was Bez.' So I just said, 'Oh, sorry.' He looked a bit like the American rapper DMX and had a similar accent, and he then went, *'You just done it again you motherfucker!!'* So I just said, 'Sorry, mate, I didn't mean to.' But whatever I said didn't placate him. He must have known it wasn't me, because he was looking at me and my mouth was closed, while Bez was going ten to the dozen, 'feh feh feh feh!' Then this dude just went, *'You motherfucker!'* and he pulled out this fucking gun and stuck it right in my face. It all happened in a couple of seconds. I had a bottle of beer in my hand in a paper bag, and I just remember thinking, 'This is going to have to go in your face.' But just then, the first geezer we had met miraculously appeared from nowhere like some cracked-up black guardian angel and told this cunt to leave it out and put his gun away, that we're his people, we're with him and we're cool.

Looking back, I didn't have time to shit myself. You just react instinctively in situations like that. My thought process was really simple: 'He's pulling that gun and putting it in my face and he's going to let go . . . all I've got is this forty-ounce

bottle in my hand – it's going to have to connect in his face.'
There wasn't time to be scared, and the fact that I was cracked
up probably helped in a way.

We just brushed off the incident, and didn't really think
about how serious it was, and got out of there. We got back to
the hotel only to find that, after all that, the vials we'd bought
from the other kid were just full of polystyrene balls, the type
you get in a fucking beanbag or something.

It wasn't until the next day, when we got up and went for
something to eat, that it actually hit me – how close I had come
to getting my head shot off and my face blown apart, and I was
like, 'Fuck-ing hell.' We still went back down there to score
again, though.

We were staying at the Chelsea Hotel, which was Wilson's idea.
I didn't then know the full history of the Chelsea and everyone
who had stayed or lived there, but I obviously knew that Sid
and Nancy had lived there, and Nancy had died there.

We were in New York for five nights for one show, which
was on the second night. Me and Bez had already had a proper
bollocking off Wilson for what happened the first day. During
the afternoon of the second day we turned up to the Limelight,
where we were playing, and we met this really sexy older
woman. I was twenty-four at the time and she must have been
about thirty-eight. She was quite a classy woman, and she took
a liking to me and Bez and took us back to her apartment,
where we had some really, really strong coke. She was undressing and giving us the come on, making it absolutely
blatantly obvious that she wanted a threesome, but me and
Bez were so coked up that we physically weren't capable.
We didn't even try. She was doing all the trying and we
were just sat there, completely whacked out. It wasn't the
first time we had done coke, but this was nothing like the

coke we had taken back in Manchester; it was *proper* cocaine.

By the time of the gig the two of us looked like proper coke yetis. We were absolutely flying. Completely out of it and *looking* completely out of it. Sweating profusely, with eyes on stalks, thinking this is fucking great. We thought the gig was absolutely fantastic. Tony thought it was shit. He thought it was the worst gig we had ever done. The rest of the band were all wasted as well. PD had to play the gig lying down, he was so fucked. Phil Saxe and my dad had both come to New York with us, but that didn't curtail our behaviour one bit. Not for a minute. When we had first started out we wouldn't have really done drugs in front of my dad, but by the time we got to New York that had pretty much gone out of the window. We were all on crack or Charlie, and there was no way of disguising it.

I thought New York was fucking great. Don't forget, New York in 1987 was still dirty old New York, like it was in the 70s. In fact it was possibly even worse than the 70s in 1986, because it was at the height of the crack epidemic, so it was ultra-violent. It was pretty much still like Night of the fucking Living Dead back then. Nothing like the sanitized New York of today.

We didn't really do any sightseeing. The photographer Kevin Cummins was with us and wanted to take a picture of us for a Salfordians exhibition he had coming up, so we did go on the Staten Island ferry to do a shot with the New York skyline in the background, and this became quite an iconic photo. We also went shopping at Macy's, but that was about it. Looking for crack cocaine was the only sightseeing me and Bez really wanted to do.

When we got back we shot the video for our next single, '24 Hour Party People', which was another Bailey Brothers job. It's basically us starting outside the Boardwalk and then bombing around town in an Oldsmobile, a big old American car that was owned by some guy that Tony Wilson knew who collected classic American cars. The little kid driving the car at the start is Mark Bradbury, who was the little brother of Suzy, who I was seeing at the time. He still lives round the corner from me now. He was about ten or eleven then; he's about thirty-five now and he's got about nine kids. He's actually done all right for himself, Mark. He's a businessman, a proper entrepreneur type. I'd not seen him for about ten years, but then I ran into him in the shop at the bottom of the road quite recently and he said, 'All right, Shaun?'

Back then, you didn't really expect to make a lot of money from a debut album, but even with all the gigs we were doing we weren't really earning any money. It was still a real struggle, and anything that we did make as the Mondays was ploughed back into the band. We were pretty focused in that respect. The band kept us all going for a few years, because we all really believed in it, but it didn't really seem to be getting any easier. Even though we'd started to get a bit of press and built up a bit of a following, we were still struggling to make ends meet. We were all on the dole, apart from Mark Day, and were getting sick of being skint. Thankfully, that was about to change.

CHAPTER FIVE

'good, good, good, good, good, good, good, good,
good, good, good, good, double double good,
double double good'

The summer of 1987 is when things really changed. That's when life suddenly went from black and white to technicolour. When I first had the E.

It was Bez who gave me my first one. Predictably. He said 'X, try one of these – they're fucking mega,' when we were rehearsing one day at the Boardwalk. It blew me away. It made me feel euphoric. It's pretty obvious why it was called ecstasy, but it also felt really clean and fresh. So much so that it made me want to go home and have a shower and change my clothes. Like I said before, me and Bez were garbageheads. We'd had almost every type of drug, from acid to crack; we'd take whatever was around. But the E was a totally different buzz.

The first Es we got were little white ones. They didn't have a stamp on them or anything, just a line across them sometimes. They had originally come from Amsterdam. Like I said earlier, our lot had been going to the Dam on and off for a few years, and had a few really good contacts. The first E we had came from a French guy in a gay club there. One of our lot used to score weed off him, and one night he gave my pal this pill to try. He was knocked off his feet by it and brought a few back to Manchester in a tube of toothpaste. I'm pretty sure those were the first Es to arrive in Manchester, in that tube of toothpaste. One tube of fucking Colgate changed everything.

Around this time I split up with Suzy. I was partying so much that it had ruined the relationship, so at the start of the summer I moved in with Bez and his girlfriend Debs in Fallowfield, in the basement flat of an old Victorian house on Egerton Road. That house really was where it all changed. That was the epicentre, the root of it all. The house was split into three flats. Me, Bez and Debs were in the basement; Our Matt, Pat and Karen had the top flat; and Nige, or Platty, a friend of ours from the Haçienda, was in the middle flat; and a mate of his from Blackley, Antony Murray – Muzzer – lived just round the corner. That was our core group.

People bang on about the Sex Pistols at the Free Trade Hall, and how there were only forty or so people there, but it changed everything. When we first had the E, there couldn't have been more than about a dozen of us, perhaps twenty at a push, in our corner of the Haçienda. There was me, Our Kid, Bez, Big Minny, Little Minny, Muzzer, Platty, Our Matt and Pat, Cressa, Eric Barker and a couple of other kids. We were the only ones with the E at that time. No one else had a clue what was going on. We already had our spot in the Haçienda by then. There were four alcoves under the balcony, underneath the DJ booth, and we had the first one, by the dancefloor – that was ours, although we later spilled out into the second alcove.

The lads who were bringing the E back from Amsterdam got us involved. They were importing it, and it was our job to spread the word about the E in the Haçienda, to get punters. We were actually put on wages, like proper little salesmen.

Before the E arrived we were still skint. We weren't making any dough from the band and we were still trying to keep our noses clean, or relatively clean. Sometimes, when we were really broke, we would just nip down to the Factory office on Palatine Road and fill carrier bags with cassette tapes and albums, then take them down to one of the second-hand record shops in town and sell them for a bit of dough. It was pretty easy to make sure no one at Factory spotted us doing that, although when someone looked round afterwards it was obvious that loads of stock had gone missing. We didn't have a key to the office, but we'd go in there for a meeting and then hang about and lift some gear from their little stock room when no one was watching.

After a few weeks we started to make a bit of money from the E, from introducing people to it, but it did take people a little while to get used to spending £25 on it. People weren't used to spending that amount of money on drugs, especially on one little pill. You had the hip kids that were straight on it and knew what it was about. Then you had the people with money – either rich kids or grafters. But it took a while for your normal punters to get used to paying £25 for something. I remember coming back to Little Hulton to have a meeting with one of the local drug kingpins, and saying, 'Do you want some of these? They go for twenty-five quid a pop, but we can do 'em you for this much,' and he went *'What? Twenty-five quid a pop!?* Nah, that's too dear – these will never take off.' I'm saying to him, 'Listen, it's *happening*. Trust me.' But he wasn't having any of it. Then I went back six months later and they were all at it, although the price had gone down to £20 by then. It settled at around £15 eventually.

Bez got in a bit of trouble because the lad who was boss had gone to jail for a little while and left us in charge of the pills. Bez was giving pills away and spending the money when it came in, so when the boss came out Bez owed quite a lot. Let's just say a good few thousand. It took a bit of talking to get him out of that situation.

As we had a steady supply, we started eating the E all the time. We were getting up in the morning and having one for breakfast. Well, getting up in the afternoon and having one for breakfast. Some people would just throw an E down them, some people would just have a half or a quarter and share it. The thing is, if they just took a quarter, then by the time that quarter had come on they'd already given the rest of the pill away to somebody else because they felt so good, so they'd have to get another one, or jib a quarter or half off someone else.

I got to know Ian Brown from the Stone Roses around then, as he had moved to Fallowfield the same time as me. I was already on nodding terms with him, and knew he was the singer in the Roses, but we didn't really talk until we both moved to Fallowfield. We got on great when we got to know each other. Ian was a really nice kid, and he always had that air of non-chalance, like he was too cool for school. The Roses had sprayed their name around Manchester one night, on walls everywhere, so you knew the name the Stone Roses before you knew who the band were. They'd stopped being a goth band by then. Ian was one of those kids who changed about – he was a mod, and then he was a goth – but he stopped changing his look around 1987, when he kind of found who he was, about the time they released 'Sally Cinnamon'.

McDonald's opened a drive-thru in Fallowfield in 1987, the first one to open in Manchester, and I started having my tea there, often with Ian. We didn't arrange to meet up for tea or anything, but he would go in about the same time as I would, round about five o'clock, to get something to eat, so that's how we started talking and got to know each other, over a Big Mac. I would go in there most days, if I was around, and if I got up in time. It didn't shut until eleven o'clock at night, but if I hadn't got in from the night before until one o'clock in the afternoon, then I sometimes didn't get up until eleven o'clock or midnight.

We had the last few months of 1987 to ourselves really. There were still only a few pockets of people who had turned on to what was beginning to happen. It wasn't until early 1988 that the E scene really started to kick off, and by the summer of '88 we blew the roof off the Haçienda. Mike Pickering says he could see the E spread like a tidal wave across the Haçi, from our alcove across the club.

As people got switched on to the E, they knew to come to us for it. We were the source. We would come out of the Haçienda, which shut at 2am then, and by the time we got back to Fallowfield there would be a bigger queue outside our gaff than there was to get in the Haçi. It went right down the street. I mean, talk about bringing it on top. This was just people who had found out where we lived. When you need to buy weed or a bit of gear or something, you always find out where the people live who are selling it if you need to. At that particular time no one else really had the E in Manchester; we were the source, so people found out where we lived. I would look out the window and the queue would go right down Egerton Road. There could be a hundred people queuing up and we were selling it at £25 a pop. We weren't paying anything like that for the pills, so we were making some serious money.

It did come on top for us though, because we were attracting so much attention. Egerton Road is in a student area, so most of the houses on the street were split into rented flats. It wasn't a quiet residential area, but even so you can't have a hundred people outside your gaff several times a week without the police taking an interest – although at that stage they still didn't have a clue what was going on, so they probably just thought we were having big house parties. They didn't realize it was drug-related because they still didn't know what ecstasy was. But we did have a few run-ins with other gangs from round there – Asian gangs, and gangs that were dealing heroin – because we were also bringing it on top for them. We had fights and arguments with other groups because they didn't want those queues there and the attention that it brought on the area. Neither did we actually, but they just kept coming – there was nothing we could do about it.

That's really where the whole idea to go and break into a warehouse or somewhere and have a party started. We had a hundred people outside our gaff at two or three in the morning, all on really good E, and they're not going home. So people started breaking into cellars or disused buildings and putting little parties on. The only places to go at that time of night really were the shebeens in Moss Side and a couple in Hulme. The shebeens had been going on for years, mostly run by Jamaicans, but a lot of local criminals would also go there and they started taking the E.

A lot of those people who first starting buying the E off us went off and started their own things and their own nights. People would throw parties in old empty factories in Middleton or under railway arches, all sorts of little parties here and there. Some of our pals, like Muzzer and Platty, put on some of those early events, in Hulme or in town. The Donnelly brothers, Chris and Anthony, who started the Gio-Goi clothing label, did some. Eric Barker always used to have a sneaky party going on somewhere, often right in the centre of Manchester, in the basement of an old building. This was before every old warehouse in Manchester was turned into apartments, so there were still some great vacant spaces to be had. At one time, there would be a party every night of the week. It wasn't really a problem getting the word out; if anything it was a problem trying to keep it fucking secret. You didn't have to get the word out – the word was out. The police didn't have a clue at first, so you didn't have to worry too much about them.

Hulme was pretty wild back then. The Crescents had been this big experiment in social housing in the early 70s, which was supposed to be a vision of the future or something; all concrete walkways and stairwells. But by the mid-80s it had failed and been taken over by squatters, scallies and drug dealers. No one paid any rent, people just broke into flats and stayed there. Half the flats were boarded up, so if the one next to you was boarded you would just knock through and give yourself a massive extension, double the size of your flat.

There were always a couple of party flats in Hulme, and the best-known one later became known as The Kitchen. A kid called Jamie had built a bit of a recording studio and a sound system in his flat and it became a great party place. The DJs would play in the actual kitchen, hence the name. It was really dark, because they'd taken all the lightbulbs out, but the music was good, because Chris and Tomlin, the resident DJs from Konspiracy, the Manchester club, who were known as the Jam MCs, used to DJ there. It became so popular they had to knock through to the flat next door. The Kitchen was great. We used to try and make sure we got down there sharpish after the Haçienda shut to grab the only table and chairs. I remember being in there one night with Barney and Hooky and a few other Manc musicians; I think Chris Goodwin, who was in the Roses early doors then in the High, was there as well. We were all E'd up, and just got up and had an impromptu jamming session.

*

The E affected us just like it affected everyone: it changed our mindset. There had been certain people that me and my pals had never associated with, people that we'd never spoken to because we didn't like them, people that we stayed away from or didn't want knowing our business. But the E broke down those barriers. These were people that we had seen around for ten years and with the E we finally ended up speaking to them and getting on with them.

I had a really fucking lucky escape from the police with the E, early doors, just before they caught on to what was happening and to what ecstasy was. I was coming out of my house on Egerton Road and I had about thirty pills on me. It was the middle of the afternoon and I'd just got up. Unbeknown to me, somebody had just robbed the fucking post office round the corner, and the description of the robber matched me – blue anorak, jeans, trainers, short hair. So I'm walking down my road and this fucking cop car screeches up next to me and pulls me. The bizzie said, 'Who are you?' and I said, 'Er, I work for a record company.'

'Who do you work for then?'

I said, 'I work for Factory Records,' hoping that might ring a bell, but they had never heard of Factory.

'What do you do for them?'

'Er, I work in the office and do this and that and find bands and stuff.'

'Right, get in the back.'

'What for?'

'There's been a robbery at the post office and you match the description of one of the people fleeing the scene.'

'Give over.'

'Get in the car now. You're coming with us, and let's see if they identify you ... blah blah blah ... and if they don't identify you, then you can go.'

At the same time he's giving it all this, I've got my arms out and he's going through my pockets. He finds the bag of pills and says, 'What's this?'

Now, literally weeks after this, people were getting seven years for having seven E on them. So this bizzie pulls this bag of thirty pills out of my pocket, and he's like, 'What are these?' and then before I could say anything he says, 'Are they speed pills?'

'Yeah.'

'Right . . . okay.'

'What are you going do with 'em?' I asked. 'Can I have 'em back?'

As soon as I realized he thought they were just whizz-bomb pills, I started trying it on. Even if he had caught me with whizz, with powder, he would have thought it was more serious, but as soon as he thought they were just speed pills I started being a bit cheeky and giving it all: 'Come on, give us 'em back. I need them 'cos I work mad hours. Come on, give us 'em back.'

He went, 'Right, if this works out and it's not you who's done the post office, then we'll see.'

So I got in the back, we went round to this post office that's just been robbed and they say, 'No, it wasn't him.'

So they stuck me back in the car, drove round the corner and stopped on Wilmslow Road, the main drag in Fallowfield, and went 'Go on, get off.'

'What about me pills?'

The bizzie got out and went, 'Come here . . .', walked over to a grid and threw all the pills down it.

I just got off then. I was a bit pissed off at losing my pills but at least he hadn't nicked me. Literally weeks after that, the E exploded and suddenly everyone knew what it was. The police clamped down and everyone started getting mad sentences for only having a few E. If that incident had happened to me a few weeks later I would have gone down for ten years, for sure. I was really, really lucky on that score.

Not long after that, Jeff the Chef, who worked as a chef (obviously) but also sold a few pills, got pulled when he was serving up people in the Haçienda queue. There was a big queue as normal, and Jeff the Chef was just off his nut, walking up and down the queue going, 'Anyone want any E?' and he got pulled. He had less on him than I had, because what he would do is have a stash over the road and just run across and get some more when he'd sold out. So he only had a few on him, but he got five years. Everyone knew people who were getting locked up with these mad sentences. Seven years for seven E – it was madness.

James Anderton, the chief of Greater Manchester Police, had started to get pressure from the club owners and licensees, because they realized they were losing money because everyone was on the E and hardly anyone was drinking. When the E first came in, a lot of people would just drink water, because you would sweat a lot so you would get dehydrated, and those early Es made you feel like you wanted to be clean and fresh. I still drank, but I would drink large brandies, not beer. That seemed to keep us hydrated. All the clubs had to shut at 2am back then and people were beginning to run little illegal after-hours gaffs, so the club owners were losing loads of dough. Anderton was often in the news, because he was always coming out with ridiculous statements proclaiming God was speaking to him. This is the police chief. God's Cop.

When the scene began to take off in 1988, the press started getting wind of this new thing called ecstasy and all the parties started getting in the papers. Anderton and the courts really cracked down on it and people were literally getting banged up for longer for having E than for having crack.

The mad thing about it is that when you were right in the middle of the E thing, you knew how ridiculous the reaction to it was, because it calmed down all the mad fuckers. I knew idiots who would go out and fight and stab people, people whose whole night was about going out and kicking off in a bar and having a fight, or going to the match and kicking off. That's what it was all about for them, but once they started taking the E, that fucking shit stopped. It's a cliché, but it's absolutely true.

There was all this bad press about E, but if you were right in the middle of it you could see all the football violence stopping, and this gang going for a drink with that gang, meeting up and talking with no mither. You could see everyone really loved up, and yet at the same time you're reading in the press about this killer drug being the downfall of society. It was complete bullshit and it just makes you wonder about what other bullshit they are feeding you.

By this time we had our workers all round the Haçienda selling E. We probably had a dozen workers in the club. I would also often pop round to Stuffed Olives, a gay club on South King Street, to sell a bit of E there. Paul Cons, the promoter of the Haçienda, ended up buying that club a few years later and called it South. It's still open and Clint Boon from the Inspiral Carpets DJs on Saturday nights there.

There was quite a lot of heavy petting in the Haçienda when the E came in. Not necessarily shagging, although that did happen. The E was not like crack, which just turns people into deranged crack-sex motherfuckers. It just made people more lovey and more touchy, so people would be stroking each other and shit. There was a bit of shagging going on, and I got shagged in the corner of the Haçienda, but it wasn't like a big orgy.

The E also changed the way people dressed. It made us want to be really clean and wear pristine clothes. I know all the baggy gear was coming in, but we were wearing Hugo Boss, Armani, Paul Smith, Dolce & Gabbana, Versace and Ralph Lauren. The looser bits of their gear. It was like a designer hippy vibe. Or hippy casual, if you know what I mean? It also obviously got everyone dancing, including people who had never danced before. If you want to call it dancing. Even the few people who didn't dance would be moving in some way. It got rid of everyone's inhibitions.

Late in 1987, *i-D* magazine did a piece on this new 'scene' in Manchester and called us 'Baldricks'. They actually did two pieces, because they came back and did a bigger piece early in 1988. They called us 'Baldricks' because they reckoned we had haircuts like Baldrick in *Blackadder*. The article had a picture of a few kids, including Cressa and Alan Smith, who was another lad on the scene. Cressa was a nice kid and was one of the first on the scene. He went to grammar school with Ian Brown but he looked like a little sneak. He certainly didn't look like Baldrick, because he went bald really early. He was a clever kid, but he was a bit of a drop-out. He used to do speed and marijuana, and then later ecstasy, but he didn't sell it; he was just into music.

'Baldricks' was a load of bollocks. No one in Manchester called themselves a 'Baldrick'. In Manchester, the lads would have called themselves Perry Boys earlier on, and some people called them 'Pure Boys', but by that time they were probably just 'boys'. In London they would call themselves 'casuals' and Scousers were 'scallies', which ended up being the universal term for boys or casuals. The *i-D* piece talked about the return of the flared trouser, which they said had been happening since 1984, 'or 83 if you were from Oldham or Salford'. I don't know how Oldham got into it. There was no one from Oldham wearing flares at that stage.

At the start of 1988, I moved out to Amsterdam for a few months because I felt I needed a little break from the band and Manchester. Getting our first front cover hadn't had the effect we thought it might. It didn't seem to make any difference. I was a bit disheartened. We had got some good reviews, and we did a few shows and we did this and that, but it was still pretty hard work with the band; it still seemed like a slog. We still weren't really making any money from music.

Life outside the band, however, was changing very quickly. It was actually more exciting. It had all changed since we got the E. So I went over to Amsterdam, where it was all coming from, and had the time of my life for a few months. I had a bit of money in my pocket from selling the E, I was eating nice meals and going out partying and having a good time. It wasn't like I was never going to come back, and the band was still there, I just needed a bit of a break from it. Amsterdam is like a spider's web, it draws you in and it's really hard to get out of it, to untangle yourself from it.

Amsterdam was the centre then, the hub for lads who were grafting all over Europe. People were always passing through Amsterdam wherever they were headed, or on their way back home. There were quite a few lads there that I knew from Manchester. At first me and my pals were living in hotels, as I had quite a bit of dough, and we also had a few stolen credit cards, as we still knew kids that passed on cards that went missing from the post office. We then moved into an apartment on Williamstraat. There were about five of us in that apartment, although someone was always off jibbing about somewhere. A few of you would jump in the car and go off travelling to Switzerland or somewhere, to do a few sneak jobs.

There were loads of little scams that people were up to – stolen credit cards, sneaks, robberies, and even a few jewellers got done over. I was never a big-time sneak though; I just did what I needed to do to get by when I ran out of dough. I can remember walking round the streets of Amsterdam at five in the morning, looking for shops that were opening up. The staff would sometimes open the shutters a third of the way up while they were setting up and waiting to open, and you could sneak under there.

One of the main things lads were doing out there was arranging to get the E sent back. I wasn't involved in that, but one of the Manchester lads was buying it in massive quantities and then there was a geezer out there who used to fit out the lorries with false compartments to import it all in.

We had a hairy moment when we ended up being held hostage in the apartment on Williamstraat for two days by a psychotic kid from Manchester called Skinny Vinny, who was coked out of his brain. A month or so before this, he'd been in the car with me and Platty and we stopped to get something from a shop, but when we came out of the shop he'd fucked off in Platty's precious Golf GTI and we didn't see it again for a month. Now he had a gun and was threatening to shoot us, and kept us there nearly two days with the fucking gun pointed at us. I ended up talking him down and bringing him round, then eventually someone made a move when he wasn't expecting it and just grabbed the gun off him. He was an armed robber, Skinny Vinny, and not long after that incident he ended up robbing a bank and taking three people hostage, and having a big shoot-out with the police. Last I heard he was doing a very long stretch somewhere.

There were a lot of English out there in Amsterdam, all finding a way to make a bit of dough. There were a lot of Manchester kids and a lot of Scousers, a few Geordies, some kids from Sheffield, and a few Cockneys. That was when we first met all the Cockneys who went on to do the first acid-house nights in London, like Oz, Phuture and Spectrum – kids like Ian St Paul and his mates.

A few of the kids we met in Amsterdam are now quite big players and respected businessmen – restaurant owners and property developers and doing quite well for themselves. All of the ones that I'm still in touch with have now gone legit.

The band was still there in the background; it just took a back seat for a couple of months for me, while I was E'ing my face off out there and having a great time. When the band was ready to start work on our second album, I was still out in Amsterdam, having the time of my life. I got word that I needed to come back to start writing, but to be honest I was just having too much fucking fun. In the end, Bez had to come to the Dam to get me and bring me back home.

When I got back, Phil Saxe was still managing us, but he was also still running his shop in the Arndale and his market stall, and I felt that if we were going to take things up a notch we needed someone to look after us full time. He didn't have an office, so we had to go to this shop or down to the market stall if we wanted to see him about anything. I put it to Phil that he should let Lenny, his brother, look after the market stalls and then he could manage us full time. But he made the decision that he couldn't do that, so I decided we needed to look for a new manager.

Nathan McGough had first come to see us when we supported New Order in Macclesfield a few years earlier and made no secret of the fact that he was a fan of the band. Nathan had an office on Princess Street and was managing bands like the Bodines. He was a bit of a protégé of Wilson's, as Tony knew his mum, Thelma, and Nathan had lived with

Wilson at his house on Old Broadway when he first moved to Manchester from Liverpool in the early 80s. Thelma was married to Roger McGough, the poet.

I approached Nathan in the Haçienda and told him we'd sacked Phil Saxe and made it pretty obvious I wanted him to take over. Wilson was actually against Nathan becoming our manager at first, because he knew what he was like, knew how ambitious he was for himself and the Mondays, and thought he would be too much hard work for Factory. But I liked Nathan – he was great. He was business-like, but he was still young and liked to party. He was only twenty-five or twenty-six when he took over, and he was perfect for us, just what we needed.

Phil was a bit pissed off and disappointed. But I think after he thought about it for a while he realized that was what we needed. I bump into Phil quite a lot now, and we get on fine.

Just after Nathan took over, he got us our first £1,000 show, in Scotland, I think. It was a bit of a milestone – the first gig we had got paid a grand for, and we got paid in cash. But Nathan brought a bird back to the hotel with him after the gig and when he woke up in the morning she'd gone, and so had our first £1,000. So Our Kid, Bez and PD put bars of soap in pillowcases, threw Nathan in the bath and beat him with them, which bruises you really badly. That was kind of Nathan's initiation into the Mondays in a way. We didn't mind him partying as hard as us, but not if it was going to lose us money.

The songs for our second album were coming together in rehearsals at the Boardwalk, so we went into Out of the Blue studios in Manchester to record some quick demos of tracks, which we were really happy with. It felt like we were getting closer to the sounds in our heads.

At the same time, early summer 1988, the Haçienda really began to take off. They started a Wednesday night called Hot, with Mike Pickering and Jon Da Silva DJ-ing, and that's when the roof lifted off the place. The E had now swamped the club. I remember Hooky once said, 'There weren't that many people on E in the Haçienda.' *You fucking what?? Where were you??* If there were 1,500 people in there, then 1,400 were off their fucking tits on the E, especially on Wednesday and Friday nights, and pretty soon on every night of the week. And the ones that weren't off their tits on ecstasy were on something else. It all happened quite quickly, in a matter of months, if not weeks. The difference in a year was unbelievable. It had gone from being empty early in the summer of 1987 to being rammed every night.

People might think that us selling weed and then the E was part of a constructed image, but it wasn't; it was what we needed to do to get by. We didn't really earn any decent money from music until about early 1990 when we'd done *Top of the Pops* and were stepping up to do venues like the G-Mex. Before then, almost all the dough we made, we made ourselves, sometimes through selling our own merch, or touting gigs, but for a short while most of the money that came in was through turning people on to E.

CHAPTER SIX

'And you were wet, now you're getting drier,
you used to speak the truth but now you're a liar,
you used to speak the truth but now you're clever'

As we were getting ready to record our second album for Factory, I could feel the mood towards us at the label had changed. We were no longer the new boys; we had become more accepted. That was partly down to our music, and partly because they could see we were very clearly plugged into the Haçienda scene. By introducing the E we had pretty much filled their club and now, having heard the demos for the new album, they were starting to think we might be able to sell a decent amount of records. I definitely felt we were getting treated better and taken more seriously, rather than left alone to get on with it.

It was our idea to use Martin Hannett to produce the album. Factory had fallen out with him over the Haçienda, which he thought was a waste of money, as well as a few other things. Hannett had wanted to buy a Fairlight, which was one of the first synthesizers, but they spent the money on the club instead. He'd even tried to sue them, and had pulled a gun on Wilson at the Factory offices on Palatine Road. We spoke to Alan Erasmus, the other Factory founder and director, about it first, and he spoke to Wilson. They knew Hannett was not in a great place, financially or mentally. He was in a bit of a state, so I think they saw getting him back in to work on *Bummed* as throwing him a lifeline. I'm sure they also thought he would be good to work with us. They wouldn't have done it otherwise, but it was a bit of a peace offering, an olive branch.

We recorded the album at Slaughterhouse studios in Driffield in Yorkshire, which Factory probably picked because they thought it was a small enough place that we wouldn't get into much trouble and close enough that they could keep an eye on us.

I hadn't met Hannett before we did *Bummed*, but obviously I knew all about him. I was a big fan of his production because I'd really been into Joy Division and *Unknown Pleasures*, but I also liked the other productions he'd done.

Martin could do incredible amounts of drugs. And he did. Sometimes in the studio in Driffield he would just be flunked out. Gone. He was the only producer that I've ever worked with that was more druggy than me. And madder. Shambolic. He had this nylon weatherproof BP Oil jacket that he wore all the way through the recording. He never took that jacket off. But we got on really well, and I think he preferred hanging out with us than hanging out with the rest of Factory. I became good friends with Wendy, his missus, and the whole family. Martin was always skint, even after he produced *Bummed*. While we were recording it he was on ecstasy, heroin, cocaine, acid . . . Martin took *everything*. We gave him the E, and I think it was the first time he'd had it.

Even though I had dabbled in heroin since the early 80s, I wasn't really taking it then; when the E first came around, I was just bang into the pills. It wasn't until late 1989 that heroin really got a grip of me. So I didn't smoke any gear with Hannett when we were recording *Bummed*, although I did a year or so later.

Most people we worked with on recordings we then wouldn't see again until we were back in the studio with them, but after we finished *Bummed* I used to visit Martin's house in Chorlton a lot. Our Matt and Pat became really good friends with him too. They were actually out on a massive bender with him, which lasted for days, just before he died in 1991. After that huge blowout with Our Matt and Pat, Hannett went home and died of heart failure. He was only forty-two.

Working with Hannett was a very different recording process to working with John Cale on *Squirrel and G-Man*. John Cale had recorded us live almost, but Hannett had a few more tricks up his sleeve. It wasn't just Hannett – by the time we came to do *Bummed*, we as a band were on a total different vibe as well. Because we were on the E, we were permanently in massive party mode. When we recorded *Squirrel* it was pretty much just the band in London, but when we did *Bummed* we had the E, so all our pals came across to Driffield to party with us while we were recording.

The E had a big influence on the music. At that time we wouldn't necessarily put the house music we were hearing in the clubs on at home, but then we were never *at* home. Most of our lives at the time were spent in nightclubs or at parties, so that was where we heard the majority of the music we were soaking up. We were either out or we were in the studio, and we would play that music in the studio because we were on the E. We also had all the records the DJ Paul Oakenfold had played in Ibiza that summer at the studio with us, because one of my pals had bought them all off Oakey in Ibiza at the end of the season. Tony Wilson later said he came across to see us when we were recording and just found us in a room in the dark, lying about on the floor with hundreds of vinyl records scattered around us.

Musically, the interesting thing for me about *Bummed* is that it came about just as the E had hit, so quite a few of the songs had been written beforehand. I'm pretty sure that Our Kid, Mark Day and Gaz Whelan hadn't tried an E when we were first writing the songs, and hadn't started going to Hot at the Haçienda on a Wednesday night, like the rest of us. Me and Bez had, and PD had a bit, but the other three weren't on it yet. In fact, at first they were even a bit like, 'What the fuck are you up to?' We would be in our rehearsal room at the Boardwalk on a Wednesday, writing the songs for *Bummed* and me, Bez and PD would go straight over to the Haçienda afterwards to get on it, and the others would be like 'What are you knobs up to?' They did get on it later; they just came to it slightly after us. By the time we came to actually record the album, they were definitely bang at it as well.

So it's hard to say exactly how much the E influenced *Bummed* overall, but it's fucking obvious on some of the later tracks. 'Do It Better' is a total E track – it's really hypnotic and even the lyrics are repetitive: 'on one, in one, did one, do one, did one, have one, in one, have one, come on, have one, did one, do one, good one, in one, have one' and 'good, good, good, good, good, good, good, good, good, good, good, good, double double good, double double good'. Everything was 'double good' to us at the time because we were on the E. 'Hey man, that's double good . . .'

I don't think Hannett was particularly a fan of house music, but he was E'd off his head during the recording, so obviously this stuff was seeping into his nut as well. That's what the E could do – music that you didn't particularly like sounded great when you were E'd up. We were pretty much just listening to house music while we were recording and there was a brilliant atmosphere in the studio. It felt like one long party, which we just happened to be recording.

Driffield was a funny place. We stuck out like a sore thumb. There was a big army base in the town and I remember being in the disco there on a Friday night when a load of squaddies came in. I was with a load of our crew from Manchester and we were all E'd up. The disco was just opposite the studio – it was part of some crappy shopping precinct, a real towny place that held about five hundred people and had a DJ just playing chart music. He played 'Push It' by Salt-N-Pepa and 'Theme From S'Express', which were all right, but everything else he played was just dire chart rubbish.

This army lot, who had just come back from Belfast, were all looking at us and obviously spoiling for a fight. Bez was there with his big starey eyes, and one particular nutty squaddie wanted to start on him, because he thought Bez was looking at him. We also had a lot of the birds in the club hanging round us, so that was pissing the squaddies off as well.

There were more of them than us, probably fifteen of them and ten of us. If it had kicked off, it would have kicked off big time, because the lads that I was with certainly wouldn't have backed down. No way. But we were all in a real party mood because we were on the E, and I tried explaining this to this ultra-violent squaddie who wanted to start on Bez. 'Listen, the kid's peaceful, he's just off his head, blah blah.' Then I just said, 'Look, have one of these – it will change your life, and you'll be looking like him before you know it,' and I literally threw an E in this soldier's mouth. He was so drunk he just took it. Now I used to give it an hour for the E to kick in, but he came back over smiling in much less than that, going '*Wowwwww!!!!! Gimme some more for my mates! Gimme some more for my mates!*' So I gave him a few more and they ended up buying some off us too. Soon all of these squaddies were off their faces and they're all hugging each other, saying, 'I don't want to go back fighting wars' and 'I don't want to go back in the army.' These are the same guys that had earlier been boasting about going to Ireland on a tour of duty, and they're now all on this peaceful hippy vibe. Fucking hilarious.

It was just as funny invading Driffield during the day. Obviously the E hadn't reached this small Yorkshire town, so they hadn't seen anyone dressing like or acting like us lot, which you were beginning to see around Manchester. When our pals came to Driffield, they brought a consignment of E that should have been for the consumption of everyone in Manchester. So all our lot were E'd up the whole time. We would be in the car at traffic lights on the high street, in broad daylight, then next thing a top tune would come on the car stereo, and we'd all jump out the car and start dancing round it. Me, Muzzer and Bez and everyone just dancing round the car in the middle of the afternoon. Then when the tune finished, we'd get back in the car and drive off.

The locals would just be staring. We also looked totally alien to them as well, with our designer hippy gear going on. We would march into the pie shop in Driffield like we were in a Madness video or something. You know that thing that Madness do in their videos when they're all marching together? We'd be off our tits walking into the pie shop like that together, but thinking we were just behaving normal, you know what I mean? The old Yorkshire bird behind the counter would be like, 'Aren't you a nice bunch of cheery chaps?' as we were dancing in the middle of the shop. The yokels had no fucking idea what to make of us.

That was the thing with the whole E scene; it also changed the way people looked. If you look at the pictures of us before we all started taking pills, we all have crew cuts and stuff – that

Perry Boy/casual look. That was what the police would look out for back then – crew cuts and casual gear like Burberry jackets or whatever. If you looked like that, you were going to get nicked for something. When the E kicked in, we started growing our hair a bit longer, into a centre parting like curtains, or even a pony tail, and our clothes were also getting a bit looser, and all of a sudden the police didn't look at us. We no longer fitted their stereotype image of the lads who were knocking out drugs or trying to sneak a shop for a till or something. The police didn't give you a second look. You could be walking down the street with your curtains and your loose-fitting gear on, or even dancing down the street like we were half the time, and you didn't even register with them. You were off their radar now because they were still looking for the crew-cut scallies. Which was great, because our lot were knocking out more drugs than before, but getting stopped much less. For a while anyway. We probably had at least six months to ourselves, a little window when it was almost like walking round in disguise really, because no one else was on it yet.

It really was a small circle, a tight-knit group of people, who got into E in those very early days. There might have been a couple who worked in trendy shops, but most of those involved at that stage were not exactly normal working people. They didn't have jobs, but always seemed to have money. Even if they weren't selling drugs, they had their own ways and means. Some of those kids would just sneak any way they could.

I had grown a lot more confident in my lyrics by the time *Bummed* came around. It was just natural progression. I was arranging better and writing better lyrics. We shouldn't have been on record before *Squirrel and G-Man*, really, because we weren't ready. But by the time we came to *Bummed*, starting to record a new album almost felt like putting a pair of comfy slippers on.

The dynamic was still great in the band at this stage. They would all still listen to me, when I could tell which way a song should go, and that pretty much stayed the same until *Pills 'n' Thrills*. I always wrote the lyrics but I was also quite heavily involved in the music as well. Most of the music would come out of jams in rehearsals, and I was often kind of arranging it as we worked on stuff. Mark Day would start playing something on his guitar and I would say, 'When you do *that*, can you just do *this* instead of *that* . . . and then give us three of them there,' and he would listen and go, 'You mean like *that*?' and do it. Then I would say to Our Kid, 'You know what you're doing there? Well just lay off that, and go one up there or whatever . . . or do that twice, then bend it down there and bring it back up here,' and he'd quite happily do that. I might not be able to play guitar myself, or even name the notes, but I knew the sounds I was after.

It was only after we had been on *Top of the Pops* and made *Pills 'n' Thrills* that things changed. Even on *Pills 'n' Thrills* they still accepted my input. Half the songs on that album were written in the studio, and the music on at least four or five of them originated from the beats that Paul Oakenfold and Steve Osborne came up with. Our Kid would put his bass down on it, and Mark Day would put his guitar over the top. Songs like 'Loose Fit' came about like that. A lot of the keyboards on those songs were programmed as well, although PD would start thinking that he had written those keyboard parts. It was after *Pills 'n' Thrills* became a hit, and the recognition that came with it, that the egos really came out and the dynamic changed in the band.

There was no way, after *Pills 'n' Thrills*, that they were going to listen to me telling them what to do – saying, 'Can you do that?' 'Can you play it like this?' Once the band got recognition, things changed. You had other guitarists telling Mark Day how fucking great he was, people telling PD how brilliant he was, people telling Our Kid what a great bass player he was. When people started telling Mark Day, 'You're the main influence on this band,' and other people telling Our Kid, 'You're the core talent of this band,' they then started to say to me, 'I'm not listening to you – you should listen to me.' But back when we were recording *Bummed*, the dynamic in the band was still working and still really good.

The opening track, 'Country Song', was originally called 'Some Cunt from Preston', and is just the Mondays' own individual take on country and western. By this time we had been rehearsing in the Boardwalk for a while and were really getting it down as a band, and were able to express the different types of music that we wanted to play. Before *Bummed*, we knew the music we wanted to play in our heads, but we hadn't necessarily worked out how to get it out – both the band as musicians and me as a writer. But by this time we were all learning our craft. There is a line in 'Country Song' that says 'Better put your house up for sale, the Indians are coming', which is absolutely nothing to do with Asians or Pakistanis, in case anyone wonders. I remember thinking afterwards, 'Bloody hell, I hope no one thinks that's racist,' but no one really picked up on it.

Like on *Squirrel*, again there aren't any songs on *Bummed* that are about me, necessarily, as I wouldn't write openly about myself, but there are a few lines in there that refer to me. On 'Fat Lady Wrestlers' the line 'I just got back from a year away' could be about me coming back from living out in Amsterdam. Or it could be about me coming back to normality after spending a year tripping my fucking tits off. Or both.

There are quite a few obvious references to *Performance*

littered throughout *Bummed*. *Performance* was a huge film for me and the rest of the band. Everything about it, from the cinematography and style, to the acid and sex scenes, to the dialogue. Every line in that film is a fucking gem really. That was us beginning to know more what we wanted to achieve in the studio; wanting to include some film references and knowing we could do what we wanted, really, that we didn't have to stick to a traditional format. 'Mad Cyril' is named after a character in *Performance*, and it includes dialogue from the film as well: 'I like that . . . turn it up!' or that Edward Fox line where he insists, 'I need a bohemian atmosphere.'

The song 'Performance' starts out with a straight rip from the dialogue of the film: 'One day he was admiring his reflection, in his favourite mirror, when he realized all too clearly, what a freaky little old man he was', and I added the 'who is, he is, you is now'. To me that is just the same as what rappers do, nicking bits of dialogue and catchphrases from here and there, like magpies, and making it their own.

Side two of *Bummed* opens with me shouting, 'You're rendering that scaffolding dangerous!' at the start of 'Brain Dead', which was a line lifted from the film *Gimme Shelter*, about the Rolling Stones gig at Altamont. A lot of those film references come from our big acid phase. We would watch the same films over and over – although *Gimme Shelter* is about three fucking hours long anyway – and pick out different lines that became sort of catchphrases to us. The lines in 'Brain Dead', like 'grass eyed, slash haired, brain dead fucker', refer to certain characters, certain people that were around on the scene at the time. 'Rips off town, steals from his brother' – I certainly knew a few people like that. But, again, they're not about one particular person; they are observations of different characters that I would put together to make the song, like a little short story.

'Wrote For Luck' was definitely an important song for me, lyrically. I surprised myself a bit when I wrote some of the lines on there, like 'You used to speak the truth, but now you're clever'. Although, to be honest, I always thought I never really finished it; to me it's still a half-finished song. It needs another verse really, I think. Having said that, 'Wrote For Luck' was definitely one of the songs that helped me feel like I was getting more to grips with writing lyrics. It's obviously very heavily influenced by the E scene and what was happening at the time. Again, it's a mish-mash of different situations – he said that and I think this about that – strung together to make a song.

'Bring a Friend' is just pure filth. 'I might be the honky, but I'm hung like a donkey'; 'Come on in, grease up your skin'. The line 'Clio and her sister Rio, were watching through the key-hole' was ripped directly from one of the porn mags that I got charged for bringing back from Amsterdam a couple of years before. There were a few naughty sex parties that went down at the time. The E wasn't necessarily a sex drug; it was more of a lovey, touchy, feely drug that would make you feel more like bloody stroking or hugging someone than fucking them. But if you mixed it with a bit of coke, then it was a different matter. Not just on lads either; it had the same effect on girls as well. They weren't necessarily planned sex parties or anything, but you would get back to someone's house for a bit of a party and one thing would lead to another. A few orgy-type situations. Like the lyrics said, 'I say yes in every situation'.

'Do It Better' was definitely heavily influenced by the E scene, like I said. It was actually even called 'E' for quite a while, although if anyone asked me why it was called 'E' I said it was because it was in the key of E.

'Lazyitis' was the last song on the album, and I had really wanted to do a track like that, a kind of off-the-wall pop song.

But I don't think we quite nailed it. There were a couple of things that I wasn't happy about on the finished album version. I was really critical about our songs and I think a few of the lyrics let me down on 'Lazyitis'. I didn't want it to be a single, but Tony was adamant. It was his idea to bring in Karl Denver later and re-record it as a single. Apparently, my dad took me to a Karl Denver gig when I was just a toddler, because he was into that sort of music, but I don't remember it. We obviously all knew him from his hit single 'Wimoweh', though.

The album title *Bummed* was just a word we used for everything at the time. You'd say, 'Oh, I'd bum that!' or 'Fucking hell, I'd bum that bird there.' It was just one of those words that we all used, like 'Sorted'. The album could easily have been called 'Sorted' or 'Mega' or 'On One'. In America they weren't sure about the title, because some people thought *Bummed* meant 'failed'. They were like, 'Hey, man, I'm not sure about that title. It sounds like it hasn't sold, y'know, like, "Hey, that album bummed!"'

The cover was a painting of my face by Central Station. Again, it was all Matt and Pat's idea. We would always just leave them to get on with the artwork, then if we didn't like what they came up with we would say something. I remember seeing it for the first time and going, 'Oh God, I don't really want this as the cover.' But Matt and Pat, and Karen, and Tony were all going, 'This is great!' I'm sure the rest of the band weren't really into just having my face on the cover either. To make it worse, Factory then plastered the outside of their new office building with posters of the cover. That was also Wilson's idea.

The inner sleeve also caused a bit of a stir, because it was an old picture of a naked bird. We all agreed on it, but it was Our Matt and Pat who found it. They're artists, so they would trawl through loads of old shit, archives and second-hand shops, looking for decent images. No one at Factory had a problem with it. But then that was the thing with Factory; they never had a problem with anything like that. They would never try and interfere. The only people who really did have a problem with it were the Americans. One pressing plant in the US refused to press the album with that inner sleeve, so we had to change it.

While we were recording in Driffield, Granada came down to film us and interview us for a schools educational programme, which was supposed to be an insight into how to get into the music business. You can see it on YouTube now. I can't remember exactly how that came about, but it must have come through Tony's Granada connections, or maybe it was something that Tony and Nathan cooked up together. Back then there was really no exposure for indie bands. It's not like now. If you look at the number of programmes playing what used to be called 'indie' now; back then there was just one MTV channel, which only really showed Bon Jovi videos, and hardly anyone had Sky anyway, before the Premier League. So when Granada wanted to do this schools programme, which followed us around as a band that was trying to make it, that was great for us. It was a weird one, because at the time we thought we were like the kings of the indie scene, but this programme really put us in our place a bit, because we were portrayed as a band that hadn't made it yet and, to the general public, we hadn't. Only a select few indie types would view us as a band that had made it at that stage. It was also a bit weird to use Factory as an example to the kids of how the music industry works, when Factory worked completely differently to any other label. But that was Wilson weaving his magic, with Nathan's seal of approval. Wilson also featured in it quite a bit and, as it was plugging his band and his label, it was a win-win-win situation for him.

When I say a kids' TV show, it was aimed at college kids, not primary-school kids, so we didn't get told to rein in our behaviour and smile for the camera, but on the other hand they didn't show us swearing or skinning up either. In those days we'd have pulled out some whizz or coke, racked a few lines out and smashed it in front of anybody – we didn't give a flying fuck. But they weren't interested in capturing that rock 'n' roll side of the band; it was about the process of making an album and releasing it. They filmed some bits with us in the studio, and they even went to the record plant to film the actual record being pressed, with a narrator throughout giving it all: 'Okay, kids, first you need to get a band together, perhaps with your mates, then you need to get a manager, then you need to play some gigs, then you need to get something called an agent . . .' and all that sort of thing, you know what I mean? 'Then you get a record contract, then you make an album and then you have a launch party . . . simple as that.'

They also filmed Wilson going to see Tony the Greek, who did our radio-plugging then. Tony the Greek's real name was Tony Michaeledes and he was an old Manchester head who'd been round for years. In the programme he complains to Wilson that we hadn't turned up for some radio interview he'd set up for us, which sounds about right.

'Wrote For Luck' was the obvious single from the album, and when it came to shoot the video for it we wanted to capture the feeling of those early acid-house days and the parties and raves that were happening, because that's what we were bang into at the time, that's where our heads were at. The Bailey Brothers did the video again and had the idea to shoot it at Legends, which is the club that Spectrum took over one night a week. We just hired it out, and all the extras in the video are just our crew and the party people that we were knocking about with at the time.

Everyone in the club was on the E that night. *Everyone.* It was still people we knew that were the main supply of E in Manchester, although I was less involved personally. But I had a pocketful of pills on the night and so did Bez. If anyone down there needed one, they just got given one. The Bailey Brothers managed to capture a real trippy, gangster rave vibe, which absolutely reflected what was going on in Manchester at the time. If you want to know what those early parties and raves were like, just watch the video for 'Wrote For Luck'. They did a great job of capturing the hedonism with a hint of menace underneath.

In the end, they also decided they had to shoot an alternative version on the same day, with schoolkids, as Factory thought ours might not get shown on TV because it was so trippy and overtly druggy. So they got some local schoolkids in during the afternoon and shot a version of it with them, and then all our lot piled down in the evening to shoot the proper version. I don't think the kids' version ever saw the light of day, though.

I really got on with the Bailey Brothers. We were on a similar vibe, and were big fans of all the same films – *Performance* and stuff like that. I remember saying to Keith Jobling once, 'Have you seen that movie *Thief*?' It was a 70s American movie about a professional thief, starring James Caan, and Keith said, 'No way, man! I've asked loads of people about that film and no one else has ever seen it!' Keith knew his films and I knew my films, and we could talk about them for ages. We were right on the same trip.

The video does look slightly edgy, but that scene was a bit edgy at the start, especially to those who weren't in it. Particularly the press, like the *Manchester Evening News* – it frightened them to death. They certainly didn't see it as a big love-in. As I've said, the *Evening News* would never really touch us as a band, before we made it, and part of that was because we were the sort of people that they would cross the street to avoid if they were coming out of a pub late at night in the centre of town. A lot of the people in the media were a little bit frightened of what was happening at that time, because they just didn't get it. They would come in and see what was going on at particular nights, and it did have an edge to it. To be fair, a lot of the people involved in those early days *were* quite edgy. They were people from a different way of life. They weren't nine-to-fivers, most of these kids, and they were never going to be.

I think all the videos we did with the Bailey Brothers were great, especially considering the small budget we had to work on. 'Tart Tart', '24 Hour Party People', 'Lazyitis', 'Wrote For Luck', 'Hallelujah', they were all great. Even right up to 'Judge Fudge', where we had to cut the gates open and were driving around and playing cards – even that had a kind of *Performance* feel to it. We filmed that in the big glass diamond building in Stockport, which you go right past when you're on the rattler to London. I think it's a bank now, but it was empty then. It had just been built but it wasn't being used for anything yet.

Around the same time as the 'Wrote For Luck' video, we had also started work on this Factory film called *Mad Fuckers* with the Bailey Brothers. We filmed a few scenes on the same day we shot the 'Wrote For Luck' video, including some scene in Legends with Donald Johnson from ACR. Me and Bez were supposed to be playing two little mad fuckers, and in that scene I was picking up a parcel from Donald, or he was dropping off a parcel with me; he was some shifty geezer and there was something going down or something like that. To be honest, I still don't really know exactly what the film was supposed to be about. We did film quite a few scenes, but it never got finished. Everybody and anybody was supposedly going to be in *Mad Fuckers*, and there was quite a buzz about it, but most of it actually only happened in the Bailey Brothers' heads. I think some people still see it as the great lost Factory film or something.

We launched *Bummed* in London and the idea was to have a gig and a rave in the same night – there was a launch at Heaven, the nightclub at Charing Cross, then we played Dingwalls in Camden, then everyone went back to party at Heaven. It was an idea that we cooked up with Nathan and Jeff Barrett, who had now taken over doing our press from Dave Harper. I don't remember much about the gig at Dingwalls, but we had a load of our crew down there and half of them ended up on stage, and people like Jeff Barrett, who do remember it, say it was a great gig. Some people think that was a bit of a turning point for the Mondays, as that was the night when a lot of people *got* it, if you know what I mean, but I think it was just as much about them getting what the whole scene was about as getting what the Mondays were about. The thing is, wherever we went at that time, there was ecstasy with us and a lot of it was sold to people who came to see us, and many of these punters hadn't had it before. So, even if the gig was a bit shit, everyone would have an incredible night and feel they were having the time of their lives. A lot of people had their first E watching the Mondays, so it was something they would always remember. Most people will always remember the first time they had E.

After Dingwalls we went back to Heaven, where Spectrum was on. There were three bouncers on the door and they wouldn't let one of our lads in, one of the top boys. He wasn't a particularly big lad to look at, only about my size, and he had blond hair with a centre parting. He looked like a mix between James Cagney and the Milky Bar Kid and used to wear Jean Paul Gaultier clobber. He didn't look like the kind of serious character that he actually is. But these three bouncers made the mistake of trying to stop him coming in, and within the blink of an eye all three of them were on the ground. *Bang, bang, bang* – he battered all three of them in a matter of seconds, and then just walked in.

We would spend quite a bit of time in London at that time, when the club scene was kicking off. A few years before, back in Amsterdam, we had met Ian St Paul, who was involved in the London club scene. He had a really, really top gaff in Covent Garden and we would crash over there sometimes.

Some of my pals also knew Paul Oakenfold, from Ibiza. Three of our lot were pretty much the main heads in the clubs out in Ibiza, and had been since the early days, so they were well connected.

I didn't have a gaff of my own at this point because I'd just come back from the Dam. I crashed at Muzzer's mam's for a bit. She lived on Rochdale Road in Blackley, the other side of Collyhurst, on the way to Middleton, just past Viccy Avenue. His mam actually came downstairs and caught me at it in her front room with Cressa's ex-girlfriend Sue one day. After Sue split with Cressa, me and her were fuck buddies for a bit, and Muzzer's mam walked in and caught us right in the middle of a particularly naughty moment. She was really religious and I think she had to say about ten thousand Hail Marys because of what she saw that day. I felt a bit guilty because she'd been really good to me, putting me up when I didn't have a place of my own.

As we started to get more dough, more disposable income, through the E, we would also stay at the Britannia Hotel in town. It just seemed easier to stay there than to bother finding a flat, because we were on the road quite a bit and if you've got a flat it needs looking after, doesn't it? The Britannia was right in town, so you could nip out and do a bit of shopping, and there was a bar right next to the hotel. Me and Muzzer must have stayed there for at least seven or eight months. All the maids and cleaners at that time were young girls who were all on E and coke themselves, out raving their tits off every night. We used to leave Es and lines chopped out on the side for them so that they'd stay out of our business, and they would tidy our clothes and stuff for us in return.

At the start of 1989, we went to France to do a few dates, which all got a bit messy. We were just about to go on stage at this gig and Muzzer gets a call to tell him that his best mate, a kid called Robbo, had jumped off the top of a block of flats back in Manchester. He had this flat on the thirteenth floor of a tower block in Blackley and it was basically one of those flats where people would always be sat round smoking or whatever. This day, Robbo had just walked into the front room where two lads were sat having a smoke, said, 'Y'all right, lads?' to them and then just walked out to the balcony and jumped off. Committed suicide. He didn't seem to be off his head or anything; he was apparently acting quite normal. But things hadn't been going too well for him in his life – a couple of things were coming on top for him and it obviously had all got too much.

Muzzer hears this news just as we're going on stage. It was his best pal from when they were kids, so obviously that does his head right in. Then some pissed-up French dick starts mouthing off, so Muzzer starts rowing with him because he's already pent up, and he gives us the shout 'Sack the gig!' and that's it then. Si Machan, our sound guy, wades in and punches some other guy who is also starting on Muzz.

It went right off. We were in the middle of a number, but we all downed our instruments, jumped off stage and waded in there. The club got absolutely smashed to bits. We ended up at the back of the club, barricaded in and trying to fight our way out. I grabbed this big metal pipe from somewhere and I was wielding that around my head. Fire extinguishers were going off and all sorts; it was proper Wild West tackle. The entire band jumped in, plus our crew and a few lads who were with us. There were probably about fifteen of us, but quite a few more of them, because some of the locals backed them up. The club was a bit bigger than the Boardwalk, maybe five hundred or seven hundred people. The riot police turned up and arrested us all, but I somehow wriggled out of it and got away with just a ticking off. Muzzer and another one of our crew were nicked and banged up, and we couldn't get him out, so we had to hang around for the weekend. A few of us went to hospital, and one of their bouncers, a big six-foot seven Rastafarian dude, was there with his arm hanging out of its socket where I'd clobbered him with the metal bar. We didn't get off that badly, really – we had a few cuts and bruises and a few black eyes, and Muzzer's ear had been slashed by a broken bottle.

The thing about it in those days was that kids we knew would be all over Europe, sneaking about, and they would turn up at the gigs. They might be somewhere else in France, but they would get to us. Basically, these kids would get a couple of cars between them and drive all the way through Europe, stopping off at little towns off the map, where they might get away with things easier, and if we were playing somewhere in Europe usually some of them would tip up there. Four or five

Salford kids and a few Manc kids were regulars at our gigs all over Europe.

In some of the clubs we were playing at that time in Europe we got shit from the other bands as well. We'd turned up at gigs in Germany and had the local bands say to us, 'You fucking pigs, you come here and steal our gigs!', which I never understood. If a German band or a French band or whatever came to play the Boardwalk in Manchester, we'd always say, 'Y'all right?' and have a chat with them. But in some parts of Germany and France their attitude was, 'You English fuckers, coming here and stealing jobs that we should have.' We weren't necessarily looking for mither, but if you come at us with that kind of attitude then you're going to get something wrapped round your head from one of us, y'know what I mean? So we always seemed to end up in quite a few fights.

At that stage, in 1989, the Manchester thing was beginning to attract attention on the continent. Most music fans in Europe seemed to think that it was just people in Manchester that were taking ecstasy for a little while, so everywhere we turned up to play, there would be people with money wanting to buy E. Even if we weren't selling it as much ourselves by then, one of our lot would be knocking it out.

At that time, the Mondays were also becoming figureheads for the acid-house scene a bit, even though our music didn't really fit with that. I think it was because the scene lacked stars, as it was mostly built around DJs and people weren't necessarily ready to see DJs as stars yet; the whole superstar DJ thing was a few years off. They needed a face for this acid-house scene or movement, or whatever you want to call it, because the music was so faceless. You knew the tunes, but you didn't have a clue who was behind them and most of them were just written by kids in their bedrooms anyway. Our faces fitted the bill.

It was a bit weird when we got slots at techno nights or mini-festivals when we really shouldn't have been there. But because we were so associated with ecstasy, people would want to book us to go on the bill before or after a techno DJ, when that's never going to really work, or it shouldn't have. But luckily most of the time everyone in the audience was just off their tits. Certainly later on. It still happens now and again. A couple of years ago we were booked on some dance bill at a festival in Ireland and when we turned up a lot of the young kids were like, 'What are these lot doing on? We want techno!'

It was at this point we re-recorded 'Lazyitis' as a single, with Karl Denver. We shot the video underneath the Mancunian Way with the Bailey Brothers. The idea was that we were all convicts, playing football in the rain in the prison yard. Quite ironic, really, considering I got nicked while trying to promote it with Karl Denver. We got hold of some prison uniforms from Strangeways, no problem, but we ended up having to get a rain machine. Must have been the only time when it didn't fucking rain in Manchester. We shot it all on one night, and we had a few of our crew in it playing football, John the Duck and people like that. It was freezing and we had the rain machine pissing down on us, so half of us ended up with colds and poor Karl Denver got pneumonia.

As 'Lazyitis' was coming out, I had to go and meet Karl in Jersey, where he was doing a season. We'd played the Kilburn National Ballroom in London the night before, and then I had to fly over in the morning to some press. I was a bit the worse for wear, and I got stopped at customs going into Jersey. The customs didn't have a clue that I was in a band. They just thought I was some Manchester scum coming over to rob the island. At that time, any Mancs or Scousers going to Jersey would get stopped and searched because that's what they presumed you were up to, just nipping over there on the rob.

The problem was I hadn't checked my bags to make sure they were clean and when they searched them they found a couple of empty bags that had had coke in them. There wasn't even any coke in there at all; they were just empty bags with a little bit of residue in them. But because there were traces they charged me with importation and locked me up. The worst thing was, they don't really give you bail in Jersey, because if they do they think you'll just do one off the island.

The place I was banged up in was unreal. It was like a proper old-school prison in some sort of castle, and we all got fucking shackled up. It was fucking medieval. I got nicked on my own, but got shackled up by the ankle to this fucking chain gang with ten other geezers – whoever else had been nicked that day. Fuck knows who the rest of them were – just ten geezers of all different ages who had been nicked for different things. Everywhere we moved on that fucking island, we had to shuffle around in a chain gang, all shackled up together. We all had to go for a piss together. We all had to go for a fucking shit together. All these pots were lined up next to each other and we all had to sit there in a line. Seriously. Proper old-school affair.

Tony Wilson had to come over to sort it all out. I think in the end we had to post eight or nine grand bail, which was a fucking fortune back then to them, and even then the only reason they would grant me bail was because I was playing a benefit gig for Hillsborough with the Mondays. The urban myth about that whole incident is that Tony came to see me in jail and said, 'We'd need to get you an advocate,' and I said something like, 'What the fuck do I want a poncey fucking southern drink for, Tony, I'm in the shit here!' but that's bollocks. I knew what a fucking advocate was by then, trust me. What actually happened is that after I'd got bail and out of jail, me and Tony were having a laugh about an advocate being a poncey southern drink, and then that joke got re-told to someone else, then someone else, and twisted, and then that version became accepted as what happened, but it's bollocks.

What did make the whole situation more problematic is that when they did a blood test on me I did actually have cocaine in my system. When I got back I had to report to Swinton police station for a few months until the trial date. At that stage the band still wasn't that well known; we certainly weren't famous. We hadn't been on *Top of the Pops* or anything, so unless you were into our sort of music, you wouldn't have a clue who we were. I could still walk around the streets and wouldn't really get recognized unless someone was specifically a Mondays fan. It's when you go on TV that things change, and you become the property of the tabloids.

When it eventually came to court, it just got dropped anyway. The judge said there wasn't enough in the empty bag to charge me with anything. It did make me more careful going through customs from then on. I already had an importation charge on me, from when I got caught bringing weed back from Amsterdam. I also had various other little charges, and even though the computer systems and records weren't all linked up like they are now, if they stopped and searched you and ended up detaining you, they could find out all that information if they really wanted to.

Even though *Bummed* was a lot closer to the sound in our heads, it still hadn't crossed over. I was still bang into Paul Oakenfold's 'Jibaro', which I'd been playing loads while we were recording *Bummed*, so I had the idea to get him to remix 'Wrote For Luck'. Nathan got it – he was pretty good on that score; he could see that there was massive potential if we could tap into what was happening in the E scene, and bridge the gap between that and the indie kids. I knew Paul Oakenfold was the man for the job. Oakey might be a world-famous DJ and producer now, but back then he hadn't produced anybody and there was no established culture of DJs remixing songs by bands. I didn't know Oakey personally at that stage. I might have met him briefly in a club in London, but I didn't really know him at all, I just knew I wanted him to remix us. If I had told any other record company that I wanted this obscure DJ from London, who plays in Ibiza but has no real form in the studio, to work with us, there is no way they would have gone for it. But Factory did.

So Oakey and Steve Osborne did one remix, which actually ended up as the B-side, even though I personally thought it was a better remix. Factory also got Vince Clarke from Erasure to do a mix, which I didn't like as much as Oakey's. Vince's was a great mix, but to me it sounded too much like other records that he had worked on and had in the charts before. Oakey's and Osborne's, on the other hand, sounded totally new. It had that whole Balearic feel to it. Factory punted out a few white labels of it to club DJs and it started to get a good reaction in the clubs.

We then went out to Valencia to do this festival called La Conjura de las Danzas. Jeff Barrett was with us and ended up scoring some mescaline for us. I don't think I'd had it before. We were E'd off our faces and on mescaline and everything. We were out partying all night, and then we went down to the beach just as the sun was coming. Me and Muzzer fell asleep – we were just fucked and fell asleep on the beach – and the rest of the band thought it would be funny to just leave us there. But we were so fucked we didn't wake up, so we lay there asleep all fucking day in the blistering sun. We both had T-shirts and shorts on and Muzzer got proper nasty sunburn, but nothing like mine. The burns on my arms and legs were like third-degree fucking burns. I was burnt to a fucking frazzle – it was horrible. I was really, really burnt, and the rest of the band thought it was fucking funny. I had to go to hospital, and in the end I actually had to go and score some gear, some smack, because the pain was that bad.

It was just after Valencia that I really developed a full-on fucking proper habit, which you could even trace back to that day. We had to do a TV show later that day, and all the Spanish cameramen and crew were laughing at me – look at the stupid fucking Englishman burnt to a frazzle. But I had to do it. That was one of the reasons I had to find some gear and have a lick, so I could bear the pain and get through that TV performance. The pain was fucking killing me and that's how I probably ended up starting to hit the gear hard. I had messed around with it for years, but I'd never had a proper habit, and although I've never really thought about it like this before, looking back now, that's probably when I started on the gear big time.

We then had a gig at about 5am. The burns were so bad that I couldn't really walk or let my clothes touch me. I had to try and lean forward into the microphone, to try and let my clothes slightly hang off me so that they were hardly touching my burnt skin. I think Gaz Whelan fell backwards off the stage at that performance as well. It was a bit of a nutty gig.

After we came back from Valencia, I really started hitting the gear. It helped me with my stage fright, and there was always money about then. Gear was relatively cheap by then as well. It wasn't £90 a gram any more, or even £70 a gram. It had halved in price – you could get it for £40 a gram or something. It depended on the strength. Not that I'd be buying grams anyway. I would buy it in bigger weights. I'd be doing more than a gram a day.

When we played a gig I would never get the promoter to get

the gear for me; I kept shit like that quiet. I'd go and score, or maybe get one of our crew to do it.

In July we went back to the States on tour, supporting the Pixies. I thought the Pixies were great. We used to have this image of American musicians being mainly college kids, but they're not. A lot of them are like us and come from some quite hardcore towns or areas. I particularly got on with Johnny, the drummer from the Pixies, and I also really got on with Kim, the bass player who later joined the Breeders. The Pixies weren't necessarily a band I had listened to much before then, but I really liked them as a live band and the music really grew on me. I thought they were great. They were a lot better live than we were, musically; they could really play. We were still winging it a little, I thought. We were just a bunch of kids who liked music.

At that time there were loads of crews of Mancs and Scousers in Los Angeles who had taken the E culture over with them. They were selling ecstasy and putting raves on. If we were playing out there, they would all tip up at the gig. Or they would even tip up at the hotel, and because they were Mancs or Scousers we'd chat to them and then end up going off partying with them.

When we played Los Angeles we met Bowie, and the Beastie Boys turned up. We were all in a club called Enter the Dragon when Bowie walked in. Gaz Whelan was off his head and started going, 'Haha – Bowie's a midget! Bowie's a midget!' Gaz is obsessed with people's height, he always was. We were trying to shut him up, because he always went over the top when he was drunk.

He also had a bit of OCD, Gaz, and it could take hours to get him into or out of a club because he would have to touch something five times or something crazy like that. The bigger the band got, and the better known we got, the more his bits of

OCD came out. He was a footballer at heart and all footballers have slight OCD, don't they? They have weird rituals about how they put their boots on and stuff like that, which they have to adhere to. When Gaz was on a tour bus and it was just us, he'd be okay, although he still hated anyone touching his food. He also smelt shit everywhere. He'd always be saying, 'Can you smell shit?' Everything smelt like shit to him. He was also a hypochondriac. One week he thought he had bowel cancer, the next week he thought he had a brain tumour. It must have been a nightmare for him. He made Gillian McKeith look normal.

When the band first started, Gaz's mam and dad lived in a house that our pal Si Davis's family had lived in before. Si's dad had died in the house and Gaz was always a bit freaked out about ghosts and stuff. His mam and dad used to leave the windows open so I would climb in the window when they were out, go into Gaz's bedroom and move things about, just to freak him out. I did it for quite a while. He'd come out and say, 'There's a ghost in that bloody house.'

There were quite a few incidents on that tour of America with the Pixies. It was pretty eventful. We always seemed to meet big-time drug dealers when we were abroad around that time. Hardcore importers or people who ran smuggling rings. We just seemed to attract them. People who happened to have a kilo of weed on them, or the odd brick. We never seemed to meet normal people who were just selling an eighth of draw or a bit of coke. Wherever we went, nice restaurants or clubs or whatever, we seemed to attract these serious characters, people who were major players in some way. I remember in Los Angeles meeting this Bonnie and Clyde couple from Mexico, who were in their late twenties and looked quite respectable, but were actually responsible for bringing a lot of the weed from Mexico into LA. They were very middle class and well-spoken, none of your 'bro' talk or anything, but they were serious importers. I can't remember how we met them, but they just gave us an ounce, as if it was nothing. I think they might have even given us an ounce each. Everyone thought 'the chronic' was the strongest weed at the time, but I can't tell you how strong this stuff was. We were staying in the Hotel Roosevelt, which is facing the Chinese Theatre on Sunset Boulevard, and me and Muzzer had planned to go across and watch *Batman*, which had just come out, but we couldn't even cross the road. It was like acid, this weed; we were tripping our fucking nuts off. Me and Muzz can handle our weed, but this tackle had knocked us sideways. You have to be pretty fucking stoned before you can't even face crossing the road, but it seemed like an impossible mission to us.

It makes me laugh when people say, 'Oh the weed nowadays is much stronger than it was twenty years ago.' Bollocks. There was skunk and chronic, or whatever you want to call it, around back then; it just wasn't necessarily available in this country. But certainly if you went to the States or Mexico or Amsterdam you could get hold of it. The Dutch would always laugh at the Brits back in the day, because as soon as they arrived in Amsterdam and hit the coffee bars, they would go straight for the skunk, or the strongest weed available, roll a spliff, smoke it, and then spend the rest of the day almost in a coma, just nodding. It really bugs the shit out of me when people say the weed wasn't strong back then. Bullshit. What a load of crap.

There was also a proper heavy incident in Cleveland. A few of us – me, Muzzer, a kid called Bones and some other lad – got a taxi to go and score. We were after some weed, and some smack for me. We pulled up in this taxi and started doing a deal with this kid, but he was being a bit of a smartarse with us and giving us a bit of aggro, so we started being a bit smartarse too, started giving him some agg back. He gave it us, we gave it him back. Next thing he just gives this kind of whistle and these kids come launching out of nowhere with guns and bats. We ran to the taxi and dived in, and they started putting the windows through and everything. The taxi was a bit like what we would now call a people carrier – fuck knows what it was called then – but it was a bit bigger than a car and had a sliding door on the side. Me and Muzzer managed to dive or fall back into the taxi as they started on us, and they started smashing the windows with baseball bats. We somehow managed to get away, to this day I don't know fucking how, but by that time every window in the cab had been smashed and two of the doors had been ripped off, and the taxi driver was just sobbing, fucking bawling his eyes out. If me and Muzzer hadn't moved so sharpish and somehow managed to get back into the taxi, we would have been dead. Absolutely no question. They were hardcore hustler kids who sold gear, probably in their mid-twenties, proper corner boys. They weren't messing about. All because we were trying to do a deal and we thought this kid was trying to rip us off.

When we got to New York, the Ritz gig was quite a crazy gig. It was filmed and quite a few of our lot came on stage for the encore 'Wrote For Luck'. That was included on our Madchester video compilation that came out later in 1989, along with most of the videos the Bailey Brothers had done for us up to then. The last date of the tour was in Chicago, and after the gig I took acid for the first time in ages. I think it was in Chicago, although admittedly I was absolutely tripping my nuts off. I ended up, in the early hours, tripping my box off in this van with what I thought were really annoying people. They might have been very nice, because they were really just punters or fans who had hung around after the gig and wanted to be friendly and had offered to take us to some party. But I was on acid and they had started to annoy me. You know that certain type of American who is probably quite a nice person, but just starts to rub you up the wrong way? So I just started taking the piss out of them really heavily, just ripping into them, and one of the kids said, 'Oh my God! You're so rude!' But the more he kept saying, 'Oh my God! He's so rude!', the more it was winding me up and I was going, 'You fucking knob!' Then, next thing, the driver just shrieks in this high-pitched voice, 'I just can't drive with this motherfucker in my van any more! *Get out of my van! GET OUT OF MY VAN!!*' I was just laughing my head off, absolutely tripping my nut off, and I said, 'I don't even want to stay in your van, you fucking knob!'

We were in the middle of nowhere and I had no idea where I was, but I didn't give a fuck. Then this sexy bird in the van said, 'Hey, you can't just leave him here, he has no idea where he is!' and next thing, she jumps out and says to me, 'I better come with you.' We walked for what seemed like miles, because I was tripping, but fortunately she knew where we were supposed to be going. I'd never met her before, but somehow she knew where we were staying. It was about five in the morning at this stage, and I was fucked. I couldn't walk any further, so I flagged down a juggernaut and just pleaded with him, 'I'm an English guy and I'm tripping my nut off. Can you give us a lift please?' This girl was laughing her head off at me, but thankfully the driver took pity on us. We climbed in the truck and the girl was trying to tell this driver where we needed to go, because I'd got no idea where I was, or what was going on, and he was laughing his tits off at me because I was absolutely flying and still slagging off the knobs in the van, going, 'Those fucking dickheads' and all that. He eventually dropped us off at the hotel and I banged the arse out of her all day. Then she got up about teatime and said, 'Right, I gotta go and get my methadone.'

*

As we started taking off and getting better known, we had to spend more time in London, doing press or TV, and we found we got in places easier. We would find ourselves in some of these gaffs in London, Browns or wherever it was at the time, which were full of different crowds – aristocratic types, proper moneyed types, and even royalty.

Actually, speaking of royalty, Muzzer once fucked one of the royals in the back of a black taxi, on the floor. Not one of the immediate Royal Family – it wasn't Princess Beatrice or anyone like that – it was someone a bit further down the line to the throne. I can't remember her name and I wouldn't tell you even if I could, but she was something like seventy-eighth or eighty-fifth in line to the throne or something. Muzzer, her and me were in the back of a black taxi going through London. We'd been to some posh gaff where everyone was off their tits, and we were on our way to some other gaff and Muzzer just shagged her on the floor of the black cab while I was sat there. You might think they're all high and mighty, but some of that posh set are right naughty little fuckers. Alex Nightingale, who used to manage Primal Scream, has got some really interesting photos of some young royals on his phone, but they should probably remain nameless here.

If you're moving in the right circles or have money, that's how things happen – you end up meeting very different people. It's always been like that. That's how all the actor types ended up mixing with the Krays in London in the 60s, because they were all in the same clubs.

By the middle of 1989 our schedule was pretty relentless. There wasn't really much of a life outside the band any more. If we weren't out on tour, we were either in the studio or writing new material, and we were out every night. No days off. But none of us minded because it felt like everything was coming together. The whole E scene was going overground, but it still felt quite special at that stage. The Es were still good and the Haçienda was rammed every night. I felt like we had made a bit of a breakthrough with *Bummed* and 'Wrote For Luck'. But I also felt like we were on the cusp of something much bigger.

CHAPTER SEVEN

'Twisting my melon man, you know you talk so hip,
you're twisting my melon man . . . call the cops!'

At the end of July 1989, Factory opened Dry Bar on Oldham
Street. The Haçienda was still rammed and smashing it and
Factory had decided they wanted a sort of pre-club bar for
people to go to. Before Dry Bar we used to drink in old men's
boozers. We would go in the City Road Inn, opposite the
Haçienda, or the Britons Protection or the Peveril of the Peak.
They were our main hang-outs in the centre of town. We'd
stopped going to the 'trendy' bars, or those bars that *thought*
they were trendy. You know those late 80s type of bars?
I suppose in London they would call them wine bars, but
no one called them wine bars in Manchester. Just shit bars,
full of mirrors and chrome and fucking dickhead beer
monsters.

Ben Kelly, the guy who had designed the Haçienda, designed
Dry Bar, and it was the first modern pre-club bar in
Manchester, if not the country. They're everywhere now, Dry
lookalikes. There's probably a Dry rip-off in Ipswich and fucking Doncaster. But Dry was the first, and when it opened it was
completely different to everywhere else. It was like going to a
nightclub that opened at 1pm. We immediately made it our

headquarters and didn't really go anywhere else. If we were in town and not on tour, we would go to Dry just after we got up, about 1pm, and we would be there until 1am. We might nip out to go to a meeting or something, but basically that was where we were based. The toilet was downstairs and people spent a lot of time down there, doing drugs and just hanging out. Sometimes I would go down to the toilet about 8pm and not come back out until it closed.

By that time, the band were more well known, but I wouldn't really get mithered in Dry because of the lads that I had round me. I might get people letting on to me, or occasionally asking for an autograph, but I didn't get approached much because the sort of crew that hung around us then weren't really the sort of crew that you would want to bother. Let's just say they were a bunch of lads that people knew they had to be a bit wary of.

By 1989 there were other clubs springing up in Manchester as well, and most of them were quite moody. Konspiracy was a club below the Corn Exchange (which is now that poncey shopping centre The Triangle), near Victoria Station, which was put together by a mate of mine, Mario. Konspiracy actually used to be Pips, the club that we went to at the end of the 70s with the Bowie room. The main DJs at Konspiracy were Chris and Tomlin, the Jam MCs, who we actually took on tour with us to America. The other gaff that opened around the same time was the Thunderdome up on Rochdale Road, but I didn't really go there much. It was a pretty moody gaff.

By the end of 1989 the gangs had started to come in the Haçienda and the club tried to clamp down on it.

Just after Dry Bar opened we played at the *Other Side of Midnight* end-of-series party at Granada. It was filmed in the afternoon and we played with Mike Pickering's T-Coy and A

Guy Called Gerald. They basically tried to re-create a rave in the afternoon in a TV studio. We did about four or five tracks, including 'Wrote For Luck', which was the track that went out on the show. Fair play to Granada for trying to expose a mainstream audience to what was going on. Tony probably had a lot to do with setting that up, along with Nathan, but Granada were actually really good when it came to stuff like that, and always have been, when you look at how they covered Dylan when he first came over, or the Doors. They even filmed a programme with Muddy Waters in Chorlton years ago. Someone at Granada always seemed to have their eye on what was happening with youth culture and they were pretty good at it. You wouldn't get anything like that from any of the other British TV companies. It's a shame they don't really cover music in the same way now.

I don't really remember the filming of that show, but that's because I was completely off my tits. *Completely.* I know Tony introduced us, and Bez wasn't there because he was stuck in Marseilles for some reason. I can't remember what happened to him that time, but there were a few occasions when there were warrants out for his arrest for non-payment of fines or maybe missing a court appearance. He got escorted off a plane not long after that when we were flying to Ireland. There was a warrant out for him, so security and police came on the plane after we'd boarded and took him off. When we got to Ireland we managed to find a cardboard cut-out of Bez from somewhere and we stuck that on stage as a replacement. In fact, thinking about it now, I don't even think it was a cardboard cut-out of Bez; I think we nicked a cardboard cut-out of a pilot from the airport when we landed, and then found a picture of Bez's face from a magazine or something and cut it out and stuck that on this pilot and put some of Bez's clothes on it. Anyway, we had this cardboard cut-out on stage as a replacement for Bez, and Macca, a pal of ours from Salford, got up and danced in his place.

Not long after that a young girl called Claire Leighton died in the Haçienda. It was the first death from ecstasy. By that time there were some pretty dodgy batches of E turning up. We always knew where our original ones had come from, but we had no idea about all the others. I remember someone giving me a pill one afternoon and saying, 'Try one of these.' It was red, I think. I necked the fucker and an hour later I was walking down Oxford Road and I collapsed. I was on my own and I just blacked out. I don't know how long I was out for and I don't think anyone actually tried to help me. When I came round there were a couple of people stood just looking at me. I got up and pulled myself together a bit and just got off. There were some pretty dodgy drugs going about at that time.

About the same time, I had another dodgy E experience when I was crashing at a pal of mine's, Dave Reddie's, in Walkden, near Little Hulton. I woke up in the middle of the night because I was being dragged off the sofa and round the living room by two big Alsatian dogs. They were pulling me round the room and ripping me apart, these two Alsatians. But while this was happening to me I sort of got my head together a bit and said to myself, 'Hang on a minute – I'm in Dave Reddie's flat, and I *know* he hasn't got his dogs any more, he's got rid of 'em.' Next thing, I find myself on the floor in the front room of his flat, having a fit, convulsing and frothing at the mouth. But before that moment of clarity, I absolutely thought my hallucination was real. He'd actually only just got rid of the dogs, so you could still smell them in the flat. I must have smelt them in my sleep, and that smell had then triggered something in my brain, and the dodgy E had given me some sort of fit.

I don't think I ever stuck three or four pills down my neck in one go. Even the ones that I knew were 100 per cent MDMA. I would probably start off with one, or even a half, and then build it up, so over a night I might do three or four. A few years later, people were saying, 'I've had seven, or eight, or nine pills.' I'd just think, 'If you had put seven of those early pills down your neck in one go, mate, the top of your head would have blown off!'

It's a cliché, but the Es were definitely stronger back then. When we first started getting them they had pure MDMA in them. A 100 per cent pure MDMA pill would go for £50 a pop. Really expensive, but pure MDMA. But all of those first ecstasy pills were really good. You could tell when they started changing because they became quite whizzy; the first ones were nothing like speed. They made you feel like you had to shower and be clean all the time, and your clothes had to be really fresh. Obviously in some of the photos of the Haçienda everyone looks really sweaty because it was so hot and you were going for it, but the vibe was all about being really clean, washing your hair often and having clean clothes and feeling fresh. If you look at pictures from that period, everyone is *obviously* off their heads, completely off their nappers; but they all look quite healthy with it. Fresh-faced. And bloody young.

I was coming out of a warehouse rave one night and I had about ten pills on me. These ones were capsules, rather than tablets, so I put them in my mouth just to get out of there, because the police were searching people. But by the time I got out, these pills had melted in my mouth. Not good. I was absolutely out of my mind, and it gave me a real shock. I was knocked sideways for days and ended up taking myself to BUPA to get checked out, but they said I was fine. I've had a few near heart attacks like that, which is one of the reasons I stopped hammering the pills and moved on to other drugs.

*

Nathan, our manager, had a girlfriend called Trish at the time, and they were always arguing. She was only sixteen years old and Nathan was two years older than me. I was always saying to Nath, 'Get rid of her! You're always arguing and she's only a kid.' She was one of them who was always moaning, 'Why aren't you taking me out tonight?' when Nathan would have a gig on, or have a meeting in London or something.

Around the same time, me and Muzz were in the Haçienda one night and I said, 'Do you know what? I'm bit fed up of just shagging birds now. I want a serious girlfriend.' So we set up a double date with two girls we knew from the Haçi who were best mates and both called Joanne. Muzzer ended up marrying his Joanne, but mine blew me out. Joanne was lovely but she wasn't going to take any nonsense. The band had just started to really take off, and she knew exactly what I was like and what she would be letting herself in for, and there's no way she would have put up with me shagging around. She was too strong a woman to put up with any shit.

So she went off and eventually got married to someone else, and had a kid, Oliver, and then got divorced a while later. But she never really went out of my life, because we always had mutual friends, and she used to come to Happy Mondays and Black Grape gigs.

After Joanne had blown me out, Nathan did finish with Trish, and I was still looking for a girlfriend so I jumped straight in there. She was quite tall, Trish, so you wouldn't necessarily know she was so young. She was from Old Trafford and went to a comprehensive school and grew up in a council house, but her family, the McNamaras, came from money, back in Ireland. Trish had two sisters, Paula and Ursula, and her old bloke had died just before she arrived. His brothers had a huge construction firm and worked on the motorways. When we were on the road, I would always spot their names when there was a construction site along the way.

I was sick of couch-surfing and living in hotels, so shortly after Trish and I got together we got a flat in Granby House. It was one of the first developments of flats in Manchester city centre. They're everywhere now. Every old mill and warehouse has been turned into flats, but back then hardly anyone lived in town. There was India House, on Whitworth Street, which was like an indoor council estate; Cromford Court on top of the Arndale; and then Granby Row. I didn't really get mithered, living in town, because it was only our pals who knew I was there and we were a discreet little crew.

Granby Row was in quite a quiet part of town. There were a few trendy designers in there, including Trevor Johnson, who was a designer for Factory, a few business heads, and a few prostitutes who were making a lot of money. It was perfect for me, because I had both the Mondays' office and Matt and Pat's office on my doorstep.

Shortly after I moved into Granby Row, Nathan and Factory encouraged me to go into rehab for the first time, at the Priory in Altrincham. I'd been using more and more over the past year, but I still didn't really see as much of a problem as others did. It was pretty much a total waste of time anyway, because I didn't really understand rehab when I first did it. As far as I was concerned, I was there to stop taking drugs, so I couldn't understand it when they wouldn't let me have a beer in there. Seriously. That's where my head was at, and how naïve I was. The whole idea of rehab was just above me at that stage. I didn't have a clue. I would make a phone call to one of our lads and say, 'Bring us a bottle of whisky in will you?' Or 'Bring us some beers in will you?', and they would bring it in for me. As far as I was concerned, I didn't have an alcohol problem – I was just bored being in bed all day. I couldn't even see why the Priory would think, 'Oh God, he really is an alcoholic, he's getting booze smuggled in here.' In the end they said to me, 'Look, even if you're not an alcoholic, there are alcoholics in here and it's bad for them to even smell alcohol. And they *will* smell it, even if you've got it stashed in your room somewhere, because they're alcoholics. One of the first rules here is that there is no alcohol.' So, me being a bit of a spoilt brat at the time, I just went, 'Fuck it then, I'm out of here,' and discharged myself.

In September, Factory released the remixes of 'Wrote For Luck' after they had had such a good reaction in the clubs. It was released as 'WFL', because the original 'Wrote For Luck' had already come out as a single. Like I said earlier, I preferred Oakey's remix, which was called the 'Think About the Future' mix. It sounded totally fresh and new and had that whole Balearic thing going on. But Factory wanted to go with Vince Clarke's mix as the A-side, because he was a bigger name. It did OK, but didn't do as well as we thought it might. I think after it came out, and the dust had settled a little bit, then Factory and Wilson came round to my way of thinking that, yeah, Vince Clarke's mix was good, but Oakey's and Osborne's mix was the one that captured the new sound that was coming up and the mood of the moment. At least that meant they were more open to us working with Oakey and Osborne again in the future.

We then went into the studio to record the next single, which was going to be 'Hallelujah' and 'Rave On'. We had written the songs before we went into the studio and they were probably the first songs that had been influenced right from the very start by the whole E scene. By the time we started to write them, everyone in the band had started eating the E, and was being totally taken over by the effects of the Wednesday nights at the Haçi. It's fucking obvious if you listen to those tracks.

We recorded at the Manor studio near Oxford, which was owned by Richard Branson and Virgin, again with Martin Hannett at the helm. Martin used to pass out a lot during recordings; he wasn't in great shape then. We recorded four songs – 'Hallelujah', 'Rave On', 'Clap Your Hands' and 'Holy Ghost', but the recording is a bit of a blur for me, un-surprisingly, because we were all so off it. Apparently I had some of our lot in the vocal booth with us when I was doing the vocals to 'Hallelujah', because we were trying to get that club vibe on the record.

Wilson was desperate for us to get a single in the charts at this stage, after 'WFL' hadn't quite done it, so Factory brought Steve Lillywhite in to work on 'Hallelujah' as well. Steve was married to Kirsty MacColl at the time, and she was a fan of the band, so she did some backing vocals on 'Hallelujah'. Kirsty was great. We hung out together for a bit, and she even ended up doing some gigs and *Top of the Pops* with us.

At the same time we were down there recording, Branson was hosting one of his hot air balloon parties there. He was on his balloon vibe at the time, trying to break some record, and he had his garden party, which everyone right up to the Queen was at. Maybe not the Queen herself, but there were certainly elements of royalty there. It was one of those sort of parties where fucking everyone turns up. A proper circus. We were even on quite good behaviour, if I remember rightly.

The EP was called the *Madchester* EP. It was the Bailey Brothers who came up with the term 'Madchester' as a bit of a joke, but we were like, 'Great, yeah, go with it,' because Manchester *was* at that time, it was fucking mad. No one used the term in Manchester, unless they were a prick, but it quickly became adopted by the media, who lapped it up. The *NME* even did a Madchester issue with me and Tony on the cover, in front of a Madchester poster outside the Factory offices.

It had only been six weeks since the 'WFL' remixes had come out, but things had moved on in that short time and it finally seemed like we were beginning to make a proper breakthrough. When it came out, the *Madchester* EP was our first Top 20 hit.

That autumn we went on a big UK tour, our biggest yet. The second date was Newcastle, and me and Muzzer turned up late. The band had set off without me to do the soundcheck, as I was waiting to score, so me and Muzz had to get a train up later and then get a taxi to the venue.

We'd just made the jump to bigger venues, so we were playing some place we'd never played before. We weren't sure where it was – we didn't have any itinerary, and this was before mobile phones, so we just asked the taxi driver to take us to the local gig venue, and we pulled up and saw a queue of people outside, so we jumped out the taxi. We ran up to the door and Muzzer was giving it, 'We're the band, we're the band . . . we're late' and the bouncers just let us through and we legged it in. We walked straight through the auditorium, and should have clocked then that it was quite a civilized crowd, not our usual crowd with everyone off their faces, but we didn't. We just jumped on stage, and as I was walking across the stage I clocked the instruments and thought, 'We haven't got a saxophone,' but it still didn't click, and I just thought it was the support band's or something. Then we saw the dressing room door and Mick Hucknall was standing there with the rest of Simply Red and I suddenly realized. *'Fuck! Wrong fucking venue!'* We had turned up at a Simply Red gig. We were actually playing the Poly, which was just round the corner, so we did one sharpish.

The Manchester date on that tour was at the Free Trade Hall, which we filmed and later released on video as *One Louder*. There was a bit of trouble at that gig, as Salford had decided they weren't paying and rushed the door. The doormen were just overwhelmed. I don't think they had ever seen anything like it. They probably clocked some of the heads that were coming in as well, and realized that it wasn't wise to try and stop them or have a go at them.

We had to cancel the Leeds date on the tour so we could do *Top of the Pops* for the first time. That was a real turning point for us. It was one of those moments. Once you'd done *Top of the Pops* back then, things changed for you. I also thought it was fucking great that it was our first *Top of the Pops* and the Stone Roses were on the same show, so it felt like Manchester was taking over. The Roses also had a double A-side out – 'Fools Gold' and 'What the World Is Waiting For'. People still talk about that *Top of the Pops* to me – it's one of the main things that people bring up, so it obviously hit a nerve. I get blokes in their forties coming up to me saying, 'I was at college when you and the Roses first did *Top of the Pops* and it was fucking brilliant!' Even Dom Joly, when we were in the jungle, was banging on about it, about being at uni and watching it with his pals.

There was absolutely no rivalry with the Roses from my side. They did used to go round giving it, 'We're the best band in the world' and all that, but I'd just think, 'Right, okay. If they like saying that, fine.' Personally, I would never have said some-thing like that, but it was fine for them to say it. The Roses were a great band. Our Paul would sometimes moan to me that my songs were shit, and I should write more like Ian Brown, but that was just Our Paul. He just had a downer on my songs sometimes. I always knew, at the time, that we were getting on and making a name for ourselves because we were different, and the Roses were making a name for themselves because they were different. Our Paul contradicted himself really, because I think part of him did want to be in the Roses, but then he would turn round and say, really bullishly, 'We're the better band.'

The Roses were all good lads. Reni was a top lad, Mani was a top lad, Ian I'd known for ages since we used to meet for our tea at the drive-thru McDonald's in Fallowfield, and John Squire was another good kid. We were pretty pally with them, but you didn't really see them out in town that much. Mani was a big party-head, and he'd go to the Haçi and The Kitchen and that, but you didn't see the rest of them much. Ian went to the Haçi a bit, but not that often; neither did John. I always thought their great move was bringing Mani in. They were always a good band, but Mani seemed to be the final link, when it all really gelled. I didn't see them live much, because we would be off doing our own thing, but I did go to their huge gig at Spike Island the following year, 1990, and I had a top day out, although I can't really remember it. Like everyone else down there I was off my face. I think I watched the gig from the side of the stage, but I can't even be sure of that.

Because we were on the same *Top of the Pops* as the Roses, and the wider general public didn't really know who we were, I wanted to mix it up a bit. I wanted Ian to front my band, me to play bass in his band, Mani to play the drums with the Mondays and so on, just all swap over and mix it up a bit. It would have been really funny, because only fans of the Mondays and Roses would have noticed and got the joke. But it was the first time we had all been on *Top of the Pops*, so the rest of them weren't really up for it. Only me and Bez were up for it in the end.

I had a bit of a run-in with the bloke who was in charge of the *Top of the Pops* studio that day and he told me that I would never work in that studio again, and never do *Top of the Pops* again. Which was funny, because by the time I went back to do it again, *he* was the one that had been fired. I wasn't even really misbehaving. He was just a pompous arse, a stuck-up TV type who tried ordering me about and I just said, '*Fuck off, knobhead!*'

He was giving it all, '*I'm* the boss, I'm in charge here!' and I said, 'I don't give a fuck who you are, you silly little cunt.'

'*You* will *never* work here again.'

'Fuck off, you dick.'

Nick Kent came down to *Top of the Pops* to do a big piece on us and the Roses for *The Face*. That was supposed to be a big deal, Nick Kent coming down, but I couldn't give a fuck. All I knew about Nick Kent was that Sid Vicious had whacked him once, so I asked him about that and he told us that story and said it was a set-up by Malcolm McLaren. He seemed an all right geezer, I suppose. I think he was on smack at the time. There was a bit of kerfuffle when the piece came out because he quoted Wilson as saying, 'I have absolutely no problem with any of these guys dying on me. Ian Curtis committing suicide is the best thing that ever happened to me. Death sells.' I know Tony was upset, and I think the editor of *The Face* eventually admitted that they didn't have him on tape saying it, but it never bothered me. He might not have said it, but even if he had – and it *was* the sort of thing that he would come out with – we wouldn't have had a problem with it. If Tony denied it, then he didn't say it. I believe Tony. But it *does* sound like his sort of humour. He had a similar sense of humour to us, and I know from experience that it doesn't necessarily come across right in print. But, like I say, none of us would have had a problem with it. It was the sort of thing we would come out with ourselves.

You could tell with certain journalists that they were desperate for some sort of controversial quote, and we'd usually give it to them, because we didn't give a fuck. I can't read a lot of interviews that I did back then now, because we were just off our heads and coming out with all sorts. The wackier and more outrageous the better. We didn't care. The only thing that bothered me was when they used to write 'fuck' as 'fook'. That used to wind me right up. Oh God, that really did my fucking head in. Not my fookin head in. I can see how posh southerners might read it, but to us, 'fook' or 'fookin' looked fucking ridiculous. Knobheads. We had long discussions about that in the Mondays, and pure hated it.

What was ridiculous was we got a slight bit of resentment from some early fans when we did *Top of the Pops*. You'd get the odd dick who thought you had sold out. We used to laugh at those sort of pricks. I'd seen it years before with bands like Adam and the Ants. All the cool kids and the students were all bang into Adam and the Ants, and thought they were the greatest band ever, all dressing up like them and wearing the make-up and everything. But as soon as they went on *Top of the Pops*, the same kids decided they didn't like them any more. What a bunch of pretentious knobs. Bands want to make a living. They want to be successful so they can continue making music, because that's what they love doing. It's all right for you fucking students in your long macs, studying whatever you're pretending to be studying, not having to work, and wanting to keep them as 'your band'.

Our mates, all our lot, and everyone from round our way, were made up that we were on *Top of the Pops*. They were like, '*Yes! Go on lads!*' How often would you get a band from Salford on *Top of the Pops*?

It was a different era then though. A lot of bands would also get offended if someone wanted to use their song on an advert. '*What?* You want to use *my* song to *advertise cheese*? You want to give me £500,000 to *advertise a Ford Fiesta, with my music?*' I never understood that. The Mondays wouldn't have had any problem with it. We never had any problem speaking to any of the tabloids either. Again, that was frowned upon. You weren't supposed to speak to the red tops because it wasn't cool; you were just supposed to speak to the *NME*. People would warn us, 'They'll just twist what you say and spit you out.' Bollocks. Once you get on *Top of the Pops* and you're in the tabloids, then you're actually getting somewhere. Any dick can be in the *NME*. Any fucking student can get their ugly mug in the *NME*. So we'd welcome speaking to the tabloids and people like Piers Morgan, which other bands wouldn't do at the time.

I think that attitude has changed over the years, partly perhaps because of the Americanization of British culture. I remember they used to say if someone saw a nice car over here they'd scratch it with a key, but if someone saw a nice car in America they'd think, 'I'm going to make something of myself so I can get a car like that one day.' No one is afraid to be a success in America, which they could be over here – it's a very British thing. British kids were never schooled in that way; they weren't encouraged to think they were going to be successful, that they could do this or that, or build a successful business. But that has changed, and kids' expectations are probably too high now. You ask a kid nowadays 'What do you think a decent wage is? Ninety thousand a year?' and they'll say 'Ninety thousand a year?? That's fucking shit. I can't live off that. I want to be on at least half a million a year, because P Diddy earns this, or Man United players earn this.'

So it has changed, and people are less likely to scratch that car now, but their expectations are often unrealistic. It's good to have big ideas, but you need a bit of realism as well.

I didn't mind being associated with the Roses, but I wasn't into being lumped in with a lot of the other Manchester bands. I always thought James were OK; we'd known them for ages and played with them quite a bit. But I was pretty fucking horrible about the Inspiral Carpets back in the day. I remember watching them early on at the Boardwalk when they had a singer with big ears, and then they got rid of him because his girlfriend was moaning about him getting a proper job, and replaced him with a singer that looked exactly the same. A couple of them were quite young, but they had this old man with a bowl haircut on keyboards who whipped them into shape. Clint Boon, who was their keyboard player, is great. He loves the whole Manchester scene and he's a lovely fella. He does a radio show on XFM now, which I've been on, and does a great job. But back then I was pretty horrible about the Inspirals because I didn't want to be roped in with them. I remember sending nasty faxes over to their office, saying 'You bunch of tossers . . .' and stuff like that. Then we started getting quite naughty faxes back, saying 'You bunch of dicks . . .' I couldn't fucking believe it when those faxes came through! It was fine for us to give them shit, but I didn't expect the cheeky fuckers to give it back. We were like, 'The cheeky bastards, we'll have them put in a box!' Then I found out, years later, that it was actually their roadie who was sending all these faxes. A certain Noel Gallagher.

Noel learnt a lot from the Inspirals about the way the industry works, which he maybe doesn't give them credit for. Maybe he didn't want to be too closely associated with them, but now we're all blokes and in our forties, I think you can drop the childishness. I'll now admit I was a real knob with the Inspirals. They were just a bunch of nice lads who were trying to make it in the music business and they had a real good shot at it. They actually made some good tunes, which I slagged off at the time, but that was me being a dick, and a child. I was just up my own arse and got drawn into all that nonsense.

I just didn't like getting roped in with all these other bands.

I didn't think we had that much in common. Back then, I would even have preferred to be roped in with Take That than Inspiral Carpets, the Mock Turtles and the High. Just because it would have been different to make that association with Take That rather than the bands people expect you to be lumped in with. It wouldn't bother me nowadays to be associated with those bands, because it wouldn't seem like a matter of life and death, but back then it did.

I remember being in Muzzer's house and this kid called Dermo came round. I think he was a painter and decorator, and he was into karate. I chatted to him for a bit and I think he left thinking, 'He's just normal. He's just like me. If he can do it, I can do it.' Next thing, he's formed a band called Northside and they've signed to Factory. I probably did make it look more achievable to people, but I would also say that if you're good at something, anything, then you make it look easy.

Northside's first gigs were buzzing, because they had a massive local following. But then when they played London or Newcastle or something, the gigs didn't have quite the buzz because their pals didn't really travel. They also had to grow up in public, which isn't easy. Paris Angels were another group who had a massive local following but never really made it. Their guitarist, Paul Wagstaff, or Wags, ended up joining up with me in Black Grape.

I did see a difference in the way we were treated after *Top of the Pops*. Before that when we were talking about taking drugs or doing this or doing that it was fine, because it was all in the music press. But once you've been on *Top of the Pops* and the red tops get interested in you, they go back and look at these things you've been saying for years without any come-back, and suddenly it's news and it's slapped on the front of a newspaper as some big shock-horror story. The good thing about us is we knew it was all part of the game; we saw all that as part of rock 'n' roll. So when the press started saying stuff like 'They're all on drugs blah blah blah' it might have ruined some bands' careers, like fucking Duran Duran or Dollar or someone, but it wasn't going to ruin the career of a band like us. It was only going to help push us further forward, which is exactly what it did. If I read in the papers that I was doing drugs, I'd be like 'Dead fucking right I am!'

The sort of sex, drugs and rock 'n' roll that I had been brought up on, from the Stones to the Pistols, hadn't been around for years. I'd read the books and seen all the films, and then I'd been peering into the music business since punk, and it had just all got really safe and dull. Somebody's career could be over because they got caught smoking a joint. I was like, 'Fucking hell, that's not fucking rock 'n' roll!' So I knew all those stories wouldn't harm us; they could only help us, and they did. We had always been rock 'n' roll – that's just how we were. We were more rock 'n' roll than most fucking bands when we were still posties. It was never an act. We truly didn't give a fuck.

The only problem was, the press tended to focus on me and Bez, and that's when the hatred started from the rest of the band. They saw how we were getting elevated, and they wanted it as well. Even though anything the press said about me and Bez would only help us all. If the situation had been reversed, I would have thought, 'Go for it, nice one.' But they just saw how attention was focused on us and it did their egos in, because they really wanted to be on the cover of this mag or that mag. Me and Bez didn't even want to fucking do it. We were like, 'Oh, for fuck's sake, we've got to do this fucking interview or photo shoot.' We would have preferred it if the focus was on the others, but people only wanted us. So we did it for the sake of the band. And making dough.

It's a fucking game at the end of the day, and we just played along with it. We weren't bothered about becoming caricatures of ourselves. All that side of the game only helped our career. One of the reasons we didn't disappear overnight like lots of bands do is because we played that side of it. What it shouldn't have done is get the rest of the band so jealous that they hated me and Bez. But it did.

The way I look at it now, if you're not having the piss taken out of you on TV, and you're not being caricatured, then you're not a player, are you? When things happen like the guys from *Little Britain* taking the piss out of you, you know that it's really happening. Stuff like that helps make the dough and pays the bills. It's not life and death.

At the start of 1990 we were asked to do a cover version for our American label, Elektra, for their anniversary. I personally never wanted to do any straight-up cover versions, but for their fortieth anniversary they wanted all the bands on their label to cover another Elektra band's song for a compilation. So we had to. They sent us a tape of Elektra songs to consider and the first or second song on there was 'Step On' by John Kongos. I'd never heard it before, but I could tell it would be easy to rip, so I just went, 'Yep, we'll do that one.' I could tell we could add some different bits and catchphrases. 'Step On' is still a cover, but I think the new elements that we brought to the song really made it our own.

I'd been watching this Steve McQueen documentary called *Man On the Edge*, which had just come out. In the documentary, one of the big-shot producers from Fox or wherever describes when he first met McQueen and says something like, 'This cool kid came in, and you could tell he was an actor. He looked like a cool street kid and he said to me, "You can't tell me what's what, man! You're twisting my melon, man!"' That's what McQueen was like, an uncompromising little fucker. This producer carried on, 'This kid spoke so hip, he didn't know what he was saying!' As I was watching it, I thought, 'I'll have that – "you're twisting my melon man, you talk so hip, you know you're twisting my melon man".' I knew that's what we needed for 'Step On', some sort of catchphrase.

McQueen was a cool fucker. He was an orphan who had joined the Marines and then got into acting because he realized it was full of birds, and posh birds at that. I actually got into McQueen before I knew anything about his background. All I knew at first was he had a great haircut and wore really cool clothes. It makes me laugh when people wank on about James Dean. Please. *James Dean?* Fuck off. James Dean wasn't even in the same league as Steve McQueen, *nowhere near* the same league. Steve McQueen was the original casual, the original Perry Boy. I was already into him, but then I watched this documentary and found out more about him, about him growing up in a kids' home and lying about his age so he could sign up at fifteen. He was only about five foot eight or something, but he was a proper handy little fucker.

The other catchphrase in 'Step On' came from this kid in the Haçienda called Bobby Gillette, who was always shouting, '*Call the cops!*' He'd stand in the Haçi with all our lot, off his nut, whistling and shouting, '*Call the cops! . . . We're here! The Mancs! Our firm! Our corner! . . CALL THE COPS!!*'

So I just decided to stick those two elements together, and I had: 'You're twisting my melon man, you talk so hip, you know you're twisting my melon man . . . call the cops!' That's exactly what I thought 'Step On' needed.

It was pretty simple to do. The band laid down their parts and then I went in to do my vocals and I fucked around with the phrasing of the lyrics and added all my new bits. I even guessed at some of the lyrics at first, because I didn't have a lyric sheet. When I did get hold of one, I'd actually misheard some of the lyrics, so I changed a few of them back to the originals and re-recorded some of the vocals. I wish I'd just kept the earlier version now. Then Paul Oakenfold and Steve Osborne fucked around with it and added that big Soul II Soul sort of bass beat, that huge booming bottom end. When they gave it back to us and we played it, it just sounded mega.

We knew it needed a little something else, though – you could almost hear a gospel type of backing vocal on it. Nathan had been approached by a girl called Rowetta in the Haçienda a few weeks earlier, who said, 'You manage Happy Mondays, don't you? I fucking love that band.' Turns out she was managed by Simply Red's manager, Elliot Rashman, so Nathan put a call in and Rowetta came down the next day and added a simple backing vocal which was the final touch it needed.

Even though 'Step On' had started life as a project we weren't even arsed about, when I heard the finished track I was like, 'D'you know what? This is too good to give to that compilation . . . this is the tune that we need to get us back in the charts. This is the single that we'll put out before we do the album.' We needed a single to release to tide us over until the next album, which would be *Pills 'n' Thrills*, and 'Step On' was perfect. And it ended up doing exactly what we wanted it to do.

So we went back to the tape that Elektra had sent us, and the next song on there was 'Tokoloshe Man', which is also by John Kongos, so we just bashed that out in pretty much the same way and gave it to Elektra to put on the compilation. Elektra didn't really mind, because 'Step On' was an Elektra song and ended up being a hit single instead of just being on a compilation that only came out in America, and they owned the publishing rights and everything; plus they also got 'Tokoloshe Man' for the album, so it was a win-win for them. I liked our version of 'Tokoloshe Man'. It was a good tune, but I didn't want to release that ourselves as well, because I was a bit paranoid about us being known for cover versions, otherwise we might as well have just got in people like Nicky Chinn and Mike Chapman from RAK records, who wrote all the hits for Mud. Most people still don't actually know that 'Step On' is a cover, because we made it our own. I actually got a message from John Kongos once saying, 'Thanks for making my song so famous.'

Bob Krasnow, who was then the main guy at Elektra Records, the president and CEO, was really sound. I got on with him, even though when me and Bez first went to meet him he said to Nathan afterwards, 'You know, they both seem like nice guys, but that guy Shaun – I can't understand a word he's saying, man.'

Nathan said, 'What, but you can understand *Bez*??'

'Yes, I can understand Mark, is it? Bez? Yeah, I can understand him, but I can't understand Shaun.'

I thought, 'Fuck me, most of the English can't understand Bez!'

I remember when me and Bez first started doing American TV they gave us subtitles. We'd be watching ourselves on MTV with subtitles. We found that piss funny. We thought, 'Wow, we must be from the hood if they have to give us subtitles!'

Elektra gave us all a £5,000 Omega watch as a thank you for contributing to the album. They were fucking great watches and they had 'Elektra 25' engraved on the back. Unfortunately, I bloody lost mine a few years later in Los Angeles when we were working on the first Black Grape album. I was rushing out of the gaff where we were staying and left it there and didn't realize until later. We'd been renting this apartment, in one of those furnished blocks. They're weird, those sorts of places. You phone up to book it and they say, 'Right, what do you want in your apartment? Do you want Variety Box A – that includes flowers, mirrors, pictures, a telephone, two beds, two settees and four televisions? Or do you want Variety Box B – that includes flowers, mirrors, pictures, a telephone, three beds, three settees, and satellite television in every room?' Then they just ship in whichever variety you chose. If I stay in a hotel room, then my watch doesn't come off my wrist, but if I'm staying in some gaff like that for any length of time, then jewellery will eventually come off at some stage. So I'd taken my watch and one of my rings off and I fucking left them there. The diamond in the ring alone was worth about £10,000.

Those sort of gaffs in LA would employ bunches of Mexicans to bring in all the furniture and set it all up, then take it away afterwards. When I realized I'd left my watch and ring there, all I could think was some Mexican dude in a poorly paid job has had a right result there. He's gone home with a watch worth about £5,000 and a diamond ring worth about £10,000. I didn't even bother phoning up to see if they had found it. Where I come from, if you leave an expensive watch and a diamond ring in an apartment which then gets cleaned, it ain't gonna be there if you phone up later. No fucking chance. If we'd found them when we were younger, there's no way we would have handed them in.

Towards the end of February it was Tony Wilson's fortieth birthday, and he said later that he took eleven different drugs that night, and alluded to the fact that it was because he was hanging out with me. I'm not sure about that. I do remember Tony driving round the centre of Manchester in his Jag, with this special sort of tray next to the steering wheel, which he used to skin up on. One of the most famous people in Manchester, and he used to drive around skinning up. He did get pulled by the cops, but they just used to let him off. I've been with him when he's smoking a joint while talking to the cop and nothing happened. The cops would turn a blind eye back then.

After I moved to Didsbury, me and Muzzer would be speeding up and down Princess Parkway into town in our BMWs and Mercs, doing 120 or 130mph. I remember flying down there one day and this car came right up my arse, so I put my foot down a bit more, and next thing the sirens come on. It was the police in an unmarked car. So I pulled over and they got out and clocked it was me and said, 'Fucking hell, it's *you*. Get back in your car and slow down, you cunt!' and just let us off.

The Old Bill can be funny. If a copper was a United fan and he caught a City player speeding like that, he could lose his licence. Likewise, if the copper was a City fan and he caught a United player, he could lose his licence. If I got caught and the cop was a fan of the Mondays, he'd just say, 'Go on, get back in your car and fuck off, you silly cunt. Just *slow down*.' I have to say, I have been one *lucky boy* with the police in Manchester and London. I should have been charged with so much stuff that I actually got away with because they liked the Mondays or Black Grape, and they let me walk. There's no need to go into those incidents now, but the number of times they just said, 'Go on, get off, and sign that while you're at it.'

At the start of March, we went on a mini European tour. We played Hamburg, Berlin and Cologne, and then went to Spain to do a few dates and film the video to 'Step On' while we were there. We did a performance at the Arts Studio in Barcelona first, and we had the usual hassle from the Spanish police. Back then, it seemed to us as if the Spanish police were just there to be bribed. They'd do stuff like sneak into your dressing room before you got there and hide behind curtains or doors and watch you doing lines of cocaine, or see you with a big chunk of hash, then they'd just step out from nowhere and say something like, 'This is worth, er, eight hundred thousand pesetas' or something like that. It usually worked out about £300–500. So we'd pay it and then about three hours later we'd get gripped by another lot. They would follow us. We'd end up going, 'Not you lot again. Fuck off!' We'd pay the bribe the first time, and even the second time, but the third time we'd tell them to fuck off and we'd be on the way to the station. But you never got charged. It was mental back then in Spain, I could never work out the law. It seemed as if at half past one in the afternoon it would be legal to smoke hash, then at three o'clock the same afternoon it would be illegal. By the time it was ten to six, it was legal again. That's what it felt like, particularly in small towns, depending on who you were dealing with. It was as mad as that. We loved it.

Sitges, outside Barcelona, became our base for a little while. It was a beautiful place, absolutely gorgeous. I haven't been back for ages, so I don't know if it's been invaded by the English yet, but then it was lovely and the place where all the cool crowd from Barcelona would go. It was the gay capital of Spain as well. I remember when we went in a club there for the first time and a few of the Spanish geezers got their cocks out and started swinging them about. We just used to laugh at that.

We filmed the video to 'Step On' while we were in Sitges, with the Bailey Brothers. We wanted to get the single out quick at the start of the summer, so not too much thought went into it. A lot of people think it's filmed in Los Angeles for some reason, maybe because there's a shot in the video that is very similar to a shot where a plane takes off in the film *Bad Boys*, which is set in LA.

'Step On' had a summery feel to it, so it made sense to film it in the sun, and we just filmed it on top of the hotel we were staying in at Sitges. I don't even think we asked their permission; we just went up on to the roof and did it. There were five massive letters spelling out 'H O T E L' and I ended up climbing up on the E. When I saw the huge E, I just thought, 'Ha, perfect. Just what we need. A shot of me on a massive E.' Kevin Cummins, the photographer, was there for the *NME*, so he took a picture of me climbing on the E and it was used as an *NME* front cover. I knew it had the potential to be an iconic image. The letters were actually illuminated, but I broke a bit of the E off when I climbed on it and it wouldn't light up any more after that. Someone else damaged the L as well, so in the end it just said 'H O T'.

There was no plot to the video, but there rarely was with the Bailey Brothers. They just approached our videos like they were shooting a load of cool guys in a movie, just hanging out. A gang of cool guys on a hotel roof, in the sun, with a bit of marijuana smoke drifting across the set, and that's it. It's almost like a rap video approach in a way; they usually don't have a plot to them, it's just hanging about.

I woke up the day after the video shoot in my hotel room and there was sick on me, so I went, 'Fuckin' hell, did I spew on myself?' and Muzzer said, 'No, that was me, sorry, I didn't make it to the toilet in time.' When we were sharing rooms on tour, me and Muz would always room together because we both had a shit sense of smell. So he couldn't smell my feet and I couldn't smell anything either. We both smoked a lot of weed but couldn't really smell much. We were the gaffers as well, really. I kind of ran the band and Muzzer's official title was Assistant Tour Manager, but he basically ran the tour.

After the 'Step On' shoot, we did a couple of dates in France, including the Bataclan in Paris. Loads of coaches came over from England for that gig.

After France, we went on to Iceland, which was our first time over there. Iceland was a weird place, but beautiful in its own way. Mad landscapes. It's like landing on Mars. We did the Blue Lagoon, the volcanic lake and all that stuff you do on your first trip to Iceland, which was brilliant. It's expensive as fuck – even though you're warned about the expense, it still shocks you. We ordered four pizzas and that cost £50, and remember this is twenty years ago now. A gram of amphetamines was over £100. A ton for a gram of speed!

The gig itself was in a kind of school hall-type venue, which was a bit weird, and there was no licence but it was a great gig. Then we went to this place afterwards called the Moon Club, where it all kicked off. All the Icelanders were *really* leathered. A lot of them seem to be already steaming when they come out at night – they probably get pissed at home before they come out because the drinks are so fucking expensive. Anyway, they were bumping into us and everyone else, and Bez started a row with this huge, wide Icelandic guy, a big yeti of a bloke who had bumped into him. Bez had given him a few digs and he'd gone down a bit, on to his knees, but then he'd sunk his teeth into Bez's leg. So I picked up this big chair and started really whack-ing him across his back and the back of his head, trying to get him to let go. I really belted him with this fucking chair, and must have hit him ten times before he finally slumped over. But they seemed to be used to that sort of thing – it didn't seem out of the ordinary for them.

I thought they were great, the Icelanders; they reminded me of people from Salford quite a lot. They had a similar attitude, in the way that you can have two guys who have a beef with each other and they will get right at it, really leathering each other, and one of them might even stab the other, but then an hour later they're having a beer together and a laugh about it. If that happened in Moss Side, one of the kids would go home and get a gun and come back and shoot the other one. But in Salford they would leather the shit out of each other, absolutely brutal stuff, but then when it's done, it's done, and they would both walk away and they're mates again. I don't know if it's the Viking in them or something, but the Icelanders seemed very similar.

The Icelanders had only just heard of these things called warehouse parties and they had no idea what they were, or how you put one on. They actually thought you had it in a normal warehouse, so after the club closed they opened up this ordinary warehouse, which was full of stock – clothing, shoes and skiing equipment – and just started partying round the stock. Now at that stage we were doing all right financially and we didn't want for anything really, but there is no way you're going to put our lot in a warehouse full of stock and expect us not to rob it. Impossible. Even though it was stuff that we didn't need. We were like kids in a candy shop. We just couldn't help ourselves.

There was another incident on the flight back from Iceland. Some really drunk guy, a video director or something, who was quite a big dude, kept hassling me. He wanted me to agree to do something or other, and kept going on and on about it. I was sat at the back of the plane, in the smoking bit – remember that, when you could smoke in the back three rows of the plane? Seems mad now that you could do that. Anyway, Muzzer came down the aisle to see what the mither was all about and told this guy to fuck off and leave me alone. This guy turned round to Muzz and said something like, 'I'm talking to the act, not his monkey.' Big mistake. Muzzer just fucking headbutted him. The guy's nose just exploded and there was blood everywhere. I think it even sprayed on to both walls of the plane. Then it all kicked off and it got to the stage where the pilot said he was going to divert the flight to Glasgow. I managed to calm the bloke down and the pilot didn't turn the plane around. *I* always seemed to end up on my toes to try and talk us out of whatever situation we'd got ourselves into.

When we got back from Iceland, it was pretty much straight on to do the G-Mex, which was our biggest gig to date. Our schedule was pretty fucking relentless at that stage. No days off. G-Mex was the biggest venue in Manchester at the time, and when someone first suggested we should play there Simon Moran, whose company SJM promoted most of our gigs from *Bummed* onwards, wasn't convinced we could sell it out. Which is why we ended up doing it in-house and putting it on ourselves. Two pals of ours, Jimmy Sherlock, who everyone knew as Jimmy Muffin, and John Kenyon, who everyone called John the Phone, promoted it. They had a company called Nighttime Promotions and they had originally done the bootleg T-shirts outside our gigs, until me and Nathan decided we wanted in on the bootleg operation as well. So we offered them the chance to do our official merchandise stalls inside the gig venues as long as they also gave us 50% of whatever they made on the street.

It did seem a little bit scary doing the G-Mex, because it was a big jump up from the Free Trade Hall, which was the biggest venue in Manchester we'd done up to then. That's how quickly things had exploded for us. At the end of 1989 we did the Free Trade Hall, which was 2,000, and then at the start of 1990 we're doing the G-Mex, which was 10,000. We missed out doing those middle-sized venues like the Apollo. Outside Manchester, it was an even bigger jump: we'd gone from doing 500-capacity venues to arenas.

The Manchester Evening News Arena wasn't built at the time, but now we've played that, if I go back to the G-Mex it looks small. But at the time, playing it was a massive thing.

Bands like us just didn't play there. But Jimmy Muffin and John the Phone got on the case with putting it on sale and promoting it, and next thing they turned round to us and said, 'Look, we've done this – it's happening. Sold out. We're going to put a second night on sale.' Which must have made Moran sit up and take notice, because they weren't even promoters, really. They were ticket touts and merch sellers, and Muffin had promoted at the Thunderdome. But they knew what would sell at street level, because they were tuned into the vibe on the street and were confident it would sell out. And they were right.

As usual, we made a little bit of extra dough on top as well, especially after it sold out. I don't remember this, but Andy Spinoza said in *City Life* magazine that he stopped me on Deansgate the afternoon of the gig and tried to grab a quick interview with me, but I told him I didn't have time because I still had some tickets to get rid of for that night's gig. We were still definitely touting our own gigs at that stage, although I would have thought we would have had someone else out on the street doing it for us.

We stayed at the Midland Hotel the weekend of the gigs, which is just across the road from the G-Mex. We knew there was potential for trouble if a lot of our fans managed to book rooms in there, or just even get in the doors. We really tried to warn the hotel, but they didn't take any notice. We didn't want it all to come back on our toes. By this time we'd had the police coming to see us about the behaviour of some of our fans and we were like, 'What can we do? We don't know anything about it.' I'm sure that when Elvis played Vegas, if something got robbed in the casino next door the cops didn't drag bloody Elvis in and question him about the behaviour of his fans, or ask him about this firm or that firm, y'know what I mean?

So we had been down to the Midland beforehand and

actually had a meeting with them and stressed: 'Watch who you sell rooms to, and watch who comes through the door, and we want you to know these people have got nothing to do with us.' But they didn't listen. They just said, 'Oh, it will be fine, we've had the Who and Frank Zappa here and that was no problem.' We tried to tell them that the Who fans are nothing compared to our lot, but they just didn't listen.

There wasn't an official after-show at the hotel or anything, but inevitably everyone piled back after the gig. Bez probably invited hundreds of people back. The bar got rinsed, and someone, I think it might have been Bobby Gillette, threw a champagne bottle that smashed a mirror. The place just got trashed. There were glass cases in the lobby with watches and jewellery in, and they all got robbed. Someone just opened them up and took everything.

The next day, of course, someone from the Midland rang up complaining to us, but we just said: 'It's nothing to do with us. Check with your area manager or whoever, because we fucking warned you this could happen.'

The gigs were filmed for Channel 4, but it's all a bit of a blur to me, though everyone says they were top gigs. Rowetta played with us again on backing vocals, and after that she pretty much played every gig with us. She was great when we played live, because she used to dress up in all this leather gear and wield a cat-o'-nine-tails, and it just gave us another visual element on stage. Inevitably, I started shagging her, and it's pretty obvious from the videos of some of the gigs that there was something going on between us. That continued almost through the whole time she was with the Mondays, even though I was with Trish and other girlfriends later on. You should never get involved with a girl in your band but, like I say, there's a certain amount of inevitability about it when you've got long drives across America and endless nights in hotel rooms. But then I found myself in the situation where I had the groupies to deal with, and then still go and sort out Rowetta. It was hard work.

A couple of days after the G-Mex gigs, we went to Marbella and Puerto Banús for a few days to chill out – all the band plus our girlfriends and wives. 'Step On' had just been released and we were waiting to hear about the chart position. I think I did a live radio interview with Annie Nightingale while we were out there. You know when they used to phone you up during the chart show to get your reaction to your chart position? It had gone in at No. 5, so I was buzzing.

While we were out in Puerto Banús, the Strangeways prison riot started back in Manchester. One of our lads, Platty, was actually doing time in Strangeways then. So we were looking on telly, trying to see if we could spot him. He was one of those that went up on the roof for the first day or so, but then was smart enough to get down before he risked getting time added on to his sentence. We were hearing all sorts of rumours about what was going on in there, about kangaroo courts and all that sort of stuff. One of Gaz Whelan's family had a bar in Figuerola – I think it was his auntie. So that's what we spent most of our time doing while we were over there, watching the Strangeways riot on telly in Gaz's auntie's bar. We were all dead proud of the riot – 'Go on lads!' – it was great. The funniest thing was this geezer in Salford, who had gone up on his house or garage roof in sympathy for the Strangeways lads. All the local TV crews were coming round filming him sat up on his roof. It was hilarious.

The riot just seemed to fit in with all the madness that was going on in Manchester at the time. The police chief was talking to God, the Haçienda was still mental, the prison was rioting, the whole city just seemed like a cartoon.

*

May was the Haçienda's eighth birthday. The Haçi was still at its peak then, and people would kill to get into birthday parties or New Year's Eve or whatever. They would pay £300 for a ticket from a tout. Ridiculous prices. And I had handfuls of them. I was still in that mindset where I couldn't help but take advantage of the chance to make a bit of extra dough. I could just be standing outside the Haçi waiting for a mate or something, and people would come up to me and say, 'Shaun, have you got any tickets? Can you sell us a ticket please?!?' They'd offer me £300 for a ticket that I was probably just going to give away to a mate, and then someone else would see that going on, and go, ''Ere, have you got another one, Shaun?' There were times when I'd literally just go outside the club for a bit of fresh air for five minutes and come back in with an extra couple of grand in my pocket.

The morning after the Haçi's birthday we were supposed to go to Paris to do some TV show, but I didn't get out of bed. I think we ended up telling people that I'd done ecstasy for the first time for quite a while and when Bez came round to get me the next day I was still too wasted. But the truth is more likely to be that I didn't have any heroin, and I wasn't going anywhere until I got some. If the gear wasn't there, I wasn't getting on a plane.

As much as we would listen to the new sounds and acid house when we went out at that time, we were still listening to old classics at home and on the tour bus. Remember we were born in the early 60s, so we were young kids when all the late 60s music first came out and it had stuck with us. We had always loved Donovan and decided to go and see him when we heard he was playing Colne, which is about forty-five minutes' drive north of Manchester. To me and Bez, Donovan was as cool as Dylan; he'd written some brilliant songs.

A lot of people don't realize who played on all those songs as well. When I got to know him later, I'd be like, 'Who played bass on that?' and it would be Noel Redding from the Jimi Hendrix Experience or someone like that. He would just write these numbers like 'Sunshine Superman' on his acoustic guitar and Noel Redding would come round and drop a bass line on it, just go 'Bum, bum, bum-bum-bum-bum' and then just get off. No fee, no publishing or anything on it; Donovan would get the lot. People like Noel Redding had just given these great bass lines away back then, whereas I had Our Kid saying, 'I wrote the bass line on that. I want seventy per cent of that tune!'

Anyway, we heard that Donovan was playing up in Colne, so me and Our Matt and a few others went up to see him. We expected a full band, but it was just him and an acoustic guitar. We had a chat afterwards and he was cool, and I think we tried to get him to come down the Haçienda, but he had to carry on the tour the next day.

When we were about to go on tour again, we decided we wanted Don on the tour and Nathan had to do the deal. The thing was, we wanted him with a full band, not just doing the solo acoustic thing, but within about a week he managed to pull this full band together, and they were great. They were all session guys and they'd never played together, or played these songs before. They only had four days to learn these classics, but they sounded exactly like they did on record. I was blown away: 'Wow, these guys are *real musicians*.' It was such a big deal to get our lot to do anything, but these guys just turn up, look at all the dots on the paper and just play it, absolutely no messing. I'm thinking, 'This is how it should be.'

Don was a real hero to us. We got on brilliantly with him. He was pretty mystical, but also quite down to earth, if that's not a contradiction in terms. Not long after we met him, Our Kid started dating his daughter, Astrella. Our Paul was driving around in one of those early 4×4s at the time, can't remember the make, but it looked really cool. Then he starts dating Astrella and a week later, the 4x4 is gone and he's driving around in a little thirty-year-old battered white two-seater MG. I was like, 'What the fuck are you doing?' But they thought it was really cool. Until it died when they'd only had it about a week. They took it back to the MG garage, just opposite the Haçienda on Little Peter Street, and the garage replaced the white knackered MG, which looked OK, with this orange one, which was fucking hanging and knackered. So then they're driving around in that and we're all thinking, 'My God, what is going on?' That was one of the Mondays' Yoko moments, really. As soon as Our Kid got with Astrella, the rumour started that he was going to leave the Mondays and set up a band with her. She played guitar and sang and had a No. 1 in Italy when she was five or something.

There had even been a bit of talk that the Mondays might write with Donovan himself, but that never amounted to anything in the end. Me, Bernard Sumner and Johnny Marr were also going to do a cover version of Donovan's 'Colours' at one stage; we even started work on it, but it didn't come to anything. I'm not sure why we were going to do that, although Bernard and Johnny were obviously working together as Electronic at that time.

That summer, we headlined Glastonbury, which was actually the first time we had played there. *NME* wanted to do a big cover story on us there, so we suggested doing a photo shoot with a mini Stonehenge, because we were all big fans of Spinal Tap and they had a mini Stonehenge. We did the shoot in Heaton Park in north Manchester. We drove up there in convoy and when we arrived Bez crashed into Gaz's car in the car park.

He was a liability behind the wheel, Bez, even though he used to slag off my driving.

I'd been to other festivals before, but I'd never been to Glastonbury. I wasn't interested in the whole mystical side of it, and the ley lines and all that bollocks. To be honest, it wasn't a completely jolly experience for me. It rained, so it was muddy, but that didn't bother me much, apart from I didn't want to get my trainers muddy. I spent almost the whole time on the tour bus. I didn't even go to the dressing room. Glastonbury in 1990 was still quite basic; it was closer to what it must have been like in the 70s than to what it's like now. When I went back recently, to headline with Gorillaz, it was a completely different experience, a much more professional set-up.

Back in 1990 we had a sleeper bus, but I also booked into a hotel so I could get off site for a bit. When I was on site, I spent most of my time underneath our bus, in the luggage hold. You know when you have a panel on the side of the coach, which lifts up and there's a big hold underneath for everyone's bags and stuff? I spent most of Glastonbury in there with about twenty other smackheads. We spent almost all weekend under the bus, just smoking gear. Stick a gram on a piece of tinfoil, smoke that; stick another gram on a piece of tin foil, smoke that. Just smoking constantly – it was a mad scene. We ended up with more and more of us under there, because someone would have to go and get some more gear, and they would come back with a few more hangers-on. I did have a break from it at one stage, when I got off to the hotel with this bird that I'd met at *Top of the Pops*. We disappeared for the night, but when we got back to the site I was straight back under the bus, and straight back to my tinfoil.

My mam has got this great photograph on her living-room wall that is taken from the back of the stage at Glastonbury while we are playing. You can see the back of me, and my Armani jeans, and then the whole of the audience and the tents behind – a great crowd shot. I can't really remember much of the actual performance though, because I was so numb from the heroin. I think the most exciting part of the weekend for me was taking the bird back to the hotel. While we were there, some of our lot were making copies from our backstage passes and banging them out. I think they even had a colour photocopier and a laminating machine on the bus.

We also had people selling snide merchandise as well as the official stalls. As ever, you couldn't stop people selling bootleg merchandise, so you might as well sell it yourself. We wanted both ends of the market. So we had a few lads out there working, and what they would do is when they had made a certain amount of dough they would go and bury it or stash it somewhere. John the Phone, the guy who had put on G-Mex with Jimmy Muffin, was heavily involved in the merch, and he actually got fucking kidnapped at Glastonbury. This biker crew – I don't know for sure if they were actual Hell's Angels, but they were a heavy biker crew anyway – kidnapped him and took him to this disused farmhouse nearby. They tied him up and had him in there for nearly two days, slapping him and torturing him. But you've got to give it to the little fucker – he told them nothing. He wouldn't tell them dick. So eventually they just let him go. He had a fair few cuts and bruises and I think they'd shaved a bit of his hair off, but he just brushed it off. Went to the place where he'd stashed the last of his money, got it and brought it back to the bus.

We got asked to leave in the end, because our lot had brought it a bit on top. They realized how many backstage passes we had knocked out, and in the end their security surrounded our bus and made us leave the site. Glastonbury had its fair share of scallies, who used to come down because they thought it was easy pickings, but they just weren't prepared for us. I didn't think much of it at the time, because I was just in a haze, but looking back, we were pretty crazy.

We went to Ibiza after Glastonbury. We were playing Ku Klub and we were supposed to be chilling out, but me and Muzzer ended up spending a week trying to get paid for the show. I was sure there was something dodgy going on and they wanted to avoid paying us. It was about £100,000, but after a few days' hanging around we eventually got the money. I think Muzzer had to throw his weight around a bit, but there was no way we were going to let them take us for a ride.

We then went back to America to do a short tour, before ending up in Los Angeles to record our next album. The tour was called *The United States of the Haçienda*, and we also had Mike Pickering, Paul Oakenfold and the Haçienda DJs Graeme Park and Dave Haslam on the tour.

The gig in New York coincided with the New Music Seminar, which is a big industry thing in the States, so Wilson was in his element. I didn't have much to do with it, but I know Wilson gave this speech giving it all 'Wake up America, you're dead!' and bigging us up. The thing with Americans is, even if they think their music scene is shit at the time, or their current president is a dick, or whatever, they might be allowed to say it themselves but they won't stand for anyone else saying it. They don't like anyone else going over to America and telling them what's what, so Tony going over there saying that was never going to go down well. Yanks like success. They're different to the British. The Brits love an underdog. Look at *X-Factor*. People love it when someone goes on and is terrible, dressed like a goon, and can't sing and makes a fool of themselves. They love someone like that Wagner bloke, the Brazilian PE teacher that was on *X-Factor*, who couldn't sing at all. The

English love someone like that. The Yanks can't stand that. They hate it.

That was partly why the British loved Bez, but the Americans never really got the idea of him. They never really grasped the concept of Bez. They would be like, 'What does that guy *do*, man? He's not a dancer – that's not dancing.' Well, he's not really a dancer, no. 'So, what does he *do*? *He doesn't sing*, he doesn't play *anything*. He just fucks about on stage off his head.' But the British loved that, and in Britain Bez almost was the Happy Mondays at one point, or at least he personified us. But the Yanks just didn't understand it, and they didn't like the way it looked, this guy with bulging eyes wandering up and down the stage. They didn't mind it so much on videos, when he's just standing around, because a lot of American videos, especially rap videos, are basically just blokes standing around. But on stage they want everybody to be doing a specific job, and they couldn't see what Bez was doing there.

Keith Allen also came out on that tour with us. He was always a Factory fan, and knew Wilson and New Order, so he just started coming to the gigs, and then he came on tour with us to the States.

We were still quite young at the time, in our mid- to late twenties, but if we thought we were mad, you should have seen Keith. He was about ten years older than us, in his late thirties, but he was still hitting it hard, and when it came to doing mad things he would put us to shame. You could be out with Keith in a bar in America and it would kick off and you would be lucky to get out alive. Keith would be sat there and if something annoyed him, he would just pick up a chair and put it through a plate-glass window. Several times I can remember being in bars with Keith in America and it going off, and us having to fight our way out of there, and Keith was usually at the centre of it, if not starting it. Seriously. People thought we were complete madheads and would love to write about what we got up to, and people would lap it up, but Keith was a mentalist. Far worse than us.

When we played the Sound Factory he was on stage for the gig, like a second Bez, apart from he'd overdone it so much that he had to get his head down halfway through the gig. On stage, in the middle of the gig, he's trying to climb in this flight case at my feet. Then he woke up again and got up for the encore, I think, for 'Wrote For Luck'. When it came to craziness at that time, I don't think even Bez had anything on Keith. He used to drive about London in a black cab that he owned, with all his kids in it. But you see him now and he seems very together, and very grown up. Although he must be nearly sixty now.

Muzzer reminded me recently about this punky-looking girl I met in New York, who had dyed red and black hair, and was really nice looking. I was sharing a room with Muzzer again, and when I took her back to the room he was in bed but I thought he was asleep. I start getting it on with this bird and she says, 'I want you to hit me.' I said, 'I don't want to hit you.' She said, 'I *want* you to hit me – I like it.' I was like, 'Nah, leave it out.' But she kept on at me, 'I *want* you to hit me. I *love* it.' So in the end I just gave a little slap, and she did love it. Then she hit me back, so I clobbered her again and so on. I picked up the phone handset and smashed her round the head with it, and that must have knocked a glass over on the bedside table because somehow some glass got in the bed and she got cut, and now there's blood everywhere, but I'm still shagging her and she was loving it. Next thing she says, 'I want you to cut me . . .', but before I could say anything, Muzzer jumped out of bed and said, 'Woah, I'm putting the fucking brakes on this *now.*'

She cleaned herself up a bit and just got off. I think she had a bit of a dent in the side of her head from the phone, but that's what she was into.

*

We eventually got to Los Angeles and we were supposed to jib up to San Francisco for one last date, but we just couldn't be arsed. We'd just got to Los Angeles, where we were going to record the album, and Soul II Soul were playing in LA that night, so we fucked off the gig in frisky Frisco. Nathan phoned up and told them that PD had an abscess, which wasn't total bollocks. He did have an abscess and it was causing him major grief, but it was also a slightly handy excuse for us. I've never been someone to pull gigs, really; it just wasn't our style. I think I've only ever pulled a handful in this country, and usually for a very good reason. I've been really, really ill with all sorts and still gone on.

There have been a few we've sacked over the years. I sacked the last Black Grape gig, because that was all going tits up, and we sacked a couple of early Mondays gigs in Spain, after the stage collapsed and the lighting rig fell in and I nearly died. I'd just gone off stage when the lighting rig collapsed, and there but for the grace of God . . . Basically, if we'd done another song it would have fallen on me. So after that happened, when we arrived at the next few gigs our tech Ed would go out there and check everything, because health and safety wasn't a massive priority in Spain back then, and if he came back and said it wasn't safe then we wouldn't do the gig. I'm sure it's not as bad now in Spain, but back then everyone would be like '*Mañana, mañana.*' Then you'd read another report in the paper of a stage collapsing and people dying.

Ed, Di and Oz, our crew, had all worked on Joy Division and New Order and when we started getting support slots they started helping us out, because up until then we just had our old fella doing the sound for us and working as a roadie, and we needed more back-up. Fair play to them, when we started gigging and were still travelling round in a transit van, Ed, Di and Oz would just dive in the back of the transit and come down to London or up to Glasgow with us, and basically work for nothing, because we weren't getting paid hardly anything for the gig. Then when we did start getting paid and we needed someone to do those jobs, the work went to them, which is how it should be. Payback for good people.

So anyway, we sacked off the gig in frisky Frisco. We had arrived in Los Angeles, the sun was shining, and the vibe was right. We just wanted to go out and see Soul II Soul and have a top night, then have a few days' chilling. Then it was down to Capitol Studios to crack on with the new album.

CHAPTER EIGHT

*'Son, I'm 30, I only went with your mother cos
she's dirty, and I don't have a decent bone in me,
what you get is just what you see, yeah'*

I can't remember who first had the idea to record *Pills 'n'
Thrills* at Capitol Studios in Los Angeles, but I was bang up for
it; I thought it was a great idea. I knew about the massive
history of the place and who had recorded there, everyone from
the Beach Boys to Beastie Boys. There was an engineer there
called Ray who had been there for years and years and worked
on a lot of the iconic albums, and he would tell us stories
of past recording sessions. The building was just as iconic as
the music, because Capitol Records Tower is a Hollywood
landmark.

I remember Ray and me were in the studio one day, soon
after we started, and we both suddenly really freaked out when
this smell hit us. Some people like putting cocaine in their
joints to smoke it and one of our guys had sparked one up. The
smell of burning cocaine is pretty instantly recognizable and it
really turns my stomach and makes me feel quite ill. Ray
started absolutely freaking out. He jumped up and started
shouting, 'Whoa, what's happening, man?!? What's going
on??!' and started having these mad flashbacks and physically

shaking. It had somehow tripped off some flashback for him, some memory of some band who must have been doing the same thing – smoking cocaine when they were recording back in the day. It totally tripped him out, and he was physically shaking like a leaf. He had to go and have a two-hour sit-down in a quiet corner and try and get his head together. That was poor old Ray's introduction to Happy Mondays.

I first had the idea to use Paul Oakenfold as the producer on *Pills 'n' Thrills* when we were recording the last album, *Bummed*, at Driffield. I loved 'Jibaro' and the great Balearic mix of beats and Spanish guitar that Oakey had on there. He had then done the remix of 'WFL' for us, which I really loved as well. So right from the early discussions about recording *Pills 'n' Thrills* I absolutely knew I wanted Paul Oakenfold from day one. The rest of the band weren't too sure at first, and neither were Tony or Factory; they still saw Oakey as a DJ rather than a producer, even after the remix of 'WFL'. At that time, Oakey was more of an ideas man than a studio man, and he worked with Steve Osborne, who would do all the knob-twiddling because Oakey was still feeling his way around the studio.

What really swung it, I think, was what he did with 'Step On'. After Factory saw how it came back when he'd finished with it, then they were like, 'Right, okay, you want him, you can have him.' Still, no major label would have done that. There is no way it would have happened with any other record company but Factory, especially as this was such a big album for us; this was the album where we really needed to make that step up. With that in mind, any other record company would have opted for an established producer, a safe pair of hands.

We all got hire cars as soon as we landed in Los Angeles, and me and Muzzer got a convertible Golf GTI, which was quite a cool car in England at the time. But not in America. The Yanks were still quite backward in their thinking in some ways, even in Los Angeles. Me and Muzz would be driving about in it and everywhere we went these beefy Americans would beep us and shout something like, '*Motherfuckin' fags! Get a proper motherfuckin' car!*' We'd just shout back, '*Fuck off, you big, daft, thick cunt!*' Our Golf GTI could blow them away if we put our foot down. *Booom!* Just leave them standing at the lights. '*You get a proper car, you fuckin' rednecks!*' Nowadays you go to LA and they're driving round in nippy little fuckers, Minis and that. But back then, everywhere we went it was the same – *Beeep, beep, 'Motherfuckin' fags!! Get a proper motherfuckin' car!*'

Bez, of course, did want a 'proper motherfuckin' American car', so he got a huge convertible Chrysler LeBaron. He wrote it off straight away. The same day we arrived I think. He piled into the back of someone, then proceeded to get out of his car and go and drag the fella he'd crashed into out of his car. This big argument went off. We had to calm Bez down and say, 'You can't hit these fuckers over here, mate, because you'll get sued for the rest of your life.' I think the dude did try suing him, but it got smoothed over. I think we might have had to give the guy a bung or something, but it got sorted out. Bez didn't even have a proper licence; he had a blag licence and he'd blagged the car from the hire company on that, I think, so we didn't want that to come on top either.

Bez's main problem when he's driving is he doesn't watch the road. You'll be in the passenger seat and he'll be driving, but he's just looking at you going, 'Right, where we gonna go and what's happening and I reckon we should do this and get some of that and blah blah de blah blah blah . . .', just looking at you and not looking at the road. Then someone in another lane will beep him and he'll turn round and start giving *them* a right mouthful, and now he's looking at them and giving it out, but still not looking where he's going. He *never* looks at the road ahead.

But then if I offer someone a lift and they're getting in a car with me, Bez will have the cheek to say, 'Don't get in a car with X – he's fucking lethal,' and I'm like, 'Fucking hell, Bez!' I'd actually never written a car off in my life at that stage.

We were staying at the Oakwood Apartments in Burbank, which is one of those gaffs that are full of musicians, actresses and porn stars. Again, it's one of those places that when you phone up to book the apartment you have to choose from a menu – 'Er, I'll have the leather settee, two televisions, a vase of flowers, a silver teaset, and two pictures – the one with the crying boy and the one with the crying swan.' Weird place.

Chris Quinten, who played Brian Tilsley in *Coronation Street*, was staying there at the same time as us, trying to make it in LA as a movie actor. He must have heard our accents, but I don't think he had a clue who we actually were, because when we clocked him and said, 'All right?' he just blanked us. I thought, 'You cheeky bastard!'

Within a few days of being in LA, we got to know the kids out there, mostly Mancs and Scousers, who were running all the early raves there and dealing the E. There were a lot of them out in LA then; there still are. Back then some of them were grafters, but some of them were just hairdressers or something, who sold a few pills and put on raves on the side. We even got to the stage with these kids where they would ask us who they should let in on the door and who they shouldn't. One night Chris Quinten turned up trying to get in and I was like, 'Well, he isn't coming in for a start, because he dissed us.' Then he was running round asking everyone, 'Why don't them lot like me?' Why don't we like you? Well, we tried to be nice and say 'All right?' to you, and you blanked us. Now you want to come to all these raves? Do one.

What made me laugh, as well, was when the Yank kids would come up chatting to us, and they didn't have a fucking clue. They'd be going, 'Hey man, I believe you all even starting raving over in England now, huh?' I just thought, 'You bunch of dicks, we've been at it for years. All these raves you go to, which you think is *your* scene, are organized by Mancs and Scousers.' They didn't have a clue.

Bez got introduced to Julia Roberts one of the first nights we were there, but he didn't really know who she was. I remember him coming over to me and saying, 'X, do you know who Julie Rouberts is? That's her over there and she's got a bodyguard called Evil.' I said, 'Yeah, you know who she is.' Bez said, 'No, I don't.' I said, 'You know that film that we watched on the plane on the way coming over, *Pretty Woman*? That's Julia Roberts.' Bez was like, 'Oh, yeah. I think she fancies me.' I think she did. She ended up going out to her car to get her driving licence to prove to Bez that she was Julia Roberts. Nothing happened between them, though. I think Bez got on better with her bodyguard, Evil.

We used to hang out all over. Venice Beach was still quite heavy back then; it didn't start getting cleaned up until the mid-90s. We went to Johnny Depp's club, the Viper Room, where River Phoenix later died. Oakey also had a residency at a club on Friday nights and we used to go down there a bit. I've hung out all over LA. When I was back there later, with Black Grape, I used to go to Billy Idol's wife's place, which was up where Danny Saber, who became part of Black Grape, lives.

While we were recording *Pills 'n' Thrills* there was this lad hanging round the studio for a few days, a Scouser, who just seemed dead normal and pretty cool, and we didn't clock who he was. It was only after a few days that we realized it was Ian Astbury from the Cult. Obviously we were aware of the Cult, but we thought they were slightly glamorous LA-style rockers. We didn't know that Ian was actually a Scouser. You couldn't really tell, because he looked the part and fitted so well into that LA scene. I really liked him. I haven't seen him much since, but back then he seemed quite cool.

I've never been tempted to move to LA full time. Over the years I've done stints when I've had to be there for months and months at a time, usually for recording purposes, and I'm always quite glad to get out of there. Particularly because of the game that I'm in, which is full of bullshit. We spent quite a bit of time out there with Black Grape, because we had American management and were signed to an American label. We did some music for films, because Gary Kurfirst, who signed Black Grape, was quite plugged into that world, and we got taken round the film sets and introduced to everyone. That world is so fake and transparent. It's like, 'Hey, here comes Tom! *Hey Tommy!* You gotta meet Tom, he's such a great guy!!' Then you might be in a restaurant five days later and Tommy walks in, but all of a sudden he's not hot any more and everyone's whispering, 'Hey, Tommy just walked in. Don't look at him,' as if he suddenly smells of shit. From hero to zero. Six days later he's hot again, and everyone's like, '*Hey, Tommy!* Great to see you man. *Looking good!*' It used to do my fucking nut in.

Even though we were in Los Angeles in the sun, and we were still quite young, all in our mid- to late twenties, we were actually quite hard-working on *Pills 'n' Thrills*. Of course we were going out partying as well, but we did really knuckle down in the studio – as we did for *Bummed* with Hannett, even though we were totally off our heads on the E, and as we'd done with *Squirrel* and John Cale. When it came down to work time, we were still really focused on the job in hand when we were in the studio.

I think we had six tracks already written and demoed when we arrived in Los Angeles, stuff that we'd written back in Manchester, and the other tracks – songs like 'Loose Fit' – started from beats that Oakey and Osborne had, which we then worked up into full songs. Those beats from Oakey and Osborne played a massive part in shaping the sound of *Pills 'n' Thrills*. I knew from 'Jibaro' the sound that I wanted to get from us working with them, to marry that Balearic beat with the Mondays sound, and they gave it to me. I generally only need a bass line and/or drums to start getting ideas to write with, so working with those beats was perfect to me. It was a really pleasurable experience making *Pills 'n' Thrills*, from start to finish. It just worked so well, and I was really confident in what we were producing.

The opening track, 'Kinky Afro', was one of the songs we had already written back in Manchester, and along with 'Step On' it kind of set the tone for the album. I wouldn't necessarily call it dance music; I just saw it as a new form of pop music. The opening lyric of 'Kinky Afro' is probably one of my most quoted lyrics – 'Son, I'm 30, I only went with your mother cos she's dirty' – although I was actually only twenty-eight when I wrote that. But 'Son, I'm 28, I only went with your mother cos she's, er, my mate' wouldn't really have worked. 'Kinky Afro', again, is just a story, a wacky comic-strip story which draws from several places. I had the opening lines, and then I had some other words I liked that didn't really mean much – that's how it often happens with me. I'll have two bits of lyrics I like that don't really relate to each other, and then find some way of linking them and making some sense of it. It's like putting a jigsaw together.

Wilson said 'Kinky Afro' was the most profound comment on parenthood since Yeats or something, but that's Wilson for you. Okay, I suppose the start of the second verse – 'I said Dad, you're a shabby. You run around and act like a baddy. You're only here just out of habit. All that's mine you might as well have it' – could be seen as a bit of a dig at my old man, but only in a jokey way. My old fella never said anything to me about it, and it wasn't really about him.

The chorus obviously rips elements of 'Lady Marmalade' with the 'Yippee-ippie-ey-ey-ay-yey-yey' bit; I think everyone can hear that. The way I saw it, my approach to ripping records was kind of what became standard in rap music – lifting or adopting the odd line that you liked or that fitted. To me, this was progression from doing cover versions. Bands before the Beatles only ever did cover versions, and even the Beatles and Stones did them when they first set off.

'Kinky Afro' was chosen as the lead single from the album, and Central Station came up with the idea of ripping an image of Michael Jackson for the cover of the single, but someone thought people might take it the wrong way, and pointed out that the lyric 'I had to crucify some brother today' might be taken the wrong way in the States.

Everything to do with the artwork was always down to Our Matt, Pat and Karen at Central Station. They would put about ten ideas in front of us, for the album cover, single cover, posters and whatever else we needed. Then we would say, 'Okay, that can be used for this, that for this single, and we'll use that for a poster, and that we don't like.' I, personally, would never have used any sort of image of Michael Jackson on a cover, because I just wasn't into that, but Our Matt and Pat really liked it. When you ripped stuff for artwork some people in the industry would get nervous. Particularly after the rise of hip hop, when artists started getting done for sampling music, people in the industry would get nervous about ripping anything – bits of music, lyrics, artwork or anything. So that might have been an argument against using the image of Jacko, but I think it was more to do with the Americans taking it the wrong way. The Yanks could easily take offence at artwork. I've already mentioned that one US pressing plant refused to handle *Bummed* because the inner sleeve was a picture of a naked woman. They also took offence at the artwork for the second Black Grape album, which was a cartoon image of a black grape with boggly eyes. The Yanks looked at it and said, 'That's derogatory to black people.' We had two black kids in the band, Kermit and Psycho, who hadn't even thought anything of it. But then white people in suits in America turn round and say, 'Oh, you've got a golliwog on the front of the album with wobbly eyes – that's offensive to black people.' Eh?! The band is called Black Grape and it's a black grape, you knobs.

People always assume that 'God's Cop' is about James Anderton, chief of Greater Manchester Police, or Mancunians do anyway, but it's more of a nod to him than a whole song about him. It's one of those songs that have several double meanings in there. The line 'Me and the chief got Soul II Soul' could mean me and the chief are into Soul II Soul, or it could mean we relate to each other, we've got soul to soul, the same views. It's a double piss-take. Like I said before, Anderton was infamous for proclaiming that he spoke to God, and that's what the line 'God made it easy on me' is a reference to. But I would also have regular chats with God myself. Well, when I say that, I mean when I was in the middle of a tricky situation, or something had gone off and it was coming on top, I would go, 'Oh God, what am I doing?' But that's not really chatting to God, is it? That's more a chat with yourself, but you're bringing God into it without even thinking about it. I'm sure loads of people do that. Does that make you as barmy as Anderton? No. That fucker was actually going round telling people he's talking to God and believing he was acting on God's orders. It seems mental now that he was the chief of police, but it somehow seemed to fit in with the madness in Manchester at the time. So, part of Anderton is there in the lyrics to 'God's Cop', and part of me as well.

'Donovan' was more of a chilled vibe. The opening lines, 'Six cheap people in an empty hotel, every last one with a story to tell, give them all pills so their heads won't swell', is basically a pun on all our lot. It was a little nod to us, staying in a hotel on tour, and then I expanded it into a story, and ripped the line 'Oh sunshine, shone brightly through my window today, could have tripped out quite easy, but I decided to stay' from Donovan's 'Sunshine Superman', which is where the title comes from. I'm not sure what Don thought of it, to be honest; I don't think I ever asked him.

'Grandbag's Funeral' is one of those songs where the title actually isn't much to do with the song. I didn't know anyone called Grandbag. My grandad, Bill Carroll, had recently died, so obviously that was fresh in my mind, but we didn't call him Grandbag, and it wasn't really about his funeral. Sometimes we'll write a song and a title will come to me that fits, but sometimes it won't for ages. Then someone will turn round and say, 'Right, c'mon, we need a title for this now,' and I'll just say whatever is on my mind that minute, or whatever is in front of me in the room, it could be 'Bottle of water' or something as simple or daft as that.

There was a nod in the lyrics of 'Loose Fit' to the Gulf War, which was happening at the time – 'gonna buy an airforce base, gonna wipe out your race' – but that was more because I was seeing images of the war on television all the time, rather than me deliberately making a big political statement. Because of the lyric 'Don't need no skin tights in my wardrobe today' some people think it's about clothes or the way I dress or something, but it isn't. I wouldn't write a song about that. 'Don't you know I've got better taste'?

The second side of the album starts with 'Dennis and Lois', which is named after a real-life American couple from Brooklyn, New York. Dennis and Lois were (they still are, they're still around) two very odd characters who liked music and really liked Mancunians for some reason, and they would turn up when we played New York. Dennis was a Vietnam vet and they collected all sorts of crap. We went back to their house once and they had all these toys that they'd collected, which they kept in the original boxes. They came over to Manchester quite a lot as well, and they would put Mancunian musicians up when they played in New York if they didn't have much dough. They were also massive Frank Sidebottom fans and Chris Sievey, Frank's creator, would stay with them when he went to the States. The song is not about them; it's just named after them. But when I named a song after them, they were made up. People would ask who Dennis and Lois were and they became mini celebs. The opening line from that song, 'We all learn to box at the Midget Club', is not about us lot. I nicked that from reading about how some London gangsters – I don't think it was the Krays, it was some other firm – all learned to box, or used to hang out, at some gym called the Midget Club. I didn't really learn to box as a kid, but friends of mine now, like Billy and Too Nice Tom, who I've known for twenty years, are in the game. Tom has been a corner man for years and has tried in the past to mould me into some form of boxer, but it's a bit late for that now.

'Bob's Your Uncle' was another track that came from my

obsession with Oakey's track 'Jibaro'. I wanted us to do a track like that with Spanish guitar, but in a Mondays style, and I just stuck all these dirty lines about your mother sucking cocks in hell, and *Exorcist*-type lyrics over it, and made it into some sort of story, and then Oakey got Rowetta to just grunt over it.

Wilson always loved 'Bob's Your Uncle' and it was actually one of the songs played at his funeral in 2007.

There might have been a slight debate about including 'Step On' on the album, because it had already been a single, but if you have a Top 5 single before the album comes out, then you put it on the album, that's standard, that's what happens. And 'Step On' fitted with the vibe of the rest of the album, totally.

'Holiday' was one of the earlier tracks that we wrote in Manchester. Our Kid wanted to rip off the chorus from Madonna's 'Holiday' – although we just ripped the 'Holiday' bit in the end, so it's hardly even a rip – and then I turned it into a little short story. It's just a little nod to what always used to happen to me before I became well known with the band – 'Hold it there, boy, is that your bag?' I could never fly into Manchester airport, or pretty much any airport, without being strip-searched. I was always being stuck on the glass toilet – 'You don't look first class you, let me look up your arse you'. Even if I went through Dover and got the ferry I would get strip-searched. I got pretty shitty treatment. The customs officers didn't stop me because they thought I was carrying my own drugs just for personal use. The fuckers took one look at me and presumed I was trying to sneak in with a few ounces of coke shoved down my nuts, or wraps of heroin inside me, like some kind of mule. That's them talking in the first verse – 'a small sneak and you've just been had'. Thankfully, that all calmed down when we got known with the band. Once you've become a bit famous they presume that if you do have drugs on you it's only going to be for personal use. And you certainly don't need the mither of taking it over the border. But back in the day, I obviously looked a likely candidate to be a mule, plus I already had that bust on my record for importation. When the band took off, we wouldn't really need to smuggle any personal drugs, because wherever we were going we'd have them waiting for us on the other side anyway. So the hassle we were getting at customs calmed down a bit.

'Holiday' then segues into 'Harmony', which is the last track on the album.

The recording process of *Pills 'n' Thrills* was quite different to *Bummed*, as *Bummed* had been to *Squirrel*. There was a lot more overdubbing with *Pills*, and a lot less recording live as a band. This time it was more a case of 'Right, let's get Paul in and get him to record his bass part for this'; it was mostly done separately. When we were finished I think we all knew it was a great album. From 'Step On', we knew we were on a roll, and working with Oakey and Osborne had just gone so well.

By then, after *Squirrel* and *Bummed*, it was kind of tradition that I came up with album titles. *Pills 'n' Thrills and Bellyaches* just came off the top of my head. Just came to me like that; there was no thought about it. *Pills 'n' Thrills and Bellyaches*, straight off the top of my head. It was one of those 'I'll have that' moments. I didn't spend days thinking about it. I hate it when I have to spend ages thinking about something. I spent a year thinking of an album title for my last album and I hated that. The album was canned and ready to go, and I still didn't have a title. Usually a title will come to me straight away, right there and then, but when it doesn't it can take for ever.

Our Paul got married to his girlfriend Alison when we were out in LA recording *Pills 'n' Thrills*. The ceremony was at this real nice gaff, out in the open air, some hotel with beautiful lawns and marquees, a nice little set-up. Unfortunately, he was pretty much divorced not long after we came back.

We had the launch party for *Pills 'n' Thrills* at London Zoo. At the time they were renting out the zoo for parties and there had been a couple of raves there already, I think. I got one of my first insights into the depths the press could stoop to at that party. Like I said before, because we'd been on *Top of the Pops*, we were out of the hands of the likes of the *NME* and we were now the property of the red tops. Halfway through the launch party I came out of the aquarium and there were three geezers lifting up a park bench and trying to throw it into one of the big fish tanks. We just thought it was some knobheads who had gatecrashed our party, so we were like, 'What the fuck are you doing, you pricks?' and this big scuffle starts. Then it turns out they had press passes, and they were tabloid hacks. They wanted the story of 'Ecstasy-takers Dump Bench in Fish Tank', or the headline 'Look What This Sick Group Did to London Zoo!' So they were throwing the bench in there themselves to create the story. We threw them out instead.

After that, we decided we needed to make friends with someone like Piers Morgan. At the time, bands didn't want to talk to people like the *Sun*, and this was before the tabloids really had dedicated showbiz pages like they do now. But my thinking was, if the tabloids are going to be pulling stunts like that, then we need to be talking to someone in there who is kind of on our side. We actually got to know Piers a few months later, when he came Rio with us, which I'll get to shortly.

After the album was released we went on the *Pills 'n' Thrills* UK tour and took Donovan and his band as support. They played all his classic 60s tunes and they sounded brilliant. We took it for granted that the kids that were coming to see us would like Donovan and get off on that kind of music, and I think they did. There was no big discussion about it, like you would have to have nowadays; we were just like, 'Listen, we want Don, he'll be great, and if any kids haven't heard of Don then they should have.'

The first date was Whitley Bay Ice Rink. Apparently there was some bomb scare that was actually just a pissed-off bouncer being a knob, but I don't remember anything about it. Mind you, at that stage, I would often not bother turning up for the soundcheck.

Around the same time, Factory opened their new offices in Manchester city centre, which they had spent a fortune on. Factory obviously had more dough, or were forecast to get a big influx of dough, so they were in a position to get mortgages or bank loans or whatever, when they hadn't been before. Before that, the company had just been run out of Alan Erasmus's flat on Palatine Road in West Didsbury. He owned the flat and rented it out to Factory as their offices.

There were arguments right from the start about the offices on Charles Street and some fucking ridiculous decisions. How anyone can try and blame the Mondays for the downfall of Factory when they spunked all that money on a fucking zinc roof for an office and shit like that is beyond me. I'm still not sure who decided to spend £25,000 on that ridiculous boardroom table that hung from the ceiling. Probably Wilson. Hooky was obviously moaning about the money they had spent on it, as usual. He probably still is. The first day I went into the boardroom and saw it, I just sat on it, as you do with a table, and *crash*, £25,000 worth of table comes flying off the ceiling. Everyone just went, '*Oh, for fuck's sake, X . . .*'

I was being asked to do more TV, and went on *Jukebox Jury* with Barbara Windsor, some bloke from *Brookside* and Tony Wilson. Barbara was great, and her and me shared a bottle of champagne after the show. If you don't remember *Jukebox Jury*, the panel had to give their verdict on that week's singles, and they would have a couple of the artists there as secret guests, but didn't reveal who it was until after you'd given your verdict on their single. They played a track by some American outfit called the Nelson Brothers and I said, 'They look like they could give a good wabosh', which means a good nosh, a blowjob. But the producers didn't know what it meant and kept it in. Actually, although I don't think they had heard it called that before, they weren't thick, so they probably had an idea of what it meant but decided to keep it in there anyway. A lot of American musicians are not wet student kids; they often come from rough parts of the States. I don't particularly know much about the Nelson Brothers, but when I said that they gave me a stare that basically said, 'Do you want a fight?' I never saw them after the show, though, so luckily nothing happened.

They also showed a Paul McCartney video and I said something like 'That looks like more of McCartney's illegitimate children,' but they cut that from the show – it never went out. Not long after that, McCartney said in an interview that he'd seen the Mondays on TV and that they reminded him of 'the Beatles in our *Magical Mystery Tour* phase', which was mega to us. For Paul McCartney to have even *heard* of us was brilliant. I was like 'Wow! Paul McCartney's heard of us!' I thought the *Magical Mystery Tour* was great as well. I don't know if McCartney does. It might have been one of the Beatles phases he wasn't that wild about, which would have changed what he meant. But I was into it, and just the fact that McCartney had even heard of us and heard our music was mega.

I met McCartney several times, a few years later, when I was in my thirties and I wasn't in great shape. It's terrible really, looking at those pictures now. He's twenty years older than me, so he must have been in his late fifties then and I was in my late thirties, but he looks much healthier and younger than I do. I look fucked. It's embarrassing. He must have wondered what the fuck I was on. He was always sound with me, though. He knew Nathan was the Mondays' manager, and there were rumours and stories in various Beatles books about Nathan's mum, Thelma Pickles, having a thing with McCartney back in the day.

At the end of 1990, I was asked to do a photo shoot for *Vox* magazine, which was like a monthly magazine version of the *NME*. They asked a few of us to be photographed with an object that had been 'particularly significant' to you in the last twelve months and explain why. Bernard Sumner chose his fake Rolex, Johnny Marr chose his Chevignon shades, and Tim Booth from James painted 'crude' on his chest in oil as some comment against the Gulf War. I chose Kit Kats and my explanation was 'They've kept me going through our long arduous tours this year.' It was a little in-joke that I thought everyone would get, but hardly anyone did. It wasn't the fucking Kit Kats that kept me going; it was the tinfoil wrapper. Think about it. If you're on tour or something, you can't necessarily buy a big roll of tinfoil at an airport or a motorway service station, because it's not stocked everywhere. But Kit Kats are. It can also bring it a bit on top if you look like me and just march into a shop somewhere just to buy a roll of tinfoil and nothing else. Unless they're pretty fucking stupid, the people in the shop will have a good idea of what you're up to. But Kit Kats are sold at garages, off-licences, everywhere, so they were a bit of a godsend. That was one of the reasons they changed the Kit Kat wrapper to the new-fangled one they have now. I think they changed it in Amsterdam first, and then they changed it over here later. The hilarious thing was, after the magazine came out fucking boxes and boxes of Kit Kats turned up at the Happy Mondays office, from Nestlé, who were made up because they thought I was bang into Kit Kats.

On Christmas Day 1990 I got a right kicking. This new party had started on Epping Walk in Hulme, which we used to go to. Like The Kitchen, it was in one of the disused flats. Two kids called Billy Caldwell and Nipper used to DJ there. I think it was the only party that was going on that Christmas Day, so me, Muzzer and our mate Foley headed down there. People forget how dodgy Hulme was back then; you had to watch your back, because it was pretty lawless. Epping Walk had not been going on long, but it was opposite this Irish boozer and they were obviously sick of the music banging out of there all night, so decided to do something about it and got a firm together. Me, Muzz and Foley were just arriving and this bunch of mother-fuckers jumped us. I've no idea how many there were, but there must have been about a dozen pretty handy Irish blokes. They just jumped us from nowhere. Foley managed to get away, but me and Muzz were getting a right kicking. I had about three of them on me and I was trying to fight them off – it was really on top. Thank fuck Muzz was there. He basically got the better of the three or four of them he was up against and then came to rescue me. In the end he almost threw me over his shoulder and we did one with Foley, but we did get a bit of a hiding from those motherfuckers.

In January, we played the Great British Music Weekend at Wembley Arena, which was broadcast on Radio One and hosted by Jonathan King. People forget how big Jonathan King was. He was huge at one stage, like Steve Wright and Paul Gambaccini rolled into one, and he wrote a lot of hits and had some big TV shows. I remember him making an obvious effort to keep his distance from us that day. He clearly didn't like us, and preferred hanging out with the younger boys in other groups. Which doesn't surprise me, knowing what we know now.

We had a slight problem with 'Step On' during the gig, which we stopped after about thirty seconds because someone fucked up, even though it was being broadcast live. We had to have a sit down with the band after the gig and decide that we weren't going to do that any more, that if there was a slight problem with the sound or something we would just carry on, otherwise it looks really unprofessional. If you make a slight mistake and carry on, half the audience won't even notice, but everyone obviously notices if you stop and start the song again. I went to see Ian Brown last year, at the Manchester Evening News Arena, and he did that twice, stopped a song because he wasn't happy, which I thought was really funny, because the way Ian does it, it's almost part of his act.

Towards the end of January, we had a mental trip to Brazil. We were playing the huge Rock in Rio gig at the Maracanã stadium. It was our first time in South America, and along with all our lot there were a few journalists on the plane with us, including James Brown from the *NME* and Piers Morgan from the *Sun*. James Brown was just starting talking about this magazine he was going to do, which was what ended up being *Loaded*. Piers actually seemed all right, considering everyone had told us that these tabloid journalists were absolute motherfuckers. He was sat near to Paul Davis on the plane at one stage, and PD just pulled out a big bag of coke and got stuck right in, there and then, on the plane. Just put a towel over his head and started snorting his little head off. Well, snorting his big head off.

We were all in first class or business class, and when we landed in Rio the plane was boarded by all these military-type geezers in sunglasses and these other serious-looking guys in dark suits. They all marched on the plane shouting, 'Who are Happy Mondays? Where iz Happy Mondays?' and we were all thinking '*Fuuuck!*' So the band and all our crew had to stand up while everyone else on the plane was still sat down, and we were marched off the plane. We were led down this corridor into the airport and through this door, and we were all whispering to each other:

'*Shhhhhh . . . who's got gear on them?*'

'*Why did you bring fucking cocaine to Brazil, you fucking prick?*'

'*What have you got on you?*'

'*Why have you brought weed with you?*'

'*What have you got up your jacksie?*'

They opened another door, and there was another room with more security guards, then we went through yet another door and down another corridor. We had to wait a bit, then we were marched off down yet another corridor and round a corner where we found our luggage waiting for us. This guy goes, 'Pick it up!', so we grab it and follow him, thinking, 'We're *fucked* here.' Then all of a sudden this door opens and all we can see is beaming sunshine. It was a real *Midnight Express* moment, you know when that guy Billy finally escapes into the daylight at the end? This guy just pointed and said, 'Your coach . . . you go now!' We couldn't believe our fucking luck. We didn't go through passport control or fuck all. They just escorted us off the plane and whisked us straight through the airport.

Then we got on the coach and there were all these screaming girls surrounding us like we're the Beatles or something, and all these women in their late twenties and thirties holding their bloody babies up to us. I just thought, *'What the fuck?!'* Bands talk about being mobbed in Japan, but I think that reception in Brazil was the maddest one we ever got.

Once we got on the road, someone handed us the local newspaper and the headline on the front page was 'ECSTASY DEALERS COME TO RIO!' Someone translated the story for us and it said something like, 'Big-time English dealers are planning to flood Rio with 25,000 ecstasy pills'. That was probably my fault. I'd done some telephone interviews with the Brazilian press before we came. I thought this one geezer I was speaking to was a music journalist, so I was just having a laugh with him on the phone. He said 'So, you will bring ecstasy with you to Brazil, yes?' and I said, 'Yeah, course mate, I'm going to bring fucking tons of it with me! Do you want some? I'll bring you some over!' I was just having a laugh with him, having a bit of a nobble. But this guy had then gone and sold it to the Brazilian equivalent of the tabloids and they'd done a huge story on it.

We found out a little later that it was a pal of ours who had arranged for us to get whisked through security. He was over in Rio and had a few business things going on there and was quite cosy with the chief of police. He saw this headline in the paper and thought, 'Uh-oh,' and could see it might be a bit on top for us when we arrived, so he made a few calls to his contacts and arranged for us to be whisked straight through the airport. What a legend.

All the bands that were playing the Rock in Rio festival were put in the same hotel, apart from us and Guns 'n' Roses; they stuck us both together, out of the way, because they thought we would be causing mither. While we were there, we went round to the Great Train Robber Ronnie Biggs's house for a barbecue. Piers Morgan actually set that up so he could get a picture for the *Sun*. Ronnie was great – we got on well because he was a fellow Leo.

Rio itself was pretty hardcore. You weren't supposed to go down to the beach or wander about town because of the danger of being mugged. At that time people were being held up with syringes full of blood. The muggers would threaten you with them because AIDS was a big concern. We were fine, though, because our pal out there had a lot of contacts and was well known as a character that you shouldn't mess with, so we got to see a lot of places where Westerners and tourists would never go.

One night we went to this club called Help, which was like nothing else I've ever seen. It was wild, and it was full of prostitutes. Jayne Houghton, who was doing our PR at the time, was with us, and because we were talking to her and she was a white girl with blonde hair, all the Brazilian prostitutes thought she was a German prostitute who was bagging all the men. Jayne is a mouthy Leeds bird, who doesn't normally take much shit, but I had to explain to her: 'Jayne, look, I know you think you're hard and you're from Leeds, but these girls will fucking kill you. I mean, actually, *literally* kill you.' She ended up getting held up at knifepoint in the toilet. I had to rescue her and I just said to her, 'Jayne, be quiet *now*. Shut your fucking mouth *now*. This is not Friday night in Leeds, this is *serious*.' It really was that on top in there. These girls would have cut Jayne's throat without even thinking about it; they were in a completely different fucking league.

Half of our lot ended up taking girls from there back with them, though. One of the lads ended up spending three days with his – she was gorgeous. These girls would do anything for you. They'd give you a bath and wash you, they'd wash your clothes, iron your clothes, give you a massage, shag you, and then you just gave them a gift at the end. One of our lads just gave his girl some chocolates and stuff out of his minibar, and I think she was happy with that.

Another one of our guys, thinking he was smart for some dickhead reason, was with one of these girls for a day and instead of just bunging her some money laced her drink with methadone so she passed out, then he did one and checked into a different hotel room. She didn't wake up until a day later, and he had robbed everything of hers – her bag, her clothes, her jewellery; the fucking lot. These birds don't mess about, so she went straight to the fucking police, who don't mess about either. She wanted revenge, because these birds don't get had over, you know what I mean? They have *you* over. She tracked him down, which wasn't that fucking hard, because he was just in another room at the hotel. It was such a fucking daft thing to have done. I had to meet her and the police and smooth it over, and bung them some dough. She got some money, dropped the charges, the police got some money and that was it. What a fucking dick.

When we eventually got to do the gig, there was a thunderstorm during our set. A proper, fucking tropical, torrential, thunderstorm. It leathered it down. I had all my lyrics written out in marker pen on paper, taped to the stage, and they just all washed away. They just turned to grey mush. Kevin Cummins, the photographer, was there, watching from the side of the stage, and says it was one of the best gigs he's ever seen me do, because I just freestyled my way through most of the verses, making up words as I went along, until we got to the chorus and I remembered it.

We were also getting bombarded on stage by stuff being

thrown from the crowd. They were throwing bottles and plastic bags and all sorts at us, and I'm going, 'Fuck off, you dicks!' But apparently, or this is what we were told afterwards, this was a sign of respect. They were celebrating the fact that we continued playing in the downpour, and didn't run off stage and not play because it was raining.

One night we went to a club where there was a Prince after-show. Everyone was told that no matter who you were, even if you were George Michael or A-Ha, you weren't allowed to look at Prince. How fucking ridiculous. So of course the first thing that we did when we got in there was stand there and stare at him. He was surrounded by security, and when he wanted to dance, four of them would stand on the four corners of the dancefloor, and then four of them would actually stand directly around him, while he danced on his own.

I loved Rio, despite a couple of hairy moments. It was great. The drugs were ridiculously cheap. Me and Muzz went out to score one day and took a taxi up into one of the favelas to this dealer's gaff. I was after some gear and Muzz was after some weed. I got my gear and did it in, and went into this real nodding state and needed to get my head down for half an hour. The problem was this dealer's gaff was pretty much just one room and there was no bed. His grandma had just died, though, and they already had the coffin there waiting for her. So I just dived in and got my head down for half an hour. He was fine with it.

Just after we got back from Rio, my first daughter, Jael, was born, on 16 February 1991. Her full name was Jael Otis Ann Ryder. Jael is a name me and Trish liked that we found in one of those baby name books. It means 'climber of mountains'. Otis was after Otis Redding and Ann was after my nana. I was there at the hospital and we played *Rubber Soul* by the Beatles.

One or two of the tabloids turned up to take a picture. I'd never really wanted kids when I was younger, but when I knew Trish was pregnant it didn't faze me at all. I felt quite ready to be a father. In fact, after Jael was born I decided I wanted to have quite a few kids – becoming a father didn't freak me out. I wasn't really ready for the responsibility, though. I think Trish expected me to grow up, but I didn't; my lifestyle didn't really change.

Now we had a kid, we decided to move out of the city centre and we bought a house in Didsbury, on Beeches Mews. It was a new-build townhouse, three storeys but only two beds. It should have been £175,000, but the developer had gone bust, so they were selling them off for £90,000. Kevin Kennedy, who played Curly Watts in *Coronation Street*, lived in the flats opposite, so he was my neighbour and we used to have a drink with him now and again in the nearby Woodstock pub.

Not long after Jael was born, we had to go on tour to the States, which would normally be a massive wrench, to leave your new baby. If I go out on tour now, I always miss my little kids, but I didn't back then because I was just anaesthetized by the drugs. Heroin doesn't allow you to miss anything except heroin.

We played with Jane's Addiction at Madison Square Garden and Perry Farrell, the lead singer, was an absolute wanker. We were slightly late turning up, through no fault of our own. We were stuck in gridlocked traffic, probably the worst traffic I've ever seen in New York; it was a fucking nightmare. But we had people from the record company with us and someone had a mobile phone and we were in touch with the venue all the way, keeping them up to date. But by the time we got there we were late and only had time to go on stage and do twenty minutes. We were only getting paid a poxy fee, about $400 or something, but we'd taken the gig because we wanted to play Madison Square Garden. We'd played venues that size in

Europe, but Jane's Addiction had never played a venue that big before, so I don't know if it was Perry Farrell getting too big for his boots, or even being nervous about the show, but when Muzzer went to get our fee they said we weren't getting paid. Perry Farrell was being a right obnoxious twat, stood there with this twenty-three-stone bouncer, this huge wide mother-fucker who looked like he lived in McDonald's, telling Muzz we're not being paid because we ran over a minute or some-thing daft. Muzz just stuck one on him. He wasn't going to take that shit from some dick.

When we got back we headlined a massive gig at Elland Road, Leeds United's ground, called Match of the Day. It was us, the Farm, the La's and Stereo MCs. I remember winding the crowd up during the gig, saying 'Are you Man U, you?', because that's what Leeds fans always used to say when they were looking for a kick off.

We'd played with the La's before and they were sound, although I hope I didn't get any of them into heroin, as I've got vague memories of staying in a dingy hotel and getting the tinfoil out – although 'There She Goes', which they'd released a couple of years before, is supposedly about heroin. John Power, who went on to form Cast, was a top lad.

We'd known the Farm for ages. They were actually on TV well before us. I remember watching them on *The Oxford Road Show* in the early 80s. Their lead singer, Peter Hooton, got a bit jealous of our success later, but I've seen him more recently and got on with him fine.

Me and Muzz decided to record our set and put it out as a bootleg live album ourselves, as we thought it would be a way to make a quick bit of extra dough, although we obviously kept it quiet that it was us who released it. We had 'Made in Sardinia' stamped on the cover, but they were actually made in Salford. I was quoted as saying, 'The people who have produced this bootleg have assured me that all the profits are going to animals and poor children.' I can assure you now that *none* of the profits went to animals and poor children. But there wasn't really any profit. We thought we were going to make the same profit as we had with drugs, but it was nothing like it. In the end, we were like, 'You know what, this ain't worth fucking doing!'

Weirdly, Factory decided to put out a live album of the gig themselves later that year, but taken from the same recording we used.

That August we played Cities in the Park, which was a two-day festival in Heaton Park in north Manchester, featuring most of the bands on Factory, and everyone from Electronic to De La Soul and the Wonder Stuff. We headlined the Sunday night, and I remember as soon as I got there someone told me Salford had bumrushed the gate and a few hundred had got in for free. Which didn't surprise me. Heaton Park is that close to Salford, you have to get the security bang on, or you're just going to get taken for a ride. Alan Wise was the promoter and was moaning about the fact that we got a hundred guest tickets and got one of our lads to flog them outside. It was full of blaggers that day. I think Alan joked he even thought about turning the stage around, because there were more blaggers backstage than there were punters out front.

When autumn came round, me and Bez edited *Penthouse*. The editor was a big Mondays fan and had reviewed the album, and Jayne Houghton got talking to him about us doing something. I'm not sure if it was just supposed to be more of a straight interview at first, and then it escalated – because when you're in the band you don't always get to know every discussion that goes on – but by the time it was suggested to us it was just, 'Do you want to guest-edit *Penthouse* and do a photo shoot for them?' and I was just like, 'Damn right we do, yeah!'

We went down to London to do it, and Trish insisted on coming with me. She said, 'I'm coming with you on *that . . .*', so she did. They call it editing, but it's quite simple, really. I've done it a couple of times, for different publications. You sit at a desk, and first you read over a couple of letters and give your opinion on them, and that's editing the letters' page. Then you look at a problem letter and you give your opinion, and that means you've done the agony-aunt page. Then you have to look at a few pictures of girls and pick a couple out for a photo shoot. Then you pose for a couple of pictures at a desk and that's it.

Linzi Drew was the main girl at the time for *Penthouse*, and she was keen to be in on the shoot. There was also a girl called Miss Whiplash, who had got her name because she was caught whipping some MP. We did the photo shoot the next day at the Holiday Inn in Swiss Cottage. We had a suite with a jacuzzi, and we all ended up in it. I think Bez had a bit of a touch and a bit of fun. I was going to wear a sports vest at first, but then it was like, 'Nah,' so we just had boxer shorts on, but you couldn't tell because they covered us up in bubbles.

Shortly after that the *News of the World* did a number on me apparently confessing I had been a rent boy. It all stemmed from an MTV interview where I had been joking with the presenter, and the *News of the World* had taken the quotes completely out of context. The thing was, not many people had Sky back in 1991, before the Premier League, so they could almost get away with doing that. Weirdly, the picture they used was from the *Penthouse* shoot of me and several busty models, which hardly matched the story of me supposedly being a rent boy. Our Paul found it hilarious, but I was fuming. That evening I went down to Dry Bar with Muzzer. I was still seething, I was off my nut and drinking too, and I walked in Dry with my 375 Magnum. I was going to blow a hole in the bloody roof of the place because I felt I had to make a point, I had to show how furious I was about the piece. But I stopped short of that in the end. I just ended up smashing the mirror with a bottle. Again, it was not like it's depicted in *24 Hour Party People*. Leroy Richardson, who used to work at the Haçienda but was then running Dry Bar, was there and he just tried to calm me down and speak to me. Muzz and I just did one.

The *News of the World* then had the fucking cheek to send the female reporter up to interview me about the whole thing, to see why I was so upset. I was still fuming and not thinking straight, so I rang up a little firm of girls I knew who were pretty naughty, who would sort someone out for you. They did that for a living. I had it all set up with these girls, who were capable of serious damage. They were hiding in the toilets of Dry Bar and they were going to leather this journalist when she walked in there, then nick her handbag and make it look like a robbery. But I had second thoughts at the last minute and decided to call it off, so I just nipped down to the women's toilets and gave them a whistle and got them out of there.

If it had been two years later, or even a year later, I would have just laughed off the whole story. I probably would have taken them to court, because we had evidence of what I had said on film, and you can clearly see I'm laughing and joking. I could easily have got damages. In the end the *News of the World* printed an apology and retracted the story, but it's one of those apologies that's about the size of a postage stamp, so hardly anyone spots it anyway. I don't know how they get away with that, the fuckers. I wasn't surprised at the recent revelations about the *News of the World*. I know what some of these reporters are like.

Whether the press were positive about us or not, they were certainly interested in us, and it was definitely me and Bez they were focusing on. If there had been simmering resentment in the band since we first got that front cover a few years previously, it was now openly coming to the boil.

CHAPTER NINE

'Tell me what you know about Cowboy Dave,
did he whistle on brown, was his woman a sex
slave?'

Yes Please! was pretty much doomed from day one.

We were sort of pushed into recording a new album because Factory's financial situation was getting more perilous by the end of 1991, and it had also been over a year already since *Pills 'n' Thrills* had been released, so it was about time for us to get back in the studio. We hadn't really had any time off in that year. We hadn't been lazing about or anything – we'd been gigging and doing press, so we hadn't really had time to write new material. Bez and I had done so much press that year that Nathan joked that the only person who'd had more coverage than us was Lady Di.

At this stage I had my heart set on working with Oakenfold and Osborne. I knew I wouldn't have to be concerned about the lack of time to prepare and write, because I found it so easy to work with them and I knew we would have got the right result again. There really was no other choice for me. We asked Oakey and Osborne and we got word back that they really wanted to do it, but they had to finish off another album they were already working on first, so we would have to wait for a couple of months. I was fine with that, but Tony kept saying, 'Yeah, but we need to go and record *now*. We *need* the album *as soon as*.' Had we worked together as a band, we might have been able to persuade Factory to wait, but sadly Our Paul, PD, Mark Day and Nathan's reaction to Oakey and Osborne was, 'They should drop what they're doing. We want them *now*!' and 'They had never produced an album before they worked with us. *We made them* – they should make us their priority!' I was like, 'Whoa. They're in the middle of a fucking job, y'know what I mean?'

Oakey and Osborne were as keen to work together again as I was, because *Pills 'n' Thrills* had gone to No. 2. It was kept off the top but went top five, so it was still a massive success. But Our Paul and Tony then started coming up with other names – 'We could get thingy to do it, or so-and-so to do it . . .' and then Chris Frantz and Tina Weymouth from Talking Heads were mentioned. I didn't want *anyone else*. I tried telling them, 'No, this is madness!' Working with Oakey and Osborne was a winning formula as far as I was concerned, but the rest of them couldn't fucking see it. They'd gone right up their own arses after the success of *Pills 'n' Thrills*.

When Chris and Tina were mentioned, Our Paul, PD and Mark Day's immediate reaction was, 'Oh yes, they're *proper* musicians.' I just said, 'NO!! Look, this is *wrong*, it just won't be right. It's a step back, not moving forward,' but they just wouldn't listen. There was a band meeting over the choice of producer, and only me and Bez were up for waiting for Oakey and Osborne, and everybody else, even Gaz, wanted to go with Tina and Chris, so Our Paul and Tony went out to Jamaica to meet them. I didn't bother going too because I knew they weren't the right people for us and there was no way I was going to meet them when the decision had virtually been made without me. I had really liked Talking Heads and I was also into the stuff they had done as Tom Tom Club but, no disrespect, I just knew they weren't right to work with us. It was a bit like when Vince Clarke remixed 'Wrote For Luck'. When somebody so famous and well known gets involved in one of your records, it starts to sound like it's them. Vince Clarke's 'WFL' mix sounded like him, because it had his signature touches on it, and I knew that this time we were going to end up sounding like Chris and Tina. Everyone else thought it was a great plan, but to me, we'd just really found our sound and identity as the Mondays, and now we were going to be taken right back.

The rest of the band didn't get it; they didn't understand that our fans liked *our* sound. They thought that if we could incorporate Chris and Tina's sound into the Mondays sound, then all the Talking Heads fans would get into it and we would break into a much bigger market. But it doesn't work like that. I tried to explain my misgivings to them, but me and Bez had been outvoted and the decision was made.

Chris and Tina aside, I felt we were being rushed into this album and were in danger of running out of ideas. I also didn't want the norm. We were now in a position to use big-name producers, but I wanted something people wouldn't expect, something more unorthodox. And the band weren't getting on either.

Mark Day had actually decided to leave the Mondays at one point, just before we started making *Yes Please!* He had pretty much decided he was off, for various reasons, mainly his missus, Jane, who was like a little Yoko. She'd say to me, 'You don't tell Mark what to do any more, blah blah blah . . .' So Mark was going to go and set up his own band: 'I don't need this, I'm off, I've had enough of Shaun, I've had enough of Bez . . .' He really didn't appreciate what we had. Mark would say, 'I don't even like the Mondays' music.' Like the rest of them, he was pissed off that he wasn't the main focus of attention, and really thought he was the important one. They had so little respect for my songwriting and what I did as a front man, or what Bez did. Gaz actually did like the Mondays' songs, but the rest of them would slag them off.

They were all having talks about going off and doing their own thing, and being the front man, which was fucking hilarious. They'd also be moaning about me and Bez being on drugs and giving it, 'Grrrrrrr, *they're* ruining the band,' but all of them were off their faces too. And the more drugs they did, the more it focused their anger on us.

At one point, I asked Johnny Marr to join the Mondays and he actually did for about twenty minutes. He came round to mine one day and agreed that he would come and work on the album, but then he drove away and must have had a change of heart, because he was back within half an hour to say he had changed his mind. When I look back, it shows how little I knew about the game then, because I don't think it would have worked. Johnny is brilliant, obviously, but him joining the Mondays wouldn't have been quite right. We would probably have done a much better album than we did with Chris and Tina, because he actually understood us, but the Mondays was all about the chemistry, and Johnny was probably so much better a musician, he would have just got frustrated. He had Electronic anyway at that point, but I hadn't really thought it through, I just thought, 'Johnny Marr plays guitar. He's from Manchester.'

Chris and Tina worked in Barbados quite a lot, because they had a house down there, and the idea was to use Eddy Grant's studio, Blue Wave. At one stage we were going to use the Bee Gees' studio in Miami to record *Yes Please!*, which I thought was a brilliant idea. But some people at Factory didn't think

Miami was the right location, or, more specifically, they thought there would be too much partying. It was a coke city, and a playground, and they basically didn't think I would behave in Miami, or in front of the Bee Gees if they happened to be around. So Barbados it was.

Everyone always says that Barbados was chosen because there was no heroin there for me, but that wouldn't have even bothered me, because if I had some methadone with me and could have got hold of some Valium or some codeine pills as well, I would have been fine without it. Anyway, the plan backfired because the one thing that no one – not Nathan or anyone at Factory – had realized was that in Barbados you could buy an ounce of crack for about a quid.

Yes, I did famously drop and smash my bottles of methadone at Manchester airport on the way out to Barbados, but the knock-on effects of that have been exaggerated. I wasn't on that much methadone – only about 20ml a day, which is quite a low dosage. I'd had methadone on and off since the early 80s, and I did have a meth habit at the time, but it wasn't like I was drinking 130ml a day – I was on a steady 20ml. I had been on a meth prescription but that had recently ended and it wasn't a maintenance prescription that gets renewed; when the prescription ended that was it. So I'd started buying it, just so I had it there as a crutch when I didn't have gear. I had two 500ml bottles in my bag, but I dropped my bag in the airport and the bottles smashed. I was on my knees, desperately trying to scoop it back up, and I did actually manage to salvage about 300ml, although it had broken glass in it. But I managed to get that into a bottle we found in the airport, and when I got to Barbados I strained it through a piece of linen to get rid of all the bits of broken glass before I drank it. That 300ml would have lasted me fifteen days, at about 20ml a day. We were going to be on the island for roughly six weeks, but fifteen days would have been more than enough time to get an alternative supply sorted, so those smashed methadone bottles aren't as important as they've been made out to be.

When we landed in Barbados there was an issue with us not having return flights. We hadn't booked them because we didn't know exactly how long we were going to be recording, but they wouldn't let us in without them, so Nathan had to buy us all flights out of there before they would let us in the country. Eventually he got it sorted, and we were there and ready to start work.

I do like Chris and Tina, personally, but right from the start it all felt wrong. Eddy Grant's studio itself was all right; it was a nice enough gaff, that wasn't a problem. We started working, but within a few days I just wasn't interested in the music they were producing, or the way the rest of the band were behaving. By this stage I had become the hate-figure for them all. Meanwhile Chris and Tina basically saw me as a non-musician and thought that Bez did nothing. Because they were from the States, they weren't that aware of how the band and me and Bez were viewed in the British press and by the British public. Mark Day was the only one of us who could read music, which Chris and Tina thought was a bit amateurish. They saw Our Kid and Mark as the best of a bad bunch, basically. So their approach was to concentrate on them, and keep telling them how good they thought they were, which they obviously loved. But the stuff they were playing was already sounding like Chris and Tina and Talking Heads. It was not what I wanted at all.

We had created this new sound with *Pills 'n' Thrills*, which was a progression from *Bummed* and really worked. I didn't just want another *Pills 'n' Thrills*, but I don't think if we had worked with Oakey and Osborne again it would have been just more of the same. There were definitely more ideas to explore with them. Because Oakey was a DJ, he was constantly mixing and had that Balearic thing going on where he could mix something like the Woodentops with some 'Jibaro' beat and make it work on the dancefloor. Oakey thought, and mixed, like I thought. That's why I knew it wouldn't have been *Pills 'n' Thrills Mk II*. Because Oakey and Osborne liked to experiment with different sounds. They had the same approach as me, which was to rip ideas and then make them your own. But with Chris and Tina it was just not happening and straight away I could see this. They just saw me as a difficult artist. They were saying to the rest of the band, 'You really should get rid of Shaun as the lead singer, you know. You should make Rowetta the lead singer.'

We had bought a pound of weed (in weight, not money) as soon as we arrived in Barbados, so straight away we were big spenders to the locals, and word got round quickly to the dealers. Which meant we very rapidly found out how cheap the crack was. By the fifth or sixth day the music was just not happening for me, and Chris and Tina were just focusing on the rest of the band, so me and Bez were like, 'Let's just go and get some stone.'

The first time I'd had crack was on our first visit to the States, when I had the gun pulled on me, back in 1987, five years previously. But when we got back home from New York it had never been my drug of choice. Crack didn't really hit Manchester anyway until about 1990. It certainly wasn't freely available. We had the odd lick on our travels, but that was about it.

The band were staying in different places in Barbados. Me and Bez were staying at the studio at first, so they could keep an eye on us, and the others were staying on this private gated estate, which was patrolled. But even though it had security, the house next to the rest of the band, where a German family was staying, got turned over by masked raiders. Basically, they got the wrong house; they thought that house was where our lot were staying, and thought we had dough because we were buying off the local dealers. Some of the locals even started calling us 'the white niggers'.

The stone was so cheap that I wouldn't just buy a couple, I'd say, 'Give me ten of 'em,' or 'Can you do me an ounce brick?' Within a week I was more interested in smoking crack than going in the studio. Our Paul was also on the stone, but he would still go in, piped off his head. I'd go into the studio and have a listen to what was being laid down, but then I would *have* to go out and get on the stone, because I just couldn't write to the music they were coming up with, those loose beats like the song that became 'Cut 'Em Loose Bruce'. I wasn't feeling it at all, so I just couldn't write lyrics to it and the nightmare just progressed. It wasn't the drugs that stopped me from being able to write to the music, it was the music itself that prevented me writing to the music, so I then turned to drugs. I just didn't like what was happening in the studio, so I went and got stoned and pissed and saw the sights, went to the beach and had run-ins with the locals.

There was a baboon on the loose in our area at the time that had been nicknamed 'Jack the Ripper' because it had ripped a family to shreds. I was walking down the beach one afternoon on my own, a bit wasted, and this fucking thing just dropped out of the tree in front of me and stood there growling, looking at me. These things can smell the fear, y'know what I mean? So basically I knew I had to front it out and just growl back. So I did, and kept telling myself 'I'm hard, I'm hard, I'm hard,' and it moved. If I had freaked out then it would have ripped me to bits. That's not the sort of thing you want really, when you're walking along the beach off your head on crack – a great big baboon dropping out of a tree and wanting to start a fight with you. But things like that would always happen to me.

We also kept hitting the bars and getting smashed on rum and generally having a good time. The only time I wasn't having a good time was when I went to the studio and heard the music that was being made, which made me physically and mentally sick. I tried to speak to the rest of the band about it, but they were so sucked into what Chris and Tina were telling them, about how great they were, and about how they should get rid of me. The funniest thing about that was, a few years later, in 1996, when they did appreciate my vocal style, Chris and Tina asked me to do guest vocals on a track for them on an album they did as the Heads.

Chris and Tina moved me to a house on the other side of the island at one stage, left me there to try and write lyrics, and made sure I had no money to buy crack with. But I still had my clothes, so I just swapped a pair of Armani jeans and some Hugo Boss T-shirts for some rock. Of course, next thing someone spotted one of the locals wearing all my gear walking along the beach, and that became another legendary Shaun Ryder crack story, although it's exaggerated. I wasn't just left sitting there in my fucking underpants, smoking crack. I had other clothes with me, obviously. The locals all wanted to wear Armani, Hugo Boss and Stone Island, but it was prohibitively expensive for them to buy in the shops out there, which made it easy for me to do a deal.

The other famous tale was that I sold the sofa from the studio for crack, but that's not strictly true either. It was actually a plastic sun-lounger from beside the swimming pool. One of the guys that I was scoring off wanted a sun-lounger, so I picked up one of these two-bob loungers to put in my car – one of the seven or eight cars that I wrote off while I was there. OK, I shouldn't have taken it, but Eddy Grant who owned the studio wasn't mithered about it. It was a plastic sun-lounger that was worth fuck all. But this American kid Bruce, who was working with Chris and Tina, stuck his nose in and said, 'Hey, man, what ya doing? You can't be taking that!' I just said, 'Fuck off, you knob,' and hit him. Although, as I was cracked up, I didn't just hit him. I threatened him with a broken bottle as well, I think, which fucking terrified him. I can't remember the exact details, but it was something like that, and he went and grassed on me: 'Shaun's stealing furniture, man.' I thought, 'You mardy-arsed dick, it's only a plastic fucking sun-lounger.'

I think the crack worked out at about 50p or £1 per rock, when it would have been £10 or £20 back home. The other thing I found you could use as currency out there was car batteries. A lot of the locals lived in shacks or huts without mains electricity, so they would run everything off car batteries – their lights and whatever they used to cook with, and so on. You could get a quarter stone or a nice bit of rock for a car battery. Every time I wrote off a car I would take the car battery out and swap it for crack. I think me and Bez wrote off the rental company's entire fleet of cars. They didn't have any left – we had written off every last one of them.

I mentioned that when we were in LA, Bez shouted to someone, 'Don't get in a car with X! He's *lethal!*', but I'd never written a car off at that stage, although I'd been in a couple of crashes. I made up for it in Barbados. Bez still wrote the first one off, though, when he drove straight across the plantation near the studio and flipped a jeep and broke his arm. That was madness doing that. There were great big ruts and holes that you couldn't see, but Bez – crazed and cracked up – decided to just speed across it. So that was the first one. I rolled a lot of cars. I rolled one late one night coming back from some barbecue at the house where the others were staying.

I'd had quite a few experiences with car crashes. One thing anyone who's been in an accident will tell you is that as soon as the car starts tipping over and flying, with you inside, it all happens in slow motion. The car is turning over and starting to roll down the bank or whatever, and you're inside trying to hang on and thinking what to do, and it seems that everything is happening in slow motion. It happened to me the first time I had a car crash, and I survived, and when it happened to me the second time I had a crash, and I survived again, I decided that the key to surviving car crashes is you know you're going to live if it starts going in slow motion. Some people might feel this is an odd way to look at it, but, you know, the way you think gets a bit distorted when you've taken large amounts of drugs.

If you think about it, the publicity that we got from the stories that leaked out of Barbados was priceless. We didn't try to milk it; things just got reported everywhere. The rest of the band could never see the benefit of the amount of exposure stories like that got us, even if it was never part of any masterplan. Nathan wasn't around in Barbados when it all started to spiral; he was back home trying to sort custody of his kid out, but to be honest I don't think it would have made that much difference if he had been around. Things were out of control.

Because crack had hit Barbados, it had also affected the music that was getting played there. Especially by the young kids. When I went out in Barbados I found this scene where the lads, the older teenagers who were on the pipe at sixteen or seventeen, or maybe eighteen or nineteen, would buy reggae 7-inches but play them at the wrong speed. They were on the pipe so they wanted the music faster, so they would play these old reggae records at 78rpm instead of 45rpm, which made it sound like early jungle – it gave it a bit of a breakbeat feel. They would then toast over it, rap over it. That was the vibe in some of the little beach bars or roadside shacks that we went into. In the centre where the yachts were moored up, or Sam Lord's Castle, which was a hotel in an old buccaneer's castle, there was a totally different vibe, but we didn't really knock about there. Most of the time we ended up in the old rum-drinking gaffs at the side of the dirt roads that were little more than shacks. Then we'd go and get our hair cut under a tree for 50p or something. There would be a guy sat there with a pair of scissors who could give you a real close crop.

There were quite a few shootings while we were there as well. I remember needing to score one night and waiting until we heard the gunfire stop before we could go out. We saw a gun battle one day – some sort of drive-by when a cop was shot. I didn't think about how dangerous it was at the time, because all I was thinking about was the drugs.

The wives and girlfriends were out in Barbados for most of the time, and our kids. We did try and keep all the drugs away from the kids, but they were only babies at that time. Trish was obviously trying to get me to stay away from the crack as well. It must have been a nightmare for Trish, to be fair; it must have been terrible.

It was a beautiful place, Barbados, it really was, but the atmosphere amongst the band was dreadful. The hatred from the band was poison. It wasn't like a bunch of mates any more. I was just getting it from all sides: 'You're *ruining* the band, you and Bez, just taking drugs and getting us bad press.' The thing is, it *wasn't* bad press, us being painted as rock 'n' roll. Even if it did make us slightly comedy figures, it still worked in favour of the band. I can't tell you how many times I sat down with them and said, 'What are you *doing*? What is this *really* all about?'

There were things I didn't notice at the time, things that Muzzer would point out to me later. We'd go down to do *Top of the Pops* and someone would open the door for me and Bez, then as we walked through it they would just let go of the door and it would close in the faces of the rest of the band, and they would have to open it again to come through. I wouldn't notice stuff like that half the time, but Muzzer is really observant when it comes to these things. He found it funny, but the rest of the band fucking hated it.

Whenever they did try to act like Charlie big potatas it would backfire on them as well. One of the first times we did *Top of the Pops*, I think it was for 'Kinky Afro', PD gave them a right run around because he didn't feel he was being treated like a superstar. The keyboard stand that they had supplied him with wasn't the exact same stand that he normally used. Like that really fucking matters. But he refused to do any shots or stuff for them until it was sorted. So they spent about four or five hours trying to find this right keyboard stand, and moving things around and changing shots and the order, all to accommodate PD. By the time we eventually came to record our performance, they had wasted about five or six hours, and when the performance went out on TV, you couldn't even see PD. I think you saw a bit of his leg at one stage and that was it. The cameramen obviously thought, 'We've had enough of this little fucker!' because he was making such a big deal about his bloody keyboard stand, and just deliberately cut him off.

The other big myth about Barbados is that I took the master tapes hostage from the studio and demanded money from Factory before I returned them. That's bollocks. But it's been reported so many times, and it was included in *24 Hour Party People*, so I gave up denying it in the end. Once something has been reported that many times, it just becomes accepted fact, so even if you know that it didn't happen there's little point in keeping protesting, because no one will believe you. It's like Napoleon. Did you know Napoleon was actually five foot seven? Which was above average height at the time. But someone said he was only five foot two, and the rumour spread, and now everyone thinks that Napoleon was this little guy, and people have started referring to a Napoleon complex.

What really happened with the master tapes is there were all these rumours that Factory was going down, that the company was going to go bankrupt, and Chris and Tina were worried about not getting paid. There were also rumours that Factory needed our album to save them from going bump, and Chris and Tina could see what was happening with me on the island, and knew there was no way Factory were going to get a finished album for a while. Plus we were in Barbados, in the sun, where it takes ages to get anything done. It's 'mañana', or 'Reggie time'. Everything takes time in those sorts of places.

So Chris and Tina really started panicking that they weren't going to get paid, and they asked me if they could say to Factory that 'Shaun wants money' and 'Shaun has got the masters and is threatening to burn them', because they knew Factory would believe them considering the stories that were coming out of Barbados. They asked me if they could say that, and I shrugged and said, 'Yeah, go on then.' Really, my loyalty should have been to Tony and Factory, but I was in a place where I didn't want to be, and I was annoyed at him for putting us with the wrong producers, and annoyed at the band, plus I was off my head on crack, so I just said, 'You know what? You say what you want. If you want to use my name, then go ahead and use it.' So that's what they did – they came up with that story, saying that I was going to torch the masters if Factory didn't send over money. If anyone wants to ask Chris and Tina about that, then go ahead and ask them. They'll tell you that's what really happened.

It wasn't even a vast amount of money – it was their wages, plus PDs (*per diems*, not Paul Davis), so it couldn't have been more than about £10,000. Maybe it was £20,000, but it was not a huge amount. Tony said he had to remortgage his house to get the money, but I'm not sure that happened. As everyone knows, Tony never let the truth get in the way of a good story. He wasn't shy of a bit of exaggeration. Not that the stuff we got up to needed any exaggeration half the time, because the stories were pretty fucking wild as it was, but you'd often find something else had been added on to the tale. It was like Chinese whispers: by the time you heard a story back, and it had been retold through six people that worked in and around Factory and the music business, what was a pretty fucking wild story anyway had turned into a ridiculously mental tale with all sorts of shit added on. Anyway, the money arrived without any problem in a couple of days.

I don't think Tina and Chris were really scared of me. I think they were really worried more than anything. By this time, Tina wasn't the rock 'n' roll chick of the 70s; she was a mother. I'm sure she must have seen a few things in her Talking Heads days, although she did later say that they were surrounded by freaks and weirdos in New York in the 70s but it was all just a show – they were all normal people underneath, and she didn't think people really lived like that until she met the Mondays. But then we really did live like that for real. If we wanted something and we didn't have the money, then we just took it. I'm not saying that's how you should live your life, and I certainly wouldn't teach my kids to live that way, but that's how we were.

I don't feel responsible for what happened to Factory records because of *Yes Please!* and Barbados. Don't forget, *Pills 'n' Thrills* had gone to the top five and been a big hit, and off the back of that, our first two albums had also started selling again, so we were bringing money *in* to Factory, not bleeding it dry. Unlike all these other acts, like Cath Carroll and the Adventure Babies, who had ridiculous amounts of money pumped into them that the company were never going to recoup. Unlike fucking zinc roofs and £25,000 boardroom tables suspended from the fucking ceiling.

I didn't put one vocal down in Barbados. Not one. I did try. I'm not a quitter, so I did try and write lyrics there, but it just wasn't happening. I was dry of inspiration. They had finished the music, but I just wasn't impressed with any of it. To me, we'd taken a step back. We'd made three interesting and different albums with *Squirrel*, *Bummed* then *Pills 'n' Thrills*, but this just took us back into safe ground, which is not where I wanted to be. I could see what Factory and Tony thought they were doing – they were hoping they were going to get an album with mass appeal that would sell worldwide, and particularly in the States with Chris and Tina's names on it, but I thought we needed another big, successful album at home before we made that push for the States.

Part of the problem about conquering America was that America wasn't ready for the Mondays just yet. They weren't ready for a couple of years more, until Black Grape came out. America hadn't really had the acid-house revolution that we'd had in Britain, even though the music originally came from the States. Their music scenes and radio stations were still very pigeonholed and genre-specific. If it was a rock radio station, then it just played rock. They did have bands like Santana and Dr John who were doing freaky stuff, but they were pigeon-holed too. If we had put out a record at that time with a sequencer and beats on it, then it wouldn't really get played on rock radio, and it wouldn't get played on dance radio either, because it had guitars on it. It was mad.

Like I say, I didn't want to make a clone copy of *Pills 'n' Thrills*, but I don't think it would have been if I had got my way. The album I had in my head then, the ideas and the sounds that I was thinking of, were basically what became the first Black Grape album. *It's Great When You're Straight . . .Yeah!* is what *Yes Please!* should have sounded like, and if the other fuckers had listened to me, that's what we would have ended up with. They would have had a critically acclaimed No. 1 album. But no, instead I was outvoted and we went with their genius idea instead, and we ended up with *Yes* fucking *Please!*

When I got back from Barbados the first thing I did was go straight into the Chelsea Charter Clinic. Well, not quite the first thing. We flew into Manchester and as soon as we landed I did one from Trish at the airport, dived straight into a taxi and went to score. But the next morning Nathan picked me up and took me down to London. We went to see a consultant and he told Nathan that I needed to be admitted for treatment. You didn't need to be a specialist to make that diagnosis, it was fucking obvious to anyone who looked at me. I was mentally and physically exhausted. I weighed about six stone because I hadn't eaten hardly anything since I had left the airport to fly to Barbados six weeks previously. I had just been drinking and smoking crack and didn't want to eat.

Unlike my previous time in rehab, I was ready for it this time and took it seriously. They got an American guy in who was a top man in his field, and he was teaching us all about what he called 'Stinkin Thinkin'. He told us that one of the things that happens when you're coming down is you start all this Stinkin Thinkin – thinking bad thoughts – and straight away I latched on to that and suddenly I'm writing songs in there, and 'Stinkin Thinkin' ended up being the lead single off *Yes Please!*

I can't really remember all my time in the clinic because I was pretty far gone, but apparently I did a phone interview with Simon Mayo or someone on Radio One while I was in there and told them I was in the Lakes and all this stuff about

me being in drug rehab was nonsense. Meanwhile, Our Paul had gone back to our mam's to try and recover there.

I was in the clinic for three weeks, then Nathan came and got me and took me down to Newquay. The idea was that I would write the lyrics for the album down there. I was pretty fragile at that stage. There's a story that I went for a meal with Nathan and I asked him what veal was and he said it was a baby calf and I got all emotional and couldn't face eating it, but that's bollocks. I'm from Salford. I grew up eating tongue and tripe, so veal wouldn't have bothered me.

After Newquay we moved to Comfort's Place in Surrey, which is owned by Andy Hill and his missus, Nicola Martin, who wrote all of Bucks Fizz's hits, to record the vocals. I didn't have all the lyrics written, but I had some bits like 'Stinkin Thinkin' going round my head. The rest of the tracks we just played and played, over and again, me and Chris and Tina, till I came up with something, and we just picked up every morning where we had left off every night. I was pretty clean, fresh out of rehab, but my head was mashed and it was just really hard work. I was drinking cans of Boddingtons, but I managed to restrict it to Boddies. It was just hard because I really didn't like the music.

I took Kermit into Comfort's Place with me, and that was the first time we worked together. Kermit, as Paul Leveridge was known, had been in a Manchester breakdance crew called Broken Glass and then formed the Ruthless Rap Assassins. Me and Kermit were smack buddies – that's how we knew each other. I can't remember where I first met him, but we were both heroin users, so you would bump into each other on the scoring scene. Ruthless Rap Assassins had also played on the same bill as us at Cities in the Park.

Comfort's Place was also where I met the most obnoxious people that I'd ever encountered. Their names were Gloria and

Nik Nicholl, and they knew Chris and Tina. If only that had been the last time I met them.

The Nicholls were tour managers at the time. I remember having a conversation with Nik and talking about Big Audio Dynamite. He started telling me the story of that Big Audio Dynamite tune 'Medicine Show', and he said, 'That could have been a great record. I tried so hard to get that rubbish off the beginning of it.'

I said, 'What rubbish?'

'All that "to hang by the neck" and all that.'

I said, *'That was what made the record!'* Because you'd be in the pub with your mates having a drink and when that bit came on, 'to hang by the neck until dead!', which is a sample from *The Good, the Bad and the Ugly*, it would start going off! It was brilliant and all the lads would fucking love it.

But Nik was like, 'Nah, that sample's rubbish. You don't want that on it.'

I just thought, 'This guy is just a fucking idiot!'

So that was my first impression of the Nicholls, at Comfort's Place. Before I knew who they were, I just thought they were obnoxious twats. More of them later, unfortunately.

We managed to finish the record, but I wasn't happy with it. I liked 'Stinkin Thinkin' – I thought that was all right, but most of the rest of the album I don't care for. I don't even like 'Sunshine And Love', which was the other single. At the end of the day, if my lyrics hadn't been so off the wall and my vocals weren't in that oggy, shouty way, then it would have been a pretty banal album. If someone had written some nice lyrics and sung them in a nice manner, then that album would have been even more underwhelming; it wouldn't have stood out at all.

For the first time, I kind of gave up, and I even let PD and Our Kid come up with some of the titles, like 'Angel' and

'Theme from Netto'. With the previous albums I had really cared about them and made sure they were right, but with *Yes Please!* I just gave up in the end. PD wanted to do an instrumental that he could call his own and he wanted to call it 'Theme from Netto', so I was like 'Fine, you want to do that? Do it.' 'Netto' meant 'nothing' to us, so the title meant 'Theme from Nothing'. Shit idea, but yeah, fine, whatever, do it. It was PD's favourite track on the album. He even wanted it as a single. *'Yeah, that will get us a number one – "Theme From Netto"!'* For fuck's sake.

The song 'Cowboy Dave' came from what happened to Dave Rowbotham, who was an old Factory musician who had been in the Durutti Column and was nicknamed Cowboy Dave. He was a mate of Martin Hannett's, and he was on the brown. He was murdered while we were making the album, found in his flat in Burnage with an axe in his head.

We all got pulled in and questioned about it by the police, because Cowboy Dave had been on Factory and involved with drugs. That's where the lyrics for the song came from – the opening line is 'Tell me what you know about Cowboy Dave?' which is the first thing the police said to me. This copper just said, 'Tell me what you know about Cowboy Dave?' and I said, 'Well, he whistled on the brown and his missus was a sex slave,' and straight away I thought, that's a fucking song. So the lyrics are just what was said in that police interview, pretty much word for word.

I always seemed to get dragged into stuff like that and questioned. After the Mondays got back together I was staying in the Renaissance Hotel in Manchester, on Deansgate. The hotel had stuck me on the top floor, obviously because they presumed I was going to be rowdy and partying. They put me next to these motherfuckers who were in and out of their room all night partying and partying. It got past 4am and I was in one of my nice heroin nods, when I heard all this screaming and screaming, 'Aaaaaaaarrggghhh!' So I looked out of the window and it was just getting light and I could see two dead bodies, one with its head twisted round the wrong way, lying on the concrete canopy over the entrance. So I rang up reception and said you better send someone up to the room next door because something's happened, and you better look outside because there's two dead bodies out there. Then I got me head down and went back to sleep for a bit. I got up a bit later and looked out of the window and there were police down there and the bodies were still there and it's a fucking crime scene now. There were also police guarding the top floor of the hotel. I had a gig that night and all I'm thinking is, 'They're going to have me in all fucking day,' questioning me and everything. No one had knocked on my door yet, so I waited until the police who were guarding the top floor were talking and had their backs turned, then I nipped out of my room with my bag to the stairs and dropped it right down the stairwell to the bottom, because I didn't want it to look like I was doing one with my bag. Then I went back to the lift and no one stopped me, because they weren't really watching and I didn't have a bag with me, so it didn't look like I was doing one.

I got downstairs and grabbed my bag, and rang Neil Mather, our tour manager, to come and pick me up right away, which he did. But when we got to the gig later that day he got a call from the hotel saying, 'Shaun has got to go and hand himself in at the police station. They know he was in that room and he did one, and they want to talk to him.' Neil said, 'Listen, he's got a show, and he wasn't involved in the incident.' They said, 'We know he's not involved, but we just want to know what he heard. Did he hear any arguments or anything like that?' I wasn't keen to speak to them, so I put it off, but in the end some Detective Inspector Somebody or Other rang Neil and said, 'Look, Shaun's got to come in, or we're going to have to come and get him. It's been four or five days.' I just told them I had heard some noise from the next room and that was about it.

I didn't know if these kids knew that I was in the room next to them, but what I heard sounded like people messing about and trying to climb across the balcony to my window. Maybe they were daring each other to see if they could get across or something, but it sounded like they were trying to get across. There was also something going on with the three of them – I think the two guys were bi and they were with the same girl or something like that. I'm not sure if they ever got to the bottom of exactly what happened, and why they fell.

When we finished the vocals for *Yes Please!*, we went to New York to mix the album, which I can't remember much about, because I was still on my way back from rehab. I remember Steven Stanley, the Jamaican guy who worked with Chris and Tina on the mixing of the record – he was sound. Our Paul was there with Astrella, who was the second Yoko in the Mondays. You had Mark Day, with his bird Jane in his ear, and now you had Astrella in Our Paul's ear, and the two of them in the corner whispering, 'We're gonna form a band together . . . we're gonna be big.'

You could read all the undertones of what was going from the interviews we did around then. Our Paul said in one that he had five favourite tracks on the album before I put the vocals on them, and then realized what he'd said, so added something like 'but then Shaun puts his vocals on and it's like the cream on top of the coffee'. What he really meant is he had five favourite tracks and then Shaun put his vocals on them and ruined them.

The title *Yes Please!* came from something Phil Saxe, the

Mondays' first manager, used to say. Whatever you used to ask him, he said, *'Yes please!'* really enthusiastically. 'Do you want a cup of tea, Phil?' *'Yes please!'*

When the press and reviews started to come in, it was pretty much the first time that the Mondays had ever got bad reviews for an album. I knew it was going to happen, I expected it, so it didn't surprise me, but the rest of them had been giving interviews saying it was the best thing they had ever done and that sort of bollocks. I know you have to have a bit of bravado and say some of that when you have an album coming out, to big it up – that's part of the game. But the rest of them actually did believe it, and I'm thinking, 'You're off your heads!' But because they had been made to feel so special by Chris and Tina, and because I hadn't got involved with asking Mark to change his guitar lines or asking Our Kid to play a different bass line, they felt it was more their record than the previous ones. I let them choose song titles, I let them choose the singles, and they felt it was more their record and they really did believe in it. So when it came out and it got hammered, they couldn't take it and started to blame me.

All the press coverage we had got about the recording of the album and all the stuff that went down in Barbados had actually built up interest in the album, but the rest of the band suddenly decided *that* was why it was a failure. Not because when people got it home and listened to it they were disappointed.

When *Yes Please!* came out, Nirvana had just made *Nevermind*, and I could see things changing. *Yes Please!* sounded soft compared to Nirvana. All I could think was that if we had worked with Oakey and Osborne we would have ended up with something completely different. They always had ideas for new beats, so they would have said, 'Let's work with this beat or that beat'; 'Put a guitar line to this and that bass line'; and we'd have gone in a different direction. That's the way I wanted to work, because it was faster and more contemporary.

I pretty much expected it to get bad reviews. It wasn't a good album. There were no catchy grooves like there had been on *Bummed* and *Pills 'n' Thrills*. It had absolutely no character. *Yes Please!* wasn't the Mondays. It could have been anyone.

Just after the album was released I got in trouble for writing off a vicar's Lada while under the influence. I'd not long been out of rehab in the Chelsea Charter Clinic, and I was trying to stay clean and stick to the steps, but things were quite bleak with the band and I knew the record was terrible, so I'd had enough one night and just necked a bottle of vodka at home. After I'd polished that off, I decided in my drunken wisdom that I was going to get some gear, because I'd not had some for a bit. At the time I had a BMW 325i Sport, and Trish had a little Peugeot for nipping to the shops and stuff. The Peugeot was blocking my BMW in, so I took that instead. I drove out of Beeches Mews and on to Barlow Moor Road, and I'd only gone about twenty-five yards when I ran straight into the back of a Lada. I didn't have my seatbelt on and my head went straight through the windscreen.

I cut my head quite badly, but I wasn't knocked out. I jumped out to check if whoever was in the Lada was OK, and it was a big bearded vicar, who was fine. The Lada was a bit knackered anyway, so it was probably only worth about £50. I had about £1,200 on me because I was going to score, so I offered him a grand in cash there and then, because I didn't want the police involved. But he was having none of it. So I just jumped back in the car and drove home. I cleaned myself up a bit, but I was still bleeding when there was a knock on the door. I answered it and it was the police.

'All right, Shaun?'

'Yeah.'

'Next time, when you do a runner from an accident, remember to pick up your number plate.'

The bloody number plate had fallen off the Peugeot and I hadn't realized. The police were actually really good to me that night. They let me make a phone call and have a brew, and even have a joint. They then took me to the hospital to get seen to, before they took me down to the station. It must have been a couple of hours before we got to the station and I was breathalysed. I was charged, but the case took a year to come to court, and I got a three-year ban and a fine.

Not long after this I split up with Trish. I was going out in town a lot at the time, knocking about with Muzzer. We'd go out round town, go clubbing and pick up some birds, and either get a hotel room or go back to theirs, and I often wouldn't get home until eight in the morning. Trish wasn't stupid – she knew what was going on. Some women will put up with their boyfriends or husbands misbehaving and being unfaithful to them if they're in a comfortable situation with a nice house and a nice car, but Trish was never going to put up with it for long; she's too strong a woman. I remember one night I got off with a bird and went back to hers, and forgot to put my undies on when I was getting dressed afterwards. When I got home, Trish saw me undressing in the bedroom and clocked I had no undies on, and she knew exactly what I'd been up to. She'd basically had enough by then, and one day not long after that she just turned round and said, 'I'm going. I've had enough.'

She left me and took Jael with her and went back to her mam's in Stretford. I made sure she had a car and money, and she enrolled in Salford University. Then when I moved to Hampstead a couple of years later, I let Trish have the house in

Didsbury. She ended up emigrating to New York with Jael and has done really well for herself. She now owns her own really successful photography agency in New York. I'm still in touch with her, when we need to speak about Jael.

We then had to go out and bloody tour *Yes Please!*, which was something I was not looking forward to. It was horrible. We had plenty of loyal fans out there who were still into the band, but it was a pretty dismal experience playing that album every night. We took Stereo MCs on tour as support, and they blew us away every night. They were on the up and they sounded fresher than the songs off *Yes Please!*

I was still on and off the gear, but during that tour I was definitely hard at it. At that time, whenever I had to do something that I really didn't want to do, I turned to heroin for solace. Heroin is the perfect drug if you don't want to have any feelings, because it just masks everything and allows you to get on and do things you really don't want to do. By the time we got to the end of the tour I would even smoke heroin at the side of the stage. I didn't give a fuck. I'd sit in Dry Bar and pull out my tinfoil. PD, Our Kid and Mark Day had their own vices too, they were just sneaky with it. I would go round to someone's house to score and they would say, 'Oh, your kid's just been here . . .'; or 'Oh, you know when you left yesterday? Paul Davis came round just after . . .'; or 'Oh, Mark Day's just been . . .' So they were all shouting at me, saying, '*You're* ruining this band, 'cos *you're* doing crack and *you're* doing heroin.' But they were all bang at the drugs. They just did it in secret. Or thought they were doing it in secret.

Our Paul was still with Donovan's daughter Astrella, so she came on the tour, and her younger sister Oriole came along for the ride as well. Oriole was only twenty and had a young kid called Sebastian, but she wasn't with the father. I wasn't interested during the tour because I was on gear and there were also a lot of birds around. But at the end of the tour, as we were getting back into Manchester, she said, 'I don't know what I'm going to do now. I've got nowhere to go.' Her son Sebastian was living with her mum and dad in Ireland, and Our Paul and Astrella didn't want her at their place. Because Trish had left, I had an empty house in Didsbury, so I said she could come stay at my place, knowing full well I would end up shagging her. Which I did, within a week or so, and then we were an item.

'Sunshine and Love' was supposed to come out as a single in October, but it was delayed for a couple of weeks because Factory couldn't find a pressing plant that would give them credit. That's how dire the situation had got. They were so broke that Tony was scrabbling around trying to borrow money from here and there to make a video for the single. He was pissed off at me because I wasn't really putting any effort into promoting it, but I just didn't believe in the record, so I couldn't do it.

When Factory finally went under a couple of weeks later, it had become almost inevitable. It didn't just happen one day; it was dragged out over a few weeks, and the writing had been on the wall for at least a year. When Factory went down, Nathan was trying to negotiate us a deal with EMI. That's when we had the infamous meeting with EMI's head of A&R, Clive Black. The myth is that I walked out of that meeting, and away from that deal, and said I was off for a KFC, meaning heroin. But, as usual, that's not even half the story. What really happened was we had a meeting in the Mondays' studio in Ancoats, and Clive Black came down to listen to some of the tunes we'd been working on. I'd laid down vocals on a few, only about four tracks, but enough to give them a flavour. There was an early version of 'Kelly's Heroes', which ended up on the first Black Grape album, and a track called 'Walking the Dog' that became 'Playground Superstar', which we eventually released twelve years later after we'd re-formed. But the only music that was played in that meeting was instrumentals. That's how deluded the rest of the band were. They thought they were the future, even though they'd fucked up on *Yes Please!*, and Si Machan, our sound guy, was trying to show off what a great producer he was.

Clive just said, 'Where's the vocals, where's Shaun's vocals?'

Si was like, 'Er . . . I've lost those tracks.'

When I walked into that meeting I was honestly up for signing the deal. It was the rest of them who pissed on the fire of that meeting, not me. They just wanted to play these instrumentals they'd written and PD was like, 'Listen to this one I've got!' and it was some plinky-plonky keyboards stuff. That's when I just went, 'Fuck this . . . I'm going to get some Kentucky.' I just went out to the car park, sat in my car and got smashed. But me walking out of that meeting wasn't me splitting the Mondays up, and no one who was in that meeting could have thought that. I was just fucking angry, furious, that they had turned up at the meeting with all these Trumpton instrumentals, and none of the tunes that I'd been working on. Clive Black made it crystal clear to Nathan after the meeting that that's what he was interested in, the stuff I'd been working on with vocals, and that pissed the others off even more.

After that meeting, it was the rest of the band that told Nathan they were splitting the Mondays. Not me. It was *their* decision. At that stage, Nathan himself decided he'd had enough. I tried talking to the other members, individually and collectively, to their faces and on the phone. Me and Bez begged them not to split the band. I even told them, 'Look, if you want to go off and do your own thing for a bit, fine. Do that. But *don't* split the Mondays.' I knew how lucky we were to have got to the stage where we were, and I could see the danger of chucking it all away. We'd had a great ride, for five or six great years, and made three good albums. We'd just had one bad album that had been slagged. And rightly slagged too.

At the time I'd have done anything for the band to stay together. Not just for me, but for the rest of them as well. As a young kid, your mates mean a lot to you. As you grow older it's more about your family and your kids, and you put them first. But when you're younger, your mates mean everything. Or they did to me. Perhaps I was naïve in that respect. But we had started off together and I really would have done anything for us to stay together.

But the rest of the band were really bitter and resentful of me and Bez, and the drugs just compounded that. Any inadequacies they had they took out on me. I was on drugs and I couldn't sing in their eyes. Guess what? They couldn't really play. They weren't virtuoso musicians, but that *didn't matter*. That's not what made the Mondays *special*, and they never seemed to fully grasp that. As a band, I thought Happy Mondays were great, but I also thought we were getting away with it to a certain extent. We were lucky that there was something in the chemistry of that bunch of lads that had turned some individually reasonably average musicians into a really great band. There are better musicians than the Mondays playing in bands all over the country, but they're in shit bands, unoriginal bands, with no spark, no chemistry. With the Mondays, the whole was always greater than the sum of the parts.

When the band split and the others walked away, me and Bez were saying, 'You're fucking mad! What the fuck are you going to do?!' But they really thought they were musical geniuses. I tried telling them, 'Stop deluding yourself and blagging yourself.' Take a long hard look in the mirror. You're *fucking lucky*. 'You're a knobhead . . . you're stupid . . . and you're up your own arse. Get fucking real.' But they just couldn't see it.

Me and Bez were seeing it as a gang – we're all in it together, and we all watch each other's backs – but they didn't have that camaraderie. I saw PD a couple of years ago when Bez's ex, Debs, got engaged to Martin Moscrop from ACR and they had an engagement party. I thought, 'PD's had fifteen years to mull it over – he must have realized the mistake they made by now.' But no. By that stage he was blaming Muzzer for not keeping some of our entourage away from the band.

There was no dough left in the pot when we split. We'd been getting over £100,000 a show at our height, but we were spending a lot as well, on everything from huge lighting rigs to catering to flying wives and girlfriends around. Various members of the band would also be saying, 'I need eight thousand pounds,' 'I need ten thousand pounds,' and putting their hands in the Mondays' pot, and when we were on tour we'd stick everything on the room and run up our room bills. Mark Day was the only one who didn't really do that, and when the Mondays finished he said, 'Where's my money? I never spent mine,' but I'm afraid the answer was, 'Well, you should have dived in like everyone else, because there ain't anything left!'

I even found out that the others had been having discussions amongst themselves about sacking me and replacing me with Rowetta, as Chris and Tina had suggested, or even Everton, our security guard. That's how little they thought of me at the end. They believed that they were musical geniuses and I was just the guy who wrote the shit words.

CHAPTER TEN

'clean up your messes'

When I realized Happy Mondays were definitely over, I was annoyed more than anything else. Annoyed at the lack of loyalty and annoyed that the others couldn't see that the only chance we had of doing anything in this game was if we stuck together. All of them, from PD, a kid who just about taught himself to play keyboards, to Mark Day, who was a great guitarist but had no vision – what else were they going to do? When he was in the Mondays, Mark was always complaining, 'This is not a proper job, it's got no pension.' Then after the split he ended up selling encyclopaedias door to door. I hope they gave him a pension.

The others started popping up in the *Manchester Evening News* saying stuff like, 'I'd rather go back on the dole than work with Shaun Ryder again.' Words that soon came back to haunt them. All of the rest of the band, apart from Mark Day, ended up on the dole. What's the saying? Be careful what you wish for.

In the aftermath of the split, I was just holed up at home in Didsbury. I didn't go spouting my mouth off like everyone else, although it would have been so easy to do. I didn't rise to the bait, and I stayed out of the press. I had various people knocking on my door, saying that I had blown it, and I had various offers from different people to work with them, but I knew I wanted to do my own thing.

I also decided to try Prozac after the split. Not because I was distraught about the band or in the depths of depression. It was more because it was being heralded as this new wonder drug, and being naturally curious about new drugs, I decided I wanted to try it. It wasn't too hard to get it on prescription at that stage. If you went to the doctors and told them you were stressed out and down and depressed, they'd usually give you Prozac. I was on and off heroin then; I would go through phases with it. I thought Prozac was great at first. It felt like someone had taken my brain out and washed it and put it back again. I grew my hair again, put a bit of weight on and even grew a moustache. I felt like being incognito for a bit.

I soon discovered you couldn't take too much Prozac without it having side effects. One of them was it could give you suicidal thoughts. Now I *never* get suicidal thoughts, but after I had been on Prozac for a while I did start thinking about it, and almost rationalized the idea of the act in my head. It was almost as if I was tripping out on Prozac, and thinking about it a little too much, half convincing myself that it really didn't matter if I was alive or dead because we're all connected in this big universe, and your soul carries on living. My brain really began to think like that, until I had a moment of clarity and pulled myself together and went, 'Woaah – hang on a fucking minute!' That's when I decided I'd better stop taking the Prozac.

I was reminded of that a couple of years later when Michael Hutchence died. Most people presumed it was a sex act gone wrong, but I knew Hutchence – I'd met him a few times and I really liked him, and I knew he was taking ridiculous amounts of Prozac, silly amounts, which there was no need to take. So bearing in mind the effect it had on me, it did make me doubt that it was just a sex act gone wrong.

Inevitably, I had got together with Oriole when she was staying in my house in Didsbury. I was still with Trish when I had crashed into the vicar's Lada, but by the time it came to court I was with Oriole, and that was our first public appearance together.

I got on well with Donovan when I was with Oriole. I saw Johnny Marr recently and he reminded me how I invited him round to my house in Didsbury because he wanted to meet Donovan and he was over staying with us. Johnny came round and Don was sat there with his famous guitar, the one with the moons and the stars on it. Johnny said I was off my nut and said, 'You two have got to jam together!' and found some old battered guitar that the kids had been playing with that was fucked – the sort of guitar that you needed fingers like fat chips to play anything on, and gave that to Johnny. He said he and Don were jamming for two hours, but I must admit I've only got a hazy memory of that happening.

I was still getting asked to do a lot of TV appearances after the Mondays split, most of which I turned down, but just after the court appearance I went on *The Word*. I was interviewed by Mark Lamarr, with Oriole sitting next to me on the couch, and it was pretty obvious to everyone watching that I was high on gear. It wasn't the greatest interview, not helped by Mark being slightly sly and trying to be a bit arch, as if I didn't know what he was doing. I talked about getting a new line-up together and mentioned they might be called 'The Mondays' rather than Happy Mondays. But it's not the interview that people remember from my appearance on *The Word*; it's the fact that at the end I got up and danced with Zippy and Bungle from the children's TV programme *Rainbow*. There was a cheesy rave version of the *Rainbow* theme out at the time by some band called Eurobop and the Rainbow Crew, and they were performing at the end of the show. Lots of people saw that as evidence of how low I'd sunk, dancing with Zippy and Bungle on *The Word*, but that didn't bother me. I think people presumed I was a bit wasted and jumped up on stage of my own accord, but actually the producers of the show had mithered and cajoled me into doing it. They would often do that on *The Word* – wind up the guests or try and embarrass them if they thought it would turn into a talking point and get publicity for the show. I think Our Paul said something like, 'Look at Our Kid – he's reduced to dancing with Zippy and Bungle.' You could say that. But another way of looking at it was that I was still being invited as a guest on TV shows, while the rest of the band were sat at home and signing on the dole, waiting for the phone to ring.

Me and Oriole decided to head off to Morocco for a decent break. I needed to get out of Manchester, away from all the bullshit, and just recharge my batteries. We wanted to go to Jajouka, which is up in the Rif mountains in northern Morocco, where Bachir Attar and the Master Musicians of Jajouka are from. Oriole's family had had links with them since the 60s. Before she met Donovan, Oriole's mother, Linda, had a child with Brian Jones from the Rolling Stones, Julian Jones. Brian had recorded an album called *Brian Jones Presents the Pipes of Pan at Joujouka* with Bachir's father, Hadj Abdesalam Attar, in 1968, when he was the leader of the Master Musicians of Jajouka.

After Linda split with Brian Jones she got together with

Donovan for a while but they split and Don married an American model called Enid Karl and had two children with her – Ione Skye, who grew up to be a film star and went out with Anthony Kiedis from the Red Hot Chili Peppers and later married Adam Horovitz from the Beastie Boys; and Don Junior, who became a model. Donovan then had big success, and a big hit with 'Sunshine Superman', and shortly after he and Linda got back together. I thought Linda was all right – we got along OK, although she was quite contradictory. On the one hand she was this quite mystical being, but on the other hand she would have dizzy fits and strops if she had to miss a shopping trip to Harrods. Their whole family were all very mystical. Linda thought it was hugely significant that she and my mam shared the same birthday. They were also one of those couples who had brought their kids up as 'little adults'. You know, those hippy couples who say, 'They're *not* children, they're *little adults* and they should be treated as such.' Bollocks. They're kids. Let them be kids and enjoy life while they can. But they didn't, which meant, ironically, that they grew up to be adults who were still kids, in a way.

We were at Donovan's house in Ireland one night and Linda had us all throwing these mystical stones across the table, and then she would work out what the stones said and the significance of it. She became increasingly frustrated, though, when these mystical stones basically told her that I was the one with leadership qualities and they should listen to me. She said, 'No, that's not right. We must have done something wrong. Let's try it again.' So we threw them again and got the same result. It was hilarious. She wanted these mystical stones to confirm she was a powerful guru or something and they kept telling her that I was the chosen one and it was doing her head in.

When me and Oriole arrived in Morocco, we had a bit of a

nightmare getting up into the Rif mountains. That's the area where a lot of Moroccan hashish comes from, or 'kif', as they call it, so like any area where a lot of drugs are grown, it's quite dangerous. We were stopped several times by the army and the police at roadblocks, but it was more for our safety than anything because it was proper bandit country. We were warned that the bandits were up in the rocks, armed with guns, watching who came and went, so they took all our details and next of kin, just in case we didn't come back.

When we got up to Jajouka it was great. It's only a small village of less than a hundred people, full of musicians, bandits and weed. We were actually staying in Bachir Attar's house, which was a small walled compound, with several rooms facing this courtyard. We had a great time there. I had taken some methadone with me, so I was off heroin and just smoking weed. The only problem we had was I got really bad food poisoning. They would kill goats or other animals and cook them straight away, and I obviously ate something that had not been cooked properly, and I was really, really ill. Fortunately, that was right at the end of our stay, when we were just coming home.

I knew I wanted to get a new band together, and within a couple of months of the Mondays splitting I pulled together a rough group at my house in Didsbury. It was quite a ramshackle crazy gang that came together for the early sessions – a mad mixture of musicians, misfits, mates and smack buddies, including, at various times, me and Our Paul; Kermit; Ged Lynch, the drummer in Kermit's old band, Ruthless Rap Assassins; Craig Gannon, who had played second guitar with the Smiths; and the two Martins from Intastella, Wright and Mitler, who played guitar and bass; plus a mate of Cressa's whose name I can't even remember, a smack buddy of ours who thought he could play bongos. Bez popped round as well. Too Nice Tom was there filming most of those early rehearsals. Tom's real name is Tom Bruggen, and I'd met him a few years earlier at a boxing match when one of my pals was fighting one of his fighters. Tom was from Burnley, but a boxing trainer at Champs Camp in Moss Side. He was also a lecturer in film and interested in pharmacology, although it was more of an academic interest with Tom, he wasn't one for getting wasted. We got on really well, and we could talk for ages about different films. Tom had wanted to make a documentary with the Mondays, but then the band split, so he filmed the birth of my new band, which didn't even have a name at that stage.

Our Paul didn't last very long. I could tell that he didn't really have any enthusiasm for the new band and still had this resentment towards me for the Mondays' split, and he thought this new band was nonsense. He came round for a rehearsal, but as soon as I started saying to him, 'Can you do this, can you do that?' it was the last straw for him, and he just flipped. He started ranting at me, 'This is shit, and you're shit!' and then he started to smash my front room up. He put a window through and then he went to the kitchen and grabbed a carving knife and came at me with it, and everyone else had to jump in and calm it down. I still didn't realize how deep his resentment or hatred towards me was at that stage. I was just putting together a new band and took it for granted that Our Paul would play bass for me, but he was obviously out after that.

Our Paul went on to have quite a tough time of it for the next few years, wrestling with his habit, and even being sectioned at one point. I didn't see much of him for a few years, but I would still see him when I called in at my mam's because he was living there most of the time.

Not long after I started pulling the band together, I got a call out of the blue from Gary Kurfirst. Kurfirst was a big influential music figure in the States. He'd organized the New York Rock Festival in 1968, with a bill including the Doors, Jimi Hendrix, Janis Joplin, which had inspired Woodstock the following year. He'd also managed the Wailers, the Ramones, Blondie, Talking Heads, B-52s, Eurythmics and Jane's Addiction. He knew me through Chris and Tina of Talking Heads, but he was also a real music fan, so he knew the Mondays. When he found out the band had split he just put a call in to me to see what I was doing and if I had any plans. I hadn't been shopping myself around or trying to speak to any labels in the UK, because it was very early doors and I was still putting the band together at that stage.

I didn't tell anyone I was speaking to Kurfirst. The rest of the Mondays were still shouting their mouth off about what they were going to do and I just kept pretty schtum, and within a couple of weeks of starting those early jams at mine, I was on a plane to New York to sort out a deal with Kurfirst.

I'd been asked to work with a few different artists and turned them all down, but I did do one track with the Manchester band Intastella. I didn't really want to do it, but agreed as a favour to them. I think part of them might have thought they were doing me a favour, the cheeky fuckers, but far from it. I'd had untold artists and different bands on the phone, asking me to work with them – much bigger artists than Intastella, but had turned them all down. But I agreed to do a track with them as the two Martins were helping me out with my demos at the time.

Because it was the first thing I had done since the Mondays split, they ended up getting the front cover of the *Melody Maker* out of it, just by me saying I was retiring from the game. Which was the only chance Intastella had of ever getting a front cover. I wore a suit on the cover and declared I was getting out of the music game, knowing full well that I'd already started what would become Black Grape, and thinking, 'Just you wait and fucking see.'

Everyone had written me off. I even had Tony Wilson and Alan Erasmus and everyone knocking on my door in Didsbury, believing what the rest of the band were saying, because they were in the press claiming they were forming a supergroup, but that was just drug talk. I think they did try, but that's when Andy Rourke rang me up in disbelief because he found out PD couldn't really play keyboards. I just kept my mouth shut, thinking, 'What are people like?'

After the jamming sessions at my house in Didsbury we went into Drone studios in Chorlton to lay down some initial tracks. This was me, Kermit, Ged Lynch and the two Martins from Intastella. Basically, after I'd done them a favour and got them on the front of the *Melody Maker*, I said, 'Now you've got to do me a favour and come in and help on these demos.' I didn't tell them at that stage that I had a deal in the pipeline from Gary Kurfirst; they just thought we were recording some demos and they couldn't really be bothered. All I got from them was a series of excuses and half-hearted commitments. 'I can do half an hour this afternoon'; 'I can come in and do an hour tomorrow'; 'I can't tonight 'cos I've got to babysit for my girl-friend'; 'I've got to take my girlfriend out for steak pie.' I just thought, 'Fucking hell, no wonder you lot are never going to make it in the game.'

Even though I didn't have the line-up settled at that stage, or a name for the band, I knew exactly what I wanted it to sound like. Upbeat Rolling Stones meets Cypress Hill, with a bit of Serge Gainsbourg, Stereo MCs and a bit of reggae thrown in, but all reinterpreted in my own style. Basically, a similar approach to *Pills 'n' Thrills* and just as diverse, but a little less

Balearic and a little more hip-hop influenced, with a deep booming bass. Which is exactly what *Yes Please!* would have sounded like if I'd had my way. Kermit thought pretty much the same as I did. He had the same approach to ripping records and knew exactly where I was coming from.

I sent Kurfirst those early demos and he liked what he heard, so before I knew it I was on a plane to America to do the deal with him.

I didn't even really have many discussions with people or labels in the UK, because Kurfirst had got in there so quick. John Price at Warners had put a good publishing offer in after hearing the early demos, but I was already dealing with Kurfirst. That was how quick it happened.

Kurfirst actually wanted to sign me as Shaun Ryder, as a solo artist, but I just wasn't ready at that time to strike out on my own; I still wanted to be part of a group. Kurfirst wanted me to sign to his record label, Radioactive Records, but he also wanted my publishing and he wanted to manage me. But one person can't do all of that, because there will be a conflict of interest. So in the end he brought in the Nicholls, Gloria and Nik, who had worked for him as tour managers, and drew up a contract to make it look like they were managing me, while the idea remained that he would still be in charge really.

Like I said previously, I didn't like the Nicholls when I first met them, through Chris and Tina when we were finishing *Yes Please!* I thought they were really obnoxious. But this was Kurfirst's idea, so I went along with it, which was to prove a huge mistake.

Gary Kurfirst quite quickly hooked us up with the American producer Danny Saber. I'd described my vision of the album to Kurfirst as the idea of merging the Stones with Cypress Hill, and he thought Danny would be the right man to produce it, especially because he had worked with Cypress Hill. He said, 'This guy would be perfect for you. He's rock and he's hip hop,' and he sent him over to Manchester for an initial session.

We booked into Spirit studio on Tariff Street in Manchester's Northern Quarter, and we got on straight away, and I could tell we could work well together. Danny could play a lot of different instruments and he was a great producer. Me and Kermit had similar approaches to ripping records, and Danny totally understood where we were coming from. In those short sessions we wrote two of the songs that would end up on the album.

The nucleus of Black Grape from then on was me, Kermit and Danny. Plus Bez, of course. Then we also had Ged Lynch on drums, Danny played bass on the record and we brought Paul Wagstaff, or Wags as everyone calls him, on guitar. Wags had been the guitarist in the Manchester band Paris Angels. I can't remember exactly who introduced me to him, but we were looking for a guitarist in Manchester, and Wags was a good one, and another smackhead, so he fitted in well.

Between the sessions at my house, Drone and Spirit, we had more than half the album written when we went down to Rockfield studio in Wales to start recording proper. Coincidentally, the Stone Roses were down there at the same time, finishing *Second Coming*. From the demos we had already laid down, we knew we were on to something and there was a great atmosphere. We had a blast down there. The sessions were quite Guinness-fuelled at first. Well, Guinness, Es and Temazepam.

We spent quite a bit of time in the local pub sticking things like Thin Lizzy and Rod Stewart on the jukebox, because that was the kind of upbeat party vibe we were after. We also had a pirate copy of *Pulp Fiction* from the States, which hadn't come out in this country yet, and we sometimes watched that several times a day, so that was also an influence. Some of the religious imagery on the album was influenced by Samuel L. Jackson's character Jules in the film, and the way he quoted biblical passages. I also thought *Pulp Fiction* was a pretty realistic depiction of the effects of heroin. The scene where John Travolta's character, Vincent Vega, has just seen his dealer and is driving down the road like he's floating in his own little bubble was pretty true to how I felt when I was on heroin. *Trainspotting* was pretty real, but that was more the dirty digging end of the scene. The most realistic portrayal of a whole drug scene, and the way it's run and organized, from street-level soldiers to the boss, is *The Wire*. From the corner boys, to the way they use burner phones, to the way money is laundered, it's spot on.

I wasn't actually on the gear when we started recording *It's Great When You're Straight . . . Yeah!* but I was back on it by the time we finished it, ironically. At first we were just on the Guinness, Es and Temazis, but let's face it, if you put me, Kermit and Wags together, there's a certain inevitability about us getting some heroin. Towards the end of recording, the sessions had to be stopped temporarily while someone nipped to Bristol to get us some gear, or we'd make a call and have someone drive it down from Manchester.

Temazis, or 'jellies', were my favourite drug at the time. I loved them. I had a mate in Manchester whose girlfriend was a psychiatric nurse, and she used to rob tubs of five hundred Temazis. People had started using them to help them come down off crack or heroin, but they then became popular as a party drug. Basically, the whole recording down there was a bit of a Temazi party, which is where the song on the album 'Tramazi Parti' came from, although we changed the spelling to avoid legal problems.

We had a few run-ins with the locals while we were there. It seemed like it was almost an established routine that whoever was recording down there would get pissed, do mad things, and then end up in the local court and get fined. It was almost a game for the locals. I can remember being in the pub with Mani in Monmouth and the local kids were trying to goad us, banging on the window and going, 'Come on!' trying to get you in a fight. Me and Kermit were nicked several times for being drunk and disorderly or something. One night we were off our heads on Temazis and E and got into another scrape, and the police turned up and I shouted at Kermit, joking, 'Go and get the guns!' That's the sort of weird nights out we had down there.

While we were making the first Black Grape album, Oriole gave birth to our daughter, Coco, on 11 April 1994. She was named after Coco Chanel, not Coco the clown. Her full name is Sean Coco Chanel Ryder. I was made up to have another daughter. Like I said earlier, after my first daughter, Jael, was born, I was quite keen on having a few kids, and me and Oriole started trying not long after we got together.

Kurfirst and Radioactive had brought Steve Lironi in as a co-producer. I didn't really understand why he was there at first, because Danny Saber knew exactly the sort of record that me and Kermit wanted to make. But Kurfirst and Radioactive were a little worried the album might be too hip hop, so they brought in Steve. He had been in Altered Images and was married to Clare Grogan, and they wanted him to ensure we kept a rock element to the album. Basically, they didn't want the album to be too black.

The most obvious example of that is 'Kelly's Heroes', which I don't think turned out as great as it could have been. I loved the song originally, but I think that huge guitar riff in the finished version that was released takes over the song. I wanted a bit of a rock lick on there, not this huge riff, but that's what the Americans love, and that's what Kurfirst and Radioactive wanted. When we wrote it, me and Kermit were really bouncing off each other in the song: 'Jesus was a black man!', 'No, Jesus was a Batman!', 'No, no, no, that was Bruce Wayne!' But when the track became a bit rockier, it lost a little bit of that energy, because it's easier to bounce off each other when you have more of a groove than a rock riff behind you. Don't get me wrong, it's a good track, but it could have been better. It should be punchier and funkier. It should be a bit tighter for the verbal sparring to really work. 'Kelly's Heroes' was a little dig at the celebrity culture, 'don't talk to me about your big, big heroes'. Although one person did once say to me, 'Why are you having a go at Serbians? Do you not like Serbians?' Which confused me, so I asked them what they meant. 'Why do you sing "Don't talk to me about heroes, most of these men stink like Serbs"?'

'No, mate, it's "subs", glug glug glug . . .'

'Reverend Black Grape' was the opener and the first single off the album, and therefore probably the first Black Grape track most people heard. It was a great introduction to the band. I wasn't trying to be deliberately controversial with the line about the Pope and the Nazis: 'Oh Pope he got the Nazis, to clean up their messes. In exchange for gold and paintings, he gave them new addresses'. Reverend Black Grape was just a fictional character. I suppose he's part me, part Kermit, a character that emerged when we were riffing off each other while we were writing it. The chorus is ripped from the hymn 'O Come All Ye Faithful', which is probably that influence from Jules in *Pulp Fiction*.

'In the Name of the Father' is again not really about anything. 'Neil Armstrong, astronaut, he had balls bigger than King Kong' – they're just little snippets or stories that I've pulled together, 'first big suit on the moon and he's off to play golf.' Although I do remember watching the first moon landing in 1969, back in Little Hulton, when I was six.

'Yeah, Yeah, Brother' was something that was left over from the Mondays. Not the whole song, but I had chunks of the lyrics. It's not necessarily about Our Paul, because I wasn't quite aware of just what a backstabber he could be at that stage, although he had walked away from the new band. It's more about all the rest of the Mondays and backstabbers in general.

I'd also been listening to quite a bit of Serge Gainsbourg, which you can hear on 'A Big Day in the North', as it's a slight rip of his song 'Initials B.B.'

'Submarine' is another track that is not really about anything in particular. 'He smoked steroids, and he got me in a headlock' isn't about anyone – it just sounded good. That was one of the last songs we recorded in that session, which you can tell because I'm a bit more magpie with my lyrics, like 'You paid a debt today, oh boy' is a slight rip from the Beatles' 'A Day In The Life'.

'Shake Your Moneymaker' is also a bit of a rip, this time from the Stones' 'Fool to Cry'. It's not a straight rip, but if you listen to the two tracks side by side you can definitely see some influence in there. That was also probably down to the feed-back we were getting from Kurfirst, because he would love tracks like that, which had some rock influence, and he would reject tracks that were a bit more hip hop – those that I thought were actually more in keeping with the album we were aiming for.

Danny would deliberately record me and Kermit adlibbing or just talking bollocks in the studio, and he added snippets of that in at the end when he was mixing tracks. Like the outro of 'Little Bob', where you've got me and Kermit just riffing off each other and talking rubbish: 'I believe everything I read . . .'; 'Speak up, speak up.' We wanted to make the record as diverse and interesting as possible, so we added little samples and unexpected references from everything, from films to the old Cresta Bear, who used to say, 'It's frothy, man' on the advert. I'd done that since *Bummed*, which was littered with quotes and references to films like *Performance* and *Gimme Shelter*, but we took it to another level with Black Grape.

By the end of our time in Wales we still hadn't settled on a name for the group, and Kurfirst had been asking me to come up with something for weeks. He then started pressurizing me for one: 'We need a name for the band. You've got to come up with one now.' Kermit had a can of black grape juice in his hand, and I just thought, 'You know what, we'll call it Black Grape,' and as soon as I said it, it just seemed to fit.

While we were recording there had been a rumour going round about me signing on the dole in Salford. Piers Morgan actually rang me and said, 'Look, we've got photos of you signing on,' and I said, 'Piers, you know me, mate. If you've got photos, *look* at them, because I'm telling you, it's *not* me, mate.' So Piers said, 'Do you need money?' and I said, 'Piers, look, between you and me, I've already done a deal and I've got a great new album coming out, which will probably go to Number One. Why would I be signing on the dole, Piers, you know what I mean? Check your source and check your photographs.' Anyway, less than two hours later, I get a phone call back from Piers agreeing it isn't me in the photos, and it's a load of bollocks, but apparently there was some kid in a dole office in Salford posing as Shaun Ryder. He was signing on and claiming for whatever he could claim for – his house, garden tools, anything he could get.

I've got a good idea of how it happened. Like I said, when the Mondays split, Paul Davis and Our Paul had all gone and signed on the dole. Now this is Salford, so if anyone had seen those three of the band go and sign on, but they ain't seen me, and don't think I'm claiming, then they'll get on the scam. It's not too hard to get any info that you need – my date of birth, address, or whatever info you need when you fill in the forms. I never found out who it was. I could have done, but what's the point? Someone was pulling a scam, it wasn't me, but it wasn't costing me. The dole were the mugs for paying out and believing it. The tabloids had actually got the story from the dole as well, so someone there really got themselves in the shit, because they sold the story and then it turned out it wasn't even me.

After we finished recording in Wales, we went to Chapel Studios in Lincolnshire to put the final touches to the record. We were a couple of tracks short, because Kurfirst had rejected one or two that he thought were too hip-hop orientated. Working with Kurfirst was the first time I found out what an executive producer does. It basically means he gets to choose what tracks go on the album.

Chapel Studios is in a weird little place called South Thoresby, which is a proper wife-swapping village. There was only one pub there, so if we got up to any mischief in there, taking Temazis or something, the whole village would know what you'd been up to. It wasn't far from Skegness and we went there one day for a photo shoot. That's where the photo on the inside of the album sleeve is taken – on top of the arcade in Skegness.

We hadn't really been listening to much new music while we were recording; we had just been in our own little bubble. When we had finished and I got to Manchester, I called in on Cressa in Chorlton and he'd just got a copy of the first Oasis album, *Definitely Maybe*. He played it to me and I was like 'Oh, okay . . .' I thought it was really good, but I was a tiny bit surprised it was straight down the line rock 'n' roll, which is not what Black Grape was about.

I went to their gig at the Haçienda when the album came out, but I didn't know Noel and Liam at the time. I never knew Noel back in the day, although, as I mentioned earlier, I found out years later it was him who had been sending those rude faxes back to us from the Inspirals' office. But I didn't meet him for years. I actually met Liam before I met Noel. Donovan was over visiting me and Oriole in Didsbury, and me and Don had popped to the Woodstock pub. Liam just happened to be in there and bowled over and introduced himself – 'Shauuunnn! Donovan!' I got on really well with him, but it was quite funny because no one in the pub seemed to have any idea who Liam was at the time, and me and Don were the ones that were getting recognized by people.

In the summer of 1994 we went out to Encore Studios in Burbank, Los Angeles, to mix the album. Kurfirst brought in a guy called Tom Lord-Alge, who was a Grammy-award-winning producer and had worked with everyone from the Stones to U2 and had about ninety-six songs in the Billboard charts at the time. Tom was a mate of Kurfirst's and he had the magic touch at the time. All the records he worked on would get radio play. He was actually working on about five different tunes at the same time as ours. The other memory I have of mixing the album is that the O. J. Simpson police chase happened then, because I remember watching it on TV when we were in the studio, this farcical low-speed car chase, with the LAPD following him down the freeway.

The album title, *It's Great When You're Straight . . . Yeah!*, came from something someone said when we were mixing the album in the studio and we didn't have any drugs. Someone just said, ironically, 'It's great when you're straight, yeah?' I thought, 'I'll have that.' We had some fun with it when the time came to do all the press for the album, but it's obviously ironic, especially with the 'Yeah?' at the end.

I was pretty confident with the album when it was finished; I felt as confident as I had when we finished *Pills 'n' Thrills*. We knew we had something really special and, more importantly, it was original.

I met Keith Richards and Ronnie Wood for the first time in Los Angeles just after we finished *It's Great When You're Straight . . . Yeah!* Someone in the Rolling Stones camp had heard a couple of early tracks from the album – I think Kurfirst must have played it to them – and loved the production, so had put forward Danny Saber's name to work with the Stones.

They wanted to meet Danny, so they invited me and him to their show in LA and sent a car to pick us up for the gig. That was actually my first ever Rolling Stones gig, and I arrived in a car and with a driver that had been sent by Keef and Ronnie. It was Hollywood Bowl, I think, and the car took us in through the private back way, and it was all set up like a rock 'n' roll circus, with pinball machines, gaming machines, huge plasma screens – it was amazing. There were huge tents set up with different themes, like Lawrence of Arabia or whatever, and this was just the backstage area. It was far out, man. It's one of the few occasions where you could actually say, with a straight face, 'This is far out.' I actually watched the gig with all the band's families, from this VIP section, and then we met them all after. Apart from Mick Jagger. He just completely disappeared, but apparently he always does that. Keef said he was probably off counting the money from the merchandise stalls: 'That fucker's probably off counting the merch money, man!'

I had a copy of the album with me, so I played it to them and when it finished Keef and Ronnie were both like, 'Put it on again, man.' So I played it again, and when it finished for the second time they both went, 'Put it on again, man!' I'm not joking, we must have listened to it about six times, and I was thinking, 'Fucking hell, this is great! Keef and Ronnie fucking Wood telling me to put my album on again and again!'

Usually when I meet people like that I tend to keep my mouth shut, and just speak when I'm spoken to, but we were having a laugh and we had a few drinks and I was a bit off my head. Later on in the evening I had a packet of Marlboro, so I started to show Keith all the supposed hidden meanings on there, the references to the Ku Klux Klan and stuff. Keef just looked at me, sighed, and said, 'Fucking hell, man, you must be bored shitless . . . that's so boring trying to figure that stuff out.' I just thought to myself, 'Right, okay, it's Keef. Shut your mouth and don't say fuck all. Just let him take the piss.'

I went round to the place where they were staying a few times, for drinks, and Danny ended up working with them on their next album, *Bridges to Babylon*. I met Ronnie's wife, Jo, and Keef's sons, and they were all really smart, cool people. At the time I was on the gear, and must have looked a bit of a state. But that's not something that they won't have come across before.

When I got back to Manchester I moved to Hampstead, and got a flat just off Hampstead High Street. I just fancied getting away from Manchester for a bit, and I'd never actually lived in London, and it made sense with all the TV stuff. Oriole was back and forth from Ireland, because Sebastian was with her parents there. The flat underneath the one I got was also going, and Muzzer fancied doing a stint in London, so he took that.

I'm not really a massive drinker, but I have had a few periods when I've been using gear and drinking at lot, usually Guinness, at the same time, and Hampstead was one of those periods. Oriole was over in Ireland a lot, so I was more or less living on my own, and if I wasn't working I would go to the pub pretty much as soon as it opened and stay there all afternoon and into the night. I wasn't even hanging out with anyone in particular; I would just drink with the locals in the pub.

Central Station did all the artwork for the release again, and they came up with this bastardized image of Carlos the Jackal, and one of Michael Jackson on the inside. The Americans had a slight problem with us using Carlos the Jackal as an image, but that was just them being overly sensitive again. They thought we were glorifying a terrorist or something like that, but it wasn't even anything to do with the band. Matt and Pat and Karen just picked it because it was a really strong image.

'Reverend Black Grape' was the obvious choice for the first single. Kurfirst brought in Don Letts to do the video, who he knew because he had managed Big Audio Dynamite. Don made total sense because he came from that background of mixing punk and reggae, which fitted perfectly with Black Grape. The video does have quite a BAD feel to it, with the religious and cowboy imagery. We filmed it on a housing estate in Ancoats in Manchester and then the interior scenes upstairs in Dry Bar. Some little fucker nicked a lovely Comme des Garçons blazer and a Gaultier jacket I had with me while we were filming in Dry Bar.

I had also had some clothes robbed previously in Marseilles on a Mondays tour. I lost a bag full of Stone Island gear, which was the same price then as it is now. Imagine trying to convince an insurance firm that you had a jacket that was worth £2,000 in the early 90s. We also caught someone sneaking on our tour bus to rob it in Brighton once. This lad had been through the whole bus and had stuff piled up at the door ready to get off, just as we came back. So we blindfolded him and took him into the hotel. Me, Our Kid, Muzz, Pat Warde, who used to do our security and a couple of others. We stripped him down to his jeans and held a kangaroo court, which went on for about two hours. Every now and then Pat would give him a dig, and someone would shout, 'There will be no brutality in this court!' We really messed with his head and he was in bits, crying and saying he had a wife and kids. But we found him guilty and his punishment was death by drowning. So we blindfolded him again and gagged him and took him down to the beach. We led him down into the sea and he really thought we were going to drown him and he was crying and pissed himself, but at the last minute we let him go. I like to think he didn't try and rob any more tour buses.

'Reverend Black Grape' went Top 10, so we got asked to do *Top of the Pops*. When we got there, I was fully expecting some producer to take me aside and say to me, 'You'll have to change that line in the song that says "Put on your Reeboks, man, and go play fucking tennis" because we don't have swearing on *Top of the Pops*,' but no one ever did. Somehow they didn't get on it. They must have presumed I said 'funky tennis' or something.

Not only was the album really strong, but we were also helped by how dated a lot of the other new music sounded at the time. Britpop was just building to a peak, and there were so many boring guitar bands, playing their dads' type of music, that it just made *It's Great When You're Straight . . . Yeah!* stand out even more. The album went to No. 1, which the Mondays have never managed, and it tasted even sweeter after I had been written off by everyone in the aftermath of the Mondays' split. We knew the album was good and had confidence in it, but I didn't expect it to go straight in at No. 1. Almost every review was really good, and talked about it as a great comeback. The *NME* gave it ten out of ten and said, 'They'll roast eternally in Hell for this bleeding classic, but what a lovely way to burn.'

We then went to do the video for the second single, 'In the Name of the Father', in Jamaica, which was Don Letts' idea. We were staying on the north coast, and that was actually my first time in Jamaica. Don had the idea to portray us as kind of missionaries, with Central Station's images of Carlos the Jackal, George Best and Pablo Escobar as our sort of religious icons. They also built a raft for me, which I floated down the river on, and we were baptized in the river.

We were there for about a week, and I just chilled out when we weren't filming. Kermit was off scoring crack while we were there, but I didn't partake for once; I just stuck to the Guinness and weed.

We didn't actually have a full Black Grape band before we needed to go on tour, because a lot of the instruments on the record were either played by Danny Saber or Steve Lironi, who both played keyboards and Hammond organ on there. Danny also played guitar and bass, and Steve had played slide guitar. Wags had played guitar on the album, Ged Lynch had played percussion and Martin Slattery, who went on to be in Joe Strummer's band The Mescaleros, had played saxophone on 'Little Bob' and 'Tramazi Parti'. So the line-up when we went on tour was me, Kermit, Bez, Wags, Martin Slattery, Ged Lynch and Danny Williams, who we brought in to play bass.

Even though the last Mondays' tour had been so horrific for me, I was well up for touring with Black Grape. The album had topped the charts, and it was such a feel-good party vibe that it was always going to be a great record to tour. Not that I can remember a great deal about that tour. Like I said, I was drinking quite a lot of Guinness at that stage and I'm not necessarily a massive boozer. But when you're on drugs like heroin and cocaine you can just drink and drink and drink, and that's when my memory gets hazy. My memory is more affected by drink than drugs. If I'm not on drugs, then I can quite happily not drink. If I'm not on drugs, I would be pissed after about four pints, I would be a mess, because I'm not a big drinker. But when I was using properly, I could drink up to twenty pints of Guinness a day. When you're using you just can.

After the tour ended, me and Oriole moved to County Cork in Ireland. Her mum and dad were living out there, so she was keen, and I just fancied a change. I had a bit of money in the bank and took a chunk of money from the proceeds of the tour, which was owed me, and bought a farmhouse out there for cash. At the time, the Church of England had been selling off some property it had in Ireland really cheaply. I found a farm-house in Ballyclough, which is about a mile from Mallow in County Cork, and not far from Donovan's place. The people I bought it from had got it at a bargain price from the church, but I still got it pretty cheap off them. I think I paid £150,000 cash, and it had six or seven bedrooms and seven or eight acres of land. It had stables, one of which they'd started converting into a recording studio. The other bonus was that at that time musicians didn't pay tax in Ireland.

I enjoyed chilling out in Ireland, although I sometimes wonder what tales Oriole was telling her old man. Some days poor old Donovan would turn up all red-faced and flustered, and I'd be thinking 'What the fuck's up with him?' Only later did I realize she must have been telling tales about what was happening or how I was misbehaving.

After the album had come out and been a success, the two Martins from Intastella popped up and started complaining that they had written part of the songs and weren't credited, even though they'd only come down to the studio for half an hour or a few hours here and there, begrudgingly, when their missus would let them. Anyway, in the end we settled that out of court by giving them a few points, which they were happy with. I actually recently saw a Black Grape royalty statement for the first time in years and thought, 'Who the fuck is that?' when I saw their names on it, until I remembered. They have probably earned far more off those few points on Black Grape songs than they ever made off Intastella, though that's not saying much. They were actually pretty lucky that we settled out of court, because a couple of people I knew couldn't quite believe they'd had the audacity to take it as far as they did and wanted to take matters into their own hands. But I wouldn't sanction it.

We were supposed to go on tour to the States in the autumn of 1995, but I couldn't get a visa. My passport had run out. I'd got a ten-year one in 1985, which was one of those old black ones. They didn't have an electronic chip in them, so your criminal record didn't automatically pop up on screen when you went through customs, so I just simply lied on all the immigration forms where they asked about convictions. But when I applied for a new passport, I got one of the new maroon EU ones that have a chip in them, and my criminal record now appeared on their screens. When we applied for visas to tour the States, I was refused one and so was Kermit. Part of the problem was my importation charge. Importation is miles worse than possession in their eyes. It didn't matter that it was only a little bit of weed; to them, importation is importation, so I might as well have been Al Capone. They checked their records and realized I had been lying to them for ten years and I got an automatic ban from the States, although Kurfirst did manage to get round that for a little while, as I'll explain shortly.

At the start of November, we did *Later with Jools Holland*. We did three songs and closed it with 'Tramazi Parti'. I really like

Later . . . and I like Jools. After Black Grape finished, he actually arranged for me to go back on my own and do a Rolling Stones cover. I much prefer singing live to miming, especially when you have to mime to an edited version, and you've got to get the timing right. When it's live, as long as you come in on the right beat you're fine, while if you're miming and you miss your cue you just look like an idiot. Gregory Isaacs, Suggs and D'Angelo were on with us as well. I ended up having a night out with Suggs afterwards, and we finished up in Browns, I think.

Shortly after that, I went on *TFI Friday* to be interviewed by Chris Evans. He said at the start of the interview, 'If you don't swear I'll give you my shoes,' and put them on his desk. I picked one up and said, 'They're Patrick Cox man, and Patrick's a good fucking . . .' before I could help myself. The show was live and after that performance I was told I was not allowed to be interviewed live on Channel 4 any more.

We then had a few European dates, where Kermit fell really ill. I think we explained it away as being from drinking dirty water at the time, but it was more likely to be dirty digging. We were in Spain, playing live, and Kermit had used the water out of the tap in his hotel room when he was cooking up. I'm not sure where he got his needle from and if that was clean, but it was a dirty dig that made him ill, and it got serious very quickly. When he got back to the UK he was hospitalized in Monsall Hospital, which is a horrible place, and we went in to see him and he looked like a skeleton. He'd always been quite a lean bloke, but he literally looked like a skeleton; there was no meat on him at all. The doctors said bits of his heart and liver were flaking off him; he was in a really bad shape. I think they even brought the priest in to give him his last rites; they really thought he was going to die at one stage.

Like I've said earlier, I've never really been a digger, and never really understood people who thought it was hard and macho to stick a needle in themselves. If you inject heroin it gets into your system quicker, but smoking is the second quickest way to get a drug into you, and you can't really over- dose by smoking heroin, because you'll mong out before you take that fatal dose. I have injected at times, when I've absolutely had to, but only when there's been no smokable gear. Even then it wasn't something I made a big ritual about – I would just want to get it over and done with. A lot of diggers love all that ritual with their works, but it's never appealed to me. If you only have a little bit of heroin, a tiny deal, and you want to make sure you get the hit you need, you would be more tempted to have a dig. But I didn't need to do that. From the time the Mondays started to became successful, I could usually lay my hands on large amounts of heroin at a reasonable price, so I could afford to smoke it.

'Kelly's Heroes' then came out as the third single from the album and we had to shoot two videos for it. The first one we shot in a club in London, with Bez dressed as Batman and me in a blond wig. Patsy Kensit is in that one, and we filmed it just before she got together with Liam Gallagher. The Americans didn't like it, so we had to shoot a different one for them, which was like an armed bank-robbery scenario. By the time we came to film the second video, Kermit was ill, so we brought in Psycho as his replacement. Psycho's real name was Carl McCarthy, and he was a mate of Kermit's from Moss Side who had come down and done some additional vocals on 'In the Name of the Father' when we were recording the album. He was still at college and a DJ, and he had the right attitude and looked great.

Because we couldn't get into America, we decided to do a press trip for the Americans to Cuba. The idea was to invite all the American press to Cuba and we could do the interviews there. Me and Oriole decided to have a little break in Mexico the week before, and went to Cancún and then on to San José. I know I was on gear at that time, because I remember going to score. I clocked someone who I knew was selling something and followed him, and then had a word with him. 'Cheeba', they call their gear out there, and it's smokable tar heroin. When you get powdered brown heroin over here, you put a light to it and it turns to black shiny tar. The *cheeba* is already turned into black tar, and comes as a lump that looks like hash. It's smokable gear – you can't inject it – and it's popular with American college kids, who don't think smoking heroin is as addictive as digging, but they all end up with habits.

We were only in Cuba for a few days, and I can't remember too much about the trip, because I wasn't too well. I did worry for a second a few years later when a mate of mine asked me if we met Castro when we were in Cuba, but I'm assured that we didn't. I don't mind only having a hazy memory of Cuba, but I would hate it if I'd met Castro and not remembered it. I do remember we stayed in a nice hotel and I enjoyed hanging about the old town, and getting my hair cut in an old-school Cuban hairdresser's.

After Kermit came back, he wasn't 100 per cent, so we decided to keep Carl. He had a good voice, and he had a lot of energy when we performed live, so he added another dimension to the band.

But then not long after Kermit came back, Bez decided he was quitting Black Grape because he thought he wasn't getting paid what he was due. Bez wanted his E bought for him, and his expensive energy drinks and this and that, and in the end we were paying about £300–400 a day, just on Bez's extras. Because we also had Kermit and Psycho in Black Grape, who were both pretty energetic on stage, I didn't think it was quite as critical when Bez left. I thought those two between them could make up for Bez's absence.

What I didn't realize is that those two would soon want out as well.

CHAPTER ELEVEN

'I've got to be sick to be ill, I've got to take my smiley pill, I've got to dress smart to kill, and it's only ever done for the thrill'

At the start of 1996, I went down to London for the Brat Awards, which was the *NME*'s equivalent of the Brit Awards. Black Grape won Best New Band, but unfortunately I ended up getting nicked right afterwards. In between the awards ceremony and the after-party I decided to go and score some gear with some Scousers I'd met. Unfortunately, the house we went to score at was under surveillance, so as soon as I walked out of there I was nicked. Thankfully I'd done my gear in there, so they took me down the station but found nothing on me, and I ended up back at the party afterwards. At some stage in the proceedings I lost my mobile phone and my award. I did a phone-in with Chris Evans on the Radio One breakfast show in the morning where I was supposed to be talking about the awards ceremony, but we just ended up talking about what had happened to me.

A couple of weeks later, Chris had us back on *TFI Friday*, where the idea was it was a kind of parody of *Stars In Your Eyes* and we did the Sex Pistols' song 'Pretty Vacant'. Never mind pretty vacant, I was pretty drunk; and even though we'd assured them I wouldn't swear because it was a live broadcast, I said 'fuck' quite a few times during the performance. Chris Evans' production company ended up being fined by the TV regulators and the programme was no longer allowed to go out live. I was banned from appearing live on any programme on Channel 4. In fact, I was the only person to be named in the Channel 4 transmission guidebook. The ban was only lifted recently, when I came out of the jungle. They kept asking me to go on Channel 4 and I had to say, 'I can't – check your rule book,' so in the end they lifted the ban.

In the spring, we managed to get into the States after Kurfirst had sorted out my visa situation. I don't know for sure how he did it, and we'll never know now, because he died a couple of years ago.

Basically, he knew someone in the American embassy and we had to pay this person $100,000. They then somehow altered my details on the system, so my previous convictions and my ban from the States didn't show up and I could get in the country. That's how much influence Kurfirst had. He managed to get round the ban for a couple of years, but after Black Grape, when I was no longer working with Kurfirst or the Nicholls, I couldn't get into the States again. The first time I got back in the States after Black Grape was when we played Coachella with the Mondays in 2006. After that I spent a couple of years on probation with the embassy, and even if I go to the States now I will be sat in immigration for three hours while all the paperwork is gone through.

The only time I tried to get in while I was banned was when Jael had an accident, just after the Mondays got back together in 1999. By that time Trish had moved out there and started a new life and I got a call from her saying, 'Jael's had an accident and she needs plastic surgery on her face.' I was still on the gear at the time, but the first thing I thought was, 'My daughter's ill, I've got to get over there.' So I plugged about seven or eight grams of smack up my arse and jumped on a fucking plane. But as soon as I arrived in the States they pulled me and realized I was banned. I was still trying to blag it, explaining my daughter was ill, but the immigration officer just said, 'If you don't turn round and get back on that plane now, I'm going to strip-search you, and you don't want me to do that.' I knew that if they did put me on the glass toilet I was going to be doing years in prison, so I just shut my beak, spun around and got back on the plane. I got another year stuck on my ban for trying to get in. Thankfully, Jael was fine. She'd just fallen over ice skating and slightly cut her face – it was just typical Americans overreacting.

When we finally got into America with Black Grape we headed to New York and did a big signing session at the Virgin Megastore on Times Square. There was an in-store DJ who kept calling us 'gangsta rave'. Whatever that is. We played Irving Plaza and I did a big photo shoot for *Q*. They dressed me in a tuxedo, which I wouldn't let them have back. The journalist started whingeing that it was only hired, but I said, 'Look, you either give it to me, or we'll take it off you – just tell the hire place your hotel room was robbed.'

The next night we played Boston and the head of Rizla came back stage. Mr Rizla was a businessman in a suit and I was just laughing with him, saying, 'Come on, you know what your Rizla papers are used for. Especially the king-size ones – you know no one uses those to make cigarettes!' I think I did actually get him to admit he knew what they were used for. I don't smoke weed any more, but when I did I never really used the king-size papers. If I wasn't in a rush, I'd always be a traditional red-papers and three-skins man. Kids today can't make a three-skin joint – they just can't. It's a lost art. They all seem to use king-size skins. Our Jake – Our Paul's oldest son, who now plays drums in my band – smokes weed like I used to, but he can't skin up with three skins.

We then had to drive overnight to Toronto, but the bus broke down. Me and Muzzer couldn't be arsed waiting, so we decided to hitch. If you've ever hitched, you'll know that the people who stop to pick up hitchhikers are the weirdest motherfuckers you'll ever meet. This guy stopped to pick me and Muzz up and he just started making all these strange grunting noises and heavy breathing. It was weird as fuck. We really thought he was going to pull out a gun or turn out to be some Hannibal Lecter type.

After the tour finished we went to Los Angeles and hired a rented house in the Hollywood Hills so we could start work writing the second album with Danny Saber. One of the first tracks we finished was 'Fat Neck', and we decided to put that out as a single to tide us over and bridge the gap between the first and second album, because we knew the follow-up was going to be a while. Johnny Marr played guitar on 'Fat Neck', so he did become a member of Black Grape for a little while, although I don't really remember the recording; that's one of my blurry periods. We had a mate called Fat Neck, whose real name was Karl Power, and he was the lad who pulled the prank at Manchester United's match against Bayern Munich in 2001. He'd got by the side of the pitch with a fake pass, and had a full kit on underneath his clothes. When the players lined up for the team photo, he just went and stood alongside them in the line-up. After that he also walked out to bat at Headingley, when England were playing Australia, jumped on Centre Court at Wimbledon and had a little rally before a Tim Henman match, and various other stunts. Karl was called

Fat Neck simply because he had a fat neck, but the song isn't about him.

Although it was only a year or so since the contract with the Nicholls had been signed, after we'd recorded the first album they more or less turned round to Kurfirst and said, 'Fuck you Gary, we've got a contract here that says we're managers, you've got conflict of interest, and we're not listening to you any more.' They had tour-managed the likes of Blondie, Talking Heads and the Ramones for him, but after that they never worked again for him. That was the start of the legal issues that would dog me for years.

After we got back from the States, I decided I had to get rid of the Nicholls as my managers. I had never liked them; I'd only gone with them because of Kurfirst, who was really supposed to be in charge, and now they'd fallen out with him so that set-up had kind of collapsed. I'd also heard all sorts of strange stories about what they were up to. I just didn't like them, and I certainly didn't trust them as far as I could throw them. If only I had known then that it would take me over twelve years to finally get rid of them.

I'm actually loath to speak about them, but unfortunately, as I couldn't get them out of my life for so long, I suppose I need to talk about it. Basically, after I sacked them they pursued me through the courts, and the court ruled that I had to pay them £150,000 damages for getting rid of them. I should have just bitten the bullet and paid it, but at the time I was off my nut on drugs and my mental state was not great, so my reaction was, 'You cheeky fuckers! Why should I pay you a hundred and fifty thousand damages? I didn't want you managing me in the first place and I'm pretty sure you've been ripping me off.' So I just ignored the judgement, and the letters asking for payment. Before I knew what was happening, they got an injunction out on me that froze half my income. Then, a couple of years later, after Black Grape split but before the Mondays re-formed, they managed to get another injunction that froze *all* my income. This went on for years and years, and in fact it's only recently been resolved.

The Nicholls used to tell me they were connected, and Gloria was always telling me she was the niece of Henry Hill, the character that Ray Liotta plays in *Goodfellas*, which I'm not sure I believed. But even if it was true, I'm not sure it's something to boast about – let's not forget that Henry Hill, at the end of the day, is just a fucking grass. If they had threatened to send someone after me I would have said, 'Listen, you put any fucking gangsters you want on a plane from New York to Salford to come and find me, and I can promise you . . . they won't get back on that fucking plane.'

I've had to go to court several times to try and resolve this situation. Before one case, Gloria threatened me outside the court as we were waiting to go in to have our case heard, issuing a veiled threat against my kids. But she was so stupid she hadn't noticed the judge standing near us. I had, so I just kept my mouth shut and pretended to start crying and, when we got into court, one of the first things the judge did was reprimand her.

I can't tell you the amount of offers I've had from people over the years to take care of them. But you have to say to yourself, 'Get real. Is it really worth it?'

I only found out quite recently that at one time the amount that I owed them had gone down to only a couple of hundred quid or something, unbeknown to me. It was out of my hands, but there was a late payment, which was not of my doing and which incurs a fine, which incurs collection fees, more solicitors' fees, which incurs interest, which incurs more solicitors' and receivers' letters and more handling fees, and so on, and before you know it I owe £20,000 again, and I'm being charged so much interest it's soon £50,000, but I could never get a straight answer about how much I owed. This went on for years and years. It's good business for the receivers when they are handling hundreds of thousands of pounds, so they don't want it being resolved. It was in everyone's best interest for the court case to drag on and on, year after year. Except mine. I'm the only fucker who was not allowed to receive and who was getting screwed. The receivers, accountants and solicitors did make more money than the Nicholls. These people have no scruples and they operate just inside the law, and even then they're bending it as much as they can. To me, those slimey cunts are far worse human beings than any criminal from the streets of Salford. At least a bank robber has the decency to put a mask or balaclava on before they go to rob you blind.

That's as far as I want to go into that really. But that's the reason I was unable to keep any money legally for years. Actually, that's not true. I was allowed to earn as much money as I wanted legally; I just wasn't allowed to keep any of it. Suffice to say I found ways and means to survive, which I don't necessarily need to go into. If there was a film voiceover at this stage of the book it would say, 'A man's got to do what a man's got to do.' Most people would hang themselves in that situation, but I dealt with it. Most people in the country would probably go bankrupt and have their house possessed if they didn't have any money coming in for two months. Try managing without any official income for twelve years.

But back to Black Grape. At the start of that summer we were asked to do a football song for Euro 96. I thought we were being asked to do the official song, but in the end they went for 'Three Lions', recorded by the Lightning Seeds with Frank Skinner and David Baddiel, so we released our song ourselves and it went Top 10. We wanted to call it England's something and I came up with 'England's Irie'. Keith Allen had heard we were doing it and volunteered himself to help out on it. I think he thought he was the patron saint of football songs or something after he had worked with New Order on 'World In Motion'. The rap that he does on 'England's Irie' he actually wrote for me, but he wrote it in what he thought was my voice. He'd tried to write it in a Mancunian accent, which sounded ridiculous, but quite funny when he did it, so I said, 'Why don't you just do it, Keith?' Joe Strummer was also on 'England's Irie', although I can't really recall the recording at Real World – it's all a bit of a blur. I do remember all wearing kilts when we shot the video in London, which was Keith's idea. We also did *Top of the Pops* and wore the kilts again, then me and Keith went out on the town wearing them afterwards. I had a really nice Armani leather jacket on with mine and some nice Patrick Cox black patent-leather shoes, so I was looking really smart. Keith was dressed pretty similar, but we didn't have anything underneath our kilts. I ended up later that night in King's Cross, scoring some gear. We walked into this off-licence and this tiny old Asian woman said, 'What have you got under kilt?' so I just flashed her. She went, 'Oooooooh, can I have another look?' It made her day.

Danny was based in Los Angeles, so me and Kermit went back out there for a while to write more material. We rented a really nice house in the Hollywood Hills for our base, but it quickly turned into a bit of a den of iniquity. We didn't really get a great amount of work done; we spent more time partying, smoking crack and drinking Guinness.

We met Dave Gahan from Depeche Mode while we were out there and me and Muzzer had a bit of a crazy night with him. We went back to his house and he had two boxes on his coffee table, one full of heroin and one full of cocaine. We ended up staying all night and for some reason Dave Gahan decided he had to go out and pick something up. I can't remember what, but it wasn't drugs, because there was no shortage of them. I was sat in his house waiting for him and he ended up getting arrested on Sunset Strip.

I also hung out with Michael Hutchence a bit while we were there, as he had been working with Danny Saber on his new album. I'd first met him when he and Paula Yates came to see us at Brixton Academy and after the gig I went back to the place they had near London Bridge. I remember me and Hutchence being in Johnny Depp's club, the Viper Room, on Sunset Strip one night and these two young American girls came over, 'Hiya, Michael. Hiya, Shaun. Can we show you our tattoos?' They lifted up their mini skirts and they had no knickers on and shamrocks tattooed on er, let's just say a delicate part of the female anatomy. One of the girls was a senator's daughter and the other one was part of Bill Clinton's administration, I think. I liked Hutchence; he was a cool guy to hang out with. I even went in and did some guest vocals on one of his album tracks, but the album never came out because shortly after that he flew back to Sydney, where he died.

Having sacked the Nicholls, I was looking for a new manager, so I spoke to a couple of different people about taking me on. I wasn't in great shape at the time as I was taking quite a lot of drugs. I remember going to see Danny Goldberg, the guy who used to manage Nirvana, and he was telling me about how he'd lost Kurt Cobain to drugs and he asked me if I was on drugs. I obviously said 'No,' but I was coked up to the eyeballs at the time and hadn't been to bed for days. It must have been blatantly obvious to him that I was off my head.

I then met Richard Bishop, who managed Henry Rollins, and who I seemed to get on with. I signed a contract with him, and he managed me for the second Black Grape album, although I didn't really have much to do with him. He liaised more with Muzzer, as Muzz and my dad had started a management company called Hot Soup and were now managing Kermit and Carl. Richard only managed me for a short while and then after the second Black Grape album we both felt it wasn't really working, so we tore up the contract by mutual consent.

Back in the UK, I presented *Top of the Pops* at the end of 1996, as Junior Jimmy, with a tracksuit on. Which I really enjoyed. There's a clip on *Grape Tapes* of me messing around back stage at *Top of the Pops* and making up a chart run-down on my favourite drugs – at No. 10, two bags of brown, and stuff like that.

I spent the first half of 1997 recording the second Black Grape album and filming the part I had landed in the Hollywood remake of *The Avengers*. That was to prove the start and the end of my Hollywood career. The main stars were Ralph Fiennes, Uma Thurman and Sean Connery; then there was me and Eddie Izzard, who wasn't as well known back then. Ralph insists on people calling him 'Rafe', but I kept forgetting and just calling him 'Ralph', especially when I saw it written down on the call-sheet. Uma was sound, but I never really spoke to her. What have I got to say to Uma Thurman? I was actually sat in her chair one day, by accident. You know when you're shooting a film and the main actors have their names on the back of the chair? I was sat in hers by accident, and she walked up and just looked at me. I moved.

My big mistake was saying I thought the film was shit when it was finished, which you just can't do. In the Hollywood game, no matter how bad the movie is, you have to go out and say you think it's great. I'm pretty much cut out of it, if you see it now. You see me briefly as a moody dude on the corner, but they've cut out all the close-ups I shot for my dying scene. They re-cut it slightly, and put more Eddie Izzard in, because he played the game right and when he was asked what he thought of it afterwards he said he thought it was great. Eddie went on to Hollywood, but I never really worked in films again.

I did get offered a part in *The 51st State*, the film they shot in Liverpool with Samuel L. Jackson, just after *The Avengers*, but I was too preoccupied with sorting out my situation with the Nicholls at the time. When I saw the film I was a bit pissed off I'd passed on it, because I thought it was great. Mind you, it was probably great because I stayed out of it.

Acting is a weird game. As soon as you start to act, or you start to do what is your idea of acting, it looks like a school play. The way real actors do it is they don't really act, or feel like they're acting; they just submerge themselves in it. They just seem to be a different breed. The Yanks are better at it, even non-actors, even musicians. Look at Eminem in *8 Mile* – he was great. Pick an English kid, or musician, and stick him in a film and he looks like he's in a school play.

Muzzer and my dad, as Hot Soup, were managing Kermit and Carl, who had a side project called Man Made. Well, I thought it was a side project, but it quickly became apparent they wanted it to be more than that. Because the first Black Grape album was a success there was interest in what they were doing, so they were offered a decent-sized publishing deal and they thought Man Made were going to be bigger than Black Grape. The American rappers Tupac and Biggie were huge at the time, and I think Kermit and Carl really wanted to be the

English answer to them. That's how it seemed to me. I felt they just wanted to get rid of the white guy. They'd been on *Top of the Pops* and done loads of interviews and TV with Black Grape, which is the first time they'd had that level of exposure and attention, and inevitably they got someone in their ear going, 'You don't need him. It's you that people come to see,' and they started to believe it. Same old story. I don't know if part of it was because they saw Black Grape more as my band because I was the one who had originally signed. But that wasn't important, really, because I was still splitting the writing credits and publishing with Kermit, and they were getting all the attention, so why did it matter?

When the time came to record the second album, it was a nightmare. We were recording down at Real World and it was impossible to get Carl and Kermit into the studio. If they were supposed to arrive on Monday, they would say they were coming Tuesday. Then they wouldn't arrive Tuesday and say they were coming Wednesday. Then Thursday would come and go. Then Friday. They would finally turn up on Saturday and stay for a night or two nights when we were supposed to be spending a week or two weeks in the studio.

What bugged me was they were never open. I would have preferred it if they'd said, 'We're leaving Black Grape because we want to concentrate on Man Made,' but they didn't. They were sort of half-heartedly in Black Grape because that's where they were getting their money and publicity, but really they were concentrating on getting Man Made going. So me and Danny Saber were left waiting in the studio for a week. I was pissed off at Muzzer as well, because he had a real conflict of interest managing Man Made. They were getting booked into a studio to work on Man Made tracks, when they should have been in the studio with me making the second Black Grape album.

After the success of the first album I really wanted to make another upbeat party album, but the vibe in the studio was hardly upbeat and it wasn't what you would call a party. Half the songs are not collaborations like they were on the first album. There is none of that infectious riotous atmosphere. *It's Great When You're Straight . . .Yeah!* sounds like the best house party. *Stupid Stupid Stupid* sounds like the morning after the house party when everyone is coming down.

It wasn't all bad; there were a couple of decent tracks. As I mentioned earlier, I loved the Marcel King track 'Reach for Love', which was one of the best tracks Factory had ever put out in my opinion, but it sank without trace when it was released in 1984. Me and Kermit decided to rip a bit of it for the track 'Get Higher', which became the single, in the hope that journalists would ask us questions about it and we could big up Marcel King and the record would end up getting re-released. Instead I got a couple of idiots complaining that I was ripping Marcel off. I said, 'I'm paying homage to it, not ripping it off, you fucking goons!' I'm trying to help it get recognized as a lost classic.

The mock Ronald Reagan speech sample on 'Get Higher' was just something that amused Danny and was for the American audience really. I also like 'Marbles', the second single; I thought that was one of the few tracks that had that infectious verbal sparring that the first album had. There was a bit of that on the chorus of 'Squeaky' as well, but generally you can tell that the band aren't really working together any more. It was my idea to do a cover version of Frederick Knight's 'I've Been Lonely for So Long', which worked out okay, but as ever we tried to rip it and make it our own rather than just do a straight cover.

The album title was what Kermit substituted when we were doing TV performances of 'Reverend Black Grape'. He couldn't say 'Talking bullshit, bullshit, bullshit!' so he said, 'stupid, stupid, stupid'.

During the recording, in the time I wasn't in the studio, I was either off getting gear or I was in bed, particularly if I was just waiting for days on end for Kermit and Carl. It really was a fucking awful time for me. The band was splintering and the music really suffered because of it. It just felt like *Yes Please!* all over again. It was a nightmare. Apart from this time it was near Bath instead of Barbados.

Just before the album came out, we released *The Grape Tapes* video, filmed by Too Nice Tom, which tracked the progress of Black Grape right from the birth of the band during the early rehearsals at my house, right through to *Stupid Stupid Stupid*, including the recording of both albums, going on tour and to America. *The Grape Tapes* is a pretty gritty, warts and all depiction of Black Grape. I haven't seen it for a couple of years now, but last time I watched it I couldn't fucking believe what I was seeing. It does capture the madness, the debauchery, the highs and the lows of Black Grape, but it doesn't always depict me in the best light.

By the time we came to tour *Stupid Stupid Stupid*, the mood in the band had really soured. If the Man Made publishing money had already appeared, I don't think Kermit and Carl would have even turned up for the tour. It was a nightmare. The atmosphere was just as bad as it had been on the last Mondays tour, and the writing was on the wall. On top of that, Oriole had gone to India to see some mystic she was into, just when I needed her. She rang me up just before the tour started and said, 'I'm going to India.'
'Why?'
'Because it's time.'
So I just thought, 'All right, fuck you then. I'm going on the

piss with the lads, and I'm going to have loads of lager and drugs . . . because it's time.'

On the second to last show in Glasgow, I had an argument with Pat Warde on the tour bus, then Pat started rowing with Muzzer. I was in a right state because I was a proper drug addict again, the second album hadn't been as good as the first one, all sorts of things were building up. Muzzer's conflict of interest with Man Made was also really winding me up, so I just did one. Muzzer had a suitcase with the tour float and takings in, which he used to sleep with, sometimes handcuffing it to himself. He was asleep on the couch with the briefcase, and I just sneaked it off him. It only had about two grand in it, so I just grabbed that. I knew that would piss him off more than anything, because he hated being sneaked.

It was all coming to an end anyway, because Kermit and Carl were convinced they were going off to be big rap superstars. It was like the end of the Mondays again. It was a sinking ship. I was pissed off at Muzzer because he'd been my pal for so long. He knew the Nicholls were pricks, which they were, and so maybe he thought he should have been managing Black Grape, but I don't think he realized how powerful Gary Kurfirst was.

Man Made then made the mistake of spending a fortune on some Motown sample, which crippled them, I think. It just never happened, which I was quietly chuffed about.

In January 1998 we made an announcement that Kermit and Carl had left, but Black Grape was going to continue. I'm not sure if even I believed it. I was in a real state by this stage. After the bitterness of the Mondays' split, and being blamed by the rest of the band, I'd made this glorious comeback with Black Grape and then it had all collapsed again. Sadly, I'd also split up with Oriole.

I really needed to get myself off the heroin and I'd heard about these new Naltrexone implants, which were supposed to be a wonder drug, and decided to give them a try. I booked myself into the clinic in London and left Ireland with a small bag and just enough clothes for a week, because I was fully intending on going back. But I never ever did. I never saw that house again.

The Naltrexone treatment was horrendous. I would not recommend it to *anyone*. I've spoken to people since who had the same implants but had only been on heroin a couple of years, and they said it wasn't quite as bad, but it was absolutely horrific for me. It sounded great, the way they sold it to you – that they would put you to sleep for twelve or twenty-four hours and speed up your withdrawal so you go through the worst while you're out of it. That's not how it worked with me.

I had the operation to sew the implants in, and then they wired me up and even stuck a catheter in so I could piss while I was still knocked out, as the Naltrexone triggered this quick withdrawal thing. I don't remember much because I was out of it, but apparently I woke up and ripped all the tubes out and started going mental. It took six or seven doctors and nurses to force me back down on the bed and sit on me. I was going berserk.

But that was just the beginning. Then I started to come round. Fuck me. It was horrific. It was terrible. It didn't matter how much Temazepam or whatever downers they gave me to help calm me down, it didn't make any difference. I was climbing the walls. Literally. It's the worst experience I've ever had in my life. It was terrifying.

Too Nice Tom had come down to pick me up and drive me back to his house in Burnley, where he kindly said I could go to recover. He really is too nice. They discharged me at 7am and Tom was there to pick me up. They gave me a big bag of

Temazepams and downers to last a fortnight, but by the time I'd got to Tom's I'd eaten the whole supply and I was still climbing the walls. Imagine the worst come-down ever and magnify it by about a thousand. I didn't even get a chance to think about the mental side of it because I was trying to cope with the physical side. I was shaking. Tingling all over. Sweating. Shitting myself, literally, because I'd lose control of my bowels. Tom is a strong bloke, because he's a professional boxing trainer, but I was just picking him up and putting him out of the way. It was a living nightmare. I was so strung out I didn't sleep for weeks. I'd go day after day and night after night without kip, awake for twenty-four hours a day, just strung out. Screaming. In so much pain, with no relief. I was on Temazis, Valium, and I had to have injections for the diarrhoea. I wasn't drinking or smoking weed, and I couldn't go out and score any gear because I had the implants, which just make you even sicker if you try and use gear.

No one knew I was at Tom's. We kept it double quiet. The worst of it probably lasted about two months, but it seemed an eternity to me. Two months with pretty much no sleep, just screaming night and day, wanting Tom to knock me out. At some points I was actually begging Tom to punch me and knock me flat out, because I knew that was the only way I could get some respite from it. The only way to make the pain go away. I was screaming, *'TOM, KNOCK ME THE FUCK OUT, PLEASE!'* Because no matter how many downers I had I couldn't get any sleep. Temazis. Valium. Sleeping pills. Nothing. Still awake. You go mad when you can't sleep for such a long time. I don't mean staying up all night partying. I mean days and days and weeks without sleep. Never under-estimate how much real sleep-deprivation can fuck with you.

Eventually we got through the worst of it and I started to sleep a little and eat a little, but at first all I wanted was cold, bland, fatty food. I would drink cold oxtail soup from a vase, and I would cook a tray of oven chips and then let them go cold, and eat them when they were limp. Thankfully Tom had a big house, because his wife and kids were there, and his wife was actually pregnant at the time. I can't thank him enough for getting me through that.

Me and Tom were also supposed to be working on a script for a film called *Molly's Idle Ways* while I was there, although I wasn't in much of a fit state. We did actually film some parts of it, including a scene with Billy Graham, the boxing trainer from Champs Camp, which we shot in a hotel.

One of Tom's friends was Tony Livesey, then editor of the *Daily Sport*, who's also from Burnley; they'd been at college together. Tony dropped round to Tom's one day when I was staying there and we all got chatting, and a couple of days later he offered me a column in the paper. I didn't have any plans to get back into music at that stage. I just needed a break from it. I hadn't walked away from it for good, but music wasn't on my mind and I was looking to do something different for a while. So when Tony suggested writing a column for the *Daily Sport* it seemed like a good idea. It wasn't my dream job, but you never know what these things can lead to. So I agreed, and they even gave me my own *Daily Sport* business cards. The first column I did was in June 1998, when I reviewed the football singles that had come out for the World Cup in France. They gave me a guy called Mark Smith from the *Sport* to work with, who would ghost-write it for me.

Radio One then asked me out to Ibiza, as they were doing some live broadcasts from there and wanted me to go on Steve Lamacq's show. Smithy came with me from the *Sport*, because the idea was we were going to do the column on the party scene in Ibiza. But as soon as we got there I was invited to the Radio

One villa, and when we were in the car on the way over there he said, 'Let's see what shit we can get on these lot,' which shocked me. I said, 'What? We've been invited into their villa, mate. Even if you do see anything going on, you don't say fuck all.' What goes on tour stays on tour. I fell out with him after that, and that was pretty much the end of our working relationship. I think he might have told Tony Livesey that I beat him up, but I didn't.

I had nothing and no one to come back to at the time. No house, no woman, no band. I met a guy out there called Nuts from Moss Side, who I got on really well with. He was a real character. He looked like a superstar and I thought he would look good in the film that me and Tom were making. So I just stayed out there and hung out with Nuts for a bit and partied hard, and before I knew it, a couple of weeks had turned into a couple of months. The *Sun* actually put missing posters up around Ibiza when they couldn't find me to do the column, although that was obviously also a bit of a publicity stunt on their behalf.

When I eventually decided I'd better come back from Ibiza, I couldn't go back to Tom's because he'd just had a new baby, so I asked him if he could sort something temporary out for me. A stopgap, just so I had somewhere to go. He fixed me up with this house about half a mile away from him in Burnley, where he thought he could keep an eye on me. It was unfurnished, but Tom stuck a mattress and a television in there for me, and then the idea was I was going to get it furnished. I'd told Tom I didn't want anywhere squalid, and the house was actually all right; there was just no furniture. It had electricity, but no hot water. If you spent a bit of money doing it up, it would have been mint. It had a massive cellar, which would have been great for throwing parties. But as it was, there was just me, a mattress on the floor in one of the bedrooms, and a television.

I'd only been in there a couple of days when there was a knock at the door. I opened it and there was a guy there, about thirty years old, and he said, 'Oh, it *is* you Shaun . . . you've been spotted going in and out of this house.' Basically, he was a local drug dealer who was a fan of the Mondays and Black Grape. He wasn't even a big drug dealer, he was just a two-bob dealer, the sort of kid who buys a few grams and knocks it out to pay for his own gear. He was stood on my doorstep and asked me to sign something, and then he waved a bag of smack under my nose and said, 'Fancy a smoke?' and I just crumbled. I let him in and we had a smoke.

That was it then. He started coming round all the time. I started smoking the gear again, then I started smoking the stone. Then a couple of other kids, smack buddies that he knew, started coming round and hanging out. The house didn't get furnished, obviously; I still only had a mattress and a TV. It just turned into a drug den. A couple of girls came knocking at the door, so they came in and we had a bit of a party, and it was all getting a bit out of hand. Burnley is a small town, and there's a lot of smack about. And a lot of the local smackheads were fans of the Mondays or Black Grape and loved the idea of taking heroin with Shaun Ryder. It was just what I didn't need, getting involved in a small-town drug scene like that.

The *Daily Sport* had given me a new guy called John Warburton to work with on my column. I got on with him, and I'm actually still friends with him. Warbie now writes for different comedy shows, like *Gavin and Stacey*. He used to come up to the house in Burnley, while all that chaos was going on, and we'd do the column from there. That was the only break from chaos, when Warbie turned up.

After a couple of months, what had started out as a bit of fun had turned into another nightmare. It was so depressing. As if that wasn't bad enough, I then had what little income I had coming in stopped. The Nicholls were already taking half of everything that I earned, but I got a call from the *Daily Sport* saying they couldn't pay me from that week because the Nicholls had got a court judgement saying they could now take *all* of my income.

I was thirty-six. Living on my own in an unfurnished house in Burnley. No income. Spending all day smoking smack. I had to get out of there. So I did one back to Manchester. Tom didn't want me to go back to town, because he thought I would resort to my old ways, but it was a bit too fucking late for that. Anyway, whatever I got up to in Manchester couldn't be any worse than the small-town smack sketch I'd got dragged into in Burnley.

CHAPTER TWELVE

'One day he was admiring his reflection, in his favourite mirror, when he realized all too clearly, what a freakin' old beasty man he was'

When I got back to Manchester from Burnley at the end of 1998 I was crashing at my mate Gaz Marsden's flat, opposite Southern Cemetery in Chorlton, while I sorted myself out somewhere to live. Within a few weeks of me arriving back in town, Simon Moran from SJM concerts rang me and asked if he could come round for a meeting. I've known Simon since he first started putting on gigs in the late 80s and always got on well with him. SJM had promoted most of the Mondays and Black Grape tours since *Bummed*, apart from the odd show, like when we first played G-Mex and Simon wasn't sure we would sell it out, so we'd put it on ourselves with Muffin and John the Phone. Like any promoter, Simon hates missing out on a gig, and SJM went on to promote Stone Roses at Spike Island, Oasis at Knebworth and most of the biggest bands in the country.

Simon came round to Gaz's flat in Chorlton and pretty much got straight to the point. He's not a man for small talk. He asked me straight out if I was interested in getting Happy

Mondays back together. I told him I hadn't thought about it for a minute. It was less than a year since Black Grape had disintegrated, and I hadn't really spoken to the rest of the Mondays since the acrimonious split seven years previously. The idea of getting the Mondays back together hadn't even crossed my mind. But Simon explained his plan and said, 'All I'm really interested in is you and Bez . . . and we'll play the Manchester Evening News Arena.' The Arena was a much bigger gig than the Mondays had ever played first time around, not including festivals, but Simon was convinced we could sell it out. It slightly amused me that the guy who didn't think we could sell out the G-Mex at the height of Madchester now thought we could sell out a venue twice the size when we'd been away for seven years. But I didn't have to think long and hard about it, I just said, 'Yeah.'

It was pretty much purely a financial decision for us. It wasn't an emotional decision about putting any unfinished business with the Mondays to bed or any such bollocks. I also never thought of it as a long-term thing, and when I first agreed to it I never thought we would make a record again. I did, however, regret that I had never got to play the Arena, as it didn't open until 1995, by which time the Mondays had long split, and Black Grape never played there. So that was part of the attraction for me.

I don't understand why bands won't admit that they're getting back together for the money. Why do they come up with these bullshit excuses about doing it for the love of it, or doing it for the fans, when it's so obvious they're only doing it for the dough? Yes, the fans want to come and see you play those songs again, especially if they never saw you first time round, but you're not doing it for them. You're doing it because someone has offered you a big fat wedge to do it. What's wrong with making a bit of money? Especially if you're on your arse and need a bit of cash.

It does my head in a bit when fans get over-protective about '*their* band'. You're watching the band; you're not in it. If you think we shouldn't be getting back together for the money, then fuck what you think. You might have been lucky enough to see us back in the day, but other people weren't. If you like the band and like the music, why would you begrudge us the chance to make some money out of it? We've got to live and pay the bills and put food on the table just the same as everyone else. If we got back together and no one wanted to come, then I would be fine with that too. If people are no longer interested, then there's not much you can do about it. But if they are, and if I still sell out venues, then I'll go and do it. People say what about the 'legacy' of the band? Please. The *legacy*? Bollocks.

Simon installed Neil Mather, who worked for SJM, as our tour manager, although Neil was much more than that really – he generally looked after us on a day-to-day basis. Then it was all about putting the band together and getting into rehearsals. Simon knew it was me and Bez that the fans would pay to see. He also knew I wouldn't want to get Mark Day or PD back in the band, so we'd have to find people to replace them. Bez had a few reservations at first, because he was still smarting a bit from the end of the Mondays and how he felt he had been treated at the end of his time in Black Grape. He was more concerned than me about the re-formed Mondays just being a cabaret act, but he had a missus and kids, and his house in Glossop, so even though he'd published an autobiography called *Freaky Dancin'*, which Debs had ghost-written for him, and done a few bits of TV and columns in the press, he couldn't really turn down the money on offer, so Simon negotiated a deal with him.

Simon had also spoken to Our Paul and Gaz Whelan. I'd not really seen much of Our Paul during the Black Grape years. He had split up with Astrella and was living back at my mam's, and having a pretty hard time of it. He'd grown a beard and had tried to come off the gear. He suffered a nervous breakdown and ended up being sectioned at one stage, admitted to the mental health unit at Meadowbank Hospital in Salford and then moved to Trafford General Hospital, but he was discharged after they found out he was still taking gear in there. He'd also robbed a lot of my stuff that I had stored at my mam's – gold records and awards – and sold them to buy drugs. On one occasion I'd been visiting my mam's on my day off on tour with Black Grape and he'd taken a load of methadone out of my bag. Despite all that, we were still on speaking terms, just about.

I was pissed off with the way both Our Paul and Gaz had acted during the Mondays split, but when Black Grape became so successful a lot of the ill feeling over the Mondays had faded away for me. So by the time Simon asked me to get the band together, I was fine with playing with Our Paul and Gaz again. I think when Gaz came back to the Mondays he realized how lucky we were and how lucky he was to be back in the game. All he needed to do to get four or five grand a night was play his drums. It's not a bad gig, is it? Playing drums for an hour or so for five grand.

Simon arranged a meeting at Jackson's Wharf in Castlefield, with me, Our Paul, Gaz and Bez, to hammer out the details. It was the first time we'd all been back in a room together since the Mondays split. It got a bit heated at one stage, but we got there in the end.

We asked Rowetta back – she didn't need much persuading – and I also decided to bring in Nuts, who I'd met in Ibiza. I was still hoping that me and Tom might get our film,

Molly's Idle Ways, off the ground, so I thought if I brought Nuts into the Mondays, then we could get some publicity for the film off the back of that. Nuts looked great and he was a real character, but he couldn't really sing, and he didn't even know the Mondays' records – it wasn't his type of music. He didn't last too long in the end, but he did a few gigs with us.

Simon then brought in Ben Leach, who had been in the Farm, on keyboards. Ben was also kind of musical director, so he needed the old master tapes of the Mondays' songs, with the different parts on, but no one knew where they were. Factory Records had gone under and London Records, who now owned our back catalogue, didn't have them. I think Ben ended up sampling some of the tracks from our albums that he had in his own CD collection and re-created them from there. We then asked Wags in to play guitar, and that was the re-formed line-up.

I never heard anything from PD or Mark Day when we re-formed. I'm not sure what they could have said anyway. By 1999, so much had changed. We'd all moved on. Mark Day had already gone back into civilian life big time and was working. He probably wouldn't have been interested anyway, because Simon wasn't providing a final salary pension. We also needed a keyboard player who could program all the samples and sequencers, and I'm not sure PD would have been up to it. Last I heard he was signing on. They still get an equal split of the Mondays' royalties, though, so hopefully their next royalty cheque was a bit bigger due to whatever uplift in sales there was after we re-formed.

We started rehearsing in a small room at Greenhouse Studios. At first Ben would rehearse with the band during the day, and then me, Rowetta and Nuts would come in at night. I think Simon thought it best to try and keep a distance between me and Our Paul to prevent the old frictions from surfacing. By coincidence, nearly a decade after we'd first been on *Top of the Pops* with the Stone Roses, Ian Brown was rehearsing next door to us at the Greenhouse for his latest solo tour.

Simon wanted us to put out a new single as a kind of announcement that we were back together and to drum up interest in the tour, so he worked out a deal with London Records to release a single and a new *Greatest Hits* album. I had writer's block at the time, and the rest of the band were pretty cabbaged, so they weren't going to come up with any decent new ideas. In the end we decided to team up with Oakey and Osborne again and do a cover of the old Thin Lizzy classic 'The Boys Are Back in Town', which we did down at Hook End Manor and Real World studios. Most people don't know the true story behind that song and its Mancunian connections. Phil Lynott was the lead singer of Thin Lizzy and his mum Phyllis used to have a late-night drinking gaff in Whalley Range in Manchester called Phyllis's, which was pretty legendary. It was a bit before my time, really; its heyday was in the mid-70s when George Best used to drink in there. A gang from Manchester called the Quality Street gang used to hang out there quite a lot, and Phil Lynott wrote 'The Boys Are Back in Town' about them. At the end of our version you can hear me give old Phyllis a shout out: 'Phyllis, this one's for you!' I didn't know Phyllis, but Arthur or Jimmy Donnelly asked me to give her a shout out. They were brothers in the Quality Street, and Arthur was the father of Chris and Anthony Donnelly, who had put on some of the early raves in town and gone on to set up the Gio-Goi clothing label.

Our version of 'The Boys Are Back in Town' was pretty terrible. Simon never liked it, and I thought it was dire, but it served a purpose. We actually got a *Top of the Pops* appearance out of it, which I couldn't fucking believe! So although it was dreadful it did at least let people know the Mondays were back together and going out on tour, and the tour sold out.

We moved into a bigger space at Greenhouse and started rehearsing the full set, but already the old jealousy towards me had resurfaced. Part of the problem was Simon wanted us to play 'Reverend Black Grape', because it was a big hit, but Our Paul didn't want to play it as it wasn't a Mondays song and he hadn't been involved in the writing of it. Because I'm not a jealous person, I didn't really understand the problem with playing a song he hadn't written, but it was tearing him apart, you could see that. Then came all the accusations about *'You're* using drugs, *you're* going to ruin this.' I *was* using. But yet again, I wasn't the only one. I was the one that admitted it. I wasn't the hypocrite. Me and Gaz used to follow Our Paul outside the rehearsal studios and he'd be sat in his car smoking gear. We'd even film him sat there in his car having a whistle on the heroin or crack. Then he would come back into rehearsals and say, *'You're* ruining this again, because *you're* doing drugs and *you're* doing that!' I'd say, 'Fucking hell, Gaz, you just stood with me watching him!'

Despite all that, rehearsals went really well and some of the songs were sounding better than they did first time round. Just before the tour started, Simon hired Birmingham National Exhibition Centre so we could do a couple of days running through the set in an arena-sized venue and get a feel for it. We were staying at the Copthorne Hotel in Birmingham and I remember Neil Mather moaning when we checked out because the band had spent well over a grand on porn channels over the couple of days we were there.

The first gig was at Hereford Leisure Centre, which Simon had stuck in as a bit of a warm-up date before we played the Manchester Evening News Arena a couple of days later. I was a bit nervous, partly because I'd not played live for a while and partly because I did quite often get a bit of stage fright, so I had to get someone to bring a tub of Valium down from Manchester for me. Then on the afternoon of the gig, a bailiff from the Nicholls arrived and tried to issue a writ on me, but he had to physically hand it to me and Neil Mather managed to keep him away from me, so it wasn't officially served.

I'm not a real football head, as I've said, but we watched United come from behind to beat Juventus before we went on stage, which had everyone buzzing and the gig was great. Afterwards, we drove up to Manchester on the tour bus, and as I didn't have anywhere to live at the time, I just slept on the tour bus for a couple of nights in the bowels of the arena.

It was a big step up from Hereford to the Manchester Evening News Arena, especially as the Mondays hadn't played for six years, and again I had a bit of stage fright, but the atmosphere was great, and you could feel the goodwill from the crowd, as if they wanted us to smash it. It was St George's Day and a Friday night, so a lot of people had been out all afternoon, which probably helped the celebratory atmosphere, but it was great. We had also reworked a few of the songs slightly, so we weren't just rehashing everything. It was packed out, and probably two thousand of the eighteen thousand were on the guest list. Because United had reached the Champions League Final in Barcelona, we played the Freddie Mercury and Montserrat Caballé song 'Barcelona' as the lights went up at the end. That wasn't my doing – that would have been Gaz or Neil Mather, who were both big Reds.

We then did the Scottish Exhibition and Conference Centre in Glasgow and two Brixton Academy dates, but after Manchester I was less nervous, because I knew the band could pull it off now, and I knew I could. The fucking Nicholls' bailiff turned up again in the early hours after one of the Brixton gigs, but Neil and our security managed to stop him getting to me, and he ended up throwing the writ at me and tried to claim he'd served it because it hit me. It was fucking ridiculous. We had to get the CCTV from the venue in the end and watch the incident to check if it actually had hit me, but it hadn't.

We then went out to Ibiza to play Manumission. The brothers who ran the club, Mike and Andy McKay, are from Manchester and started off promoting clubs in town before they got sick of being targeted by gangs. After one particularly nasty incident, they simply jumped on a plane to Ibiza and never came back. The highlight of a lot of punters' nights at Manumission was when Mike would have sex with his girlfriend, Claire, on stage in front of thousands of people. I don't remember much about the gig, but I remember Howard Marks being there. We were only supposed to be there for a couple of days and I ended up staying nearly a week.

I still didn't have anywhere to live at that point. The Mondays tour was only supposed to last a few months, but we kept getting offered more gigs. For about eighteen months from when we got back together in early 1999, if we weren't on the road I would split my time between Gaz's flat in Chorlton, the cellar of Muffin's house on Rochdale Road, which was like a little granny flat, or Rowetta's house out towards Brooklands in south Manchester, because I was still seeing her on and off.

Towards the end of that year, we were offered a nice cushy Admiral advert. I'd met the big kahuna at Admiral, Colin, who was also the big cheese at Kangol, because he was a big Mondays fan and we became quite pally. First of all Admiral sponsored my *Daily Sport* column, and then, when they were trying to launch Admiral as a fashion label rather than just a sportswear brand, he asked us to do a big ad campaign with

Terry Venables, Bobby Charlton, Stuart Hall and Emlyn Hughes. We did a couple of separate ads, one on a sort of *EastEnders* set where I passed the ball to El Tel and he kicked it through the window of a baker's that was owned by Bobby Charlton. It also had cameos by David Seaman, who was handed a brown paper bag as a joke about him being accused of accepting bribes, and Dennis Wise as a cab driver, because he'd been accused of attacking a cab driver outside El Tel's club. Then we did an ad in Stringfellows. 'Step On' was the soundtrack, and the ads went out in the cinema and on Sky Sports, and they could run them separately, or together as one long ad. We had a good time filming it and all the footballers were good sports.

At the start of 2000, I was back at the *NME* Awards to receive a Godlike Genius award. They did a quick photo with Paul McCartney, which was used on the cover of the *NME*; it's the picture I mentioned earlier. It's pretty awful to look at, because you can tell I'm on the gear as I look a bit pasty and sweaty, and I looked older than bloody Macca. God knows what he thought. Funnily enough, I then met Nathan McGough, the old Mondays manager, at the after-party. I'd not seen him since the original split, and we had a good catch-up and reminisce about the halcyon days.

Early that year I was in the Press Club late one night with a couple of pals and I met a girl called Felicia Brookes, who worked at the Palace Theatre and the Opera House. I got her number and we started seeing each other once a week. She was living with a friend of hers off Anson Road in Longsight, where the old International venue used to be. After a little while, when I got a bit of dough together, I got myself a flat up there too. It was a new block of flats, one of those gated places that look like posh student flats, but it was only five minutes out of town.

I was then approached to do a cover version of 'Barcelona' with Russell Watson. He was still up and coming at the time, Russell, and just finishing his debut album, *The Voice*. Russell and his manager then, Perry Hughes, are both from Salford and they thought it might help broaden his appeal, make him look cool and help break him into a different market if he did a song with me. Perry has a limousine service in Salford, and knew my pal Muffin, and had already loaned us some limos to go to the première of *The Faculty* at the Trafford Centre. Russell had actually already recorded 'Barcelona' for his album before Perry came up with the idea of me guesting on it. When they suggested it to me, it was a bit of a no-brainer as I didn't have to do much, so I was like, 'Yeah, no problem. Bring it on.' I just popped into the studio and laid down my vocals on the track that was already laid down, then we went to Barcelona to do the video. Obviously the video and the song weren't totally serious – it was supposed to be a bit of a joke, playing up the juxta-position of an opera singer against a bit of a wasted rock 'n' roller. If you watch that video and can't see I'm in on the joke, then you're a bit of an idiot. I'm just hamming it up, playing up to that Shaun Ryder caricature against Russell's clean-cut image.

Happy Mondays were booked to play Glastonbury that summer, but Our Paul wasn't in great shape and our relationship had deteriorated even further, if that was possible. In the end, he just walked out of rehearsals. We had to rope in Stuart Fletcher, who had played bass in John Squire's new band the Seahorses, as a replacement. The line-up of the re-formed Mondays changed quite a bit over those early noughties years, through until about 2003, when we became more settled. The 2003 line-up is pretty much the same band that I play live with now, apart from Bez and Gaz Whelan, who have both left. Gaz has been replaced on drums by Jake, Our Paul's oldest lad.

John Warburton, the journalist who was ghosting my *Daily Sport* column, then published a book called *Hallelujah! The Extraordinary Return of Shaun Ryder and Happy Mondays.* I didn't really have anything to do with it at all, but Warbie asked if he could write a book, and I said, 'Look, I'm not going to write a book about my life at this stage, but if you want to come on tour and write about what happens on tour, that's fine with me.' So it was just about the previous year, really.

There was a bit of an incident when I helped out Warbie by doing a signing at Waterstone's in town. I ended up on the front page of the *Manchester Evening News* because they claimed I pulled a gun on their reporter. Which was absolutely fucking ridiculous. Talk about sensationalism. For fuck's sake. Not only was it actually a little plastic starter pistol, it didn't *look* like anything but a daft plastic gun. I think I found it in Waterstone's or wherever we were before Waterstone's. I certainly wasn't carrying it around. It was a fucking toy; it might as well have had one of those flags that came out at the end and said 'Bang!' This journalist from the *Evening News* wanted to interview me and I just started having a bit of a nobble with him, winding him up, and then I pulled out this plastic gun and he fucking shit himself. That's all that happened.

I didn't have an issue with the *Manchester Evening News* really, even though, like I said before, they never gave us any support when we were starting out. After we had made it, every now and then we would do an interview with them and then inevitably a couple of weeks later they would stab us in the back again. I never understood why a Manchester paper couldn't get behind a Manchester band. I certainly didn't have any problem with the individual journalist who was there that day; I didn't know the kid from Adam. But it must have made his fucking day, because he went away and wrote a front-page story crying 'Shaun Ryder Pulled a Gun on Me'. He's probably lived off it ever since, telling the story at dinner parties in south Manchester. I didn't get questioned by the police or anything about the incident. If the police had seen the 'gun' they would have just laughed.

In July we supported Oasis on their stadium tour for *Standing on the Shoulder of Giants.* Johnny Marr and his band the Healers opened the bill, then us, then Oasis headlining. There was no Manchester date, but we did play Bolton's Reebok Stadium, which half of Manchester came up to, and there was a bit of an unfortunate scene when Noel and Liam's mum, Peggy, got trampled. Peggy was watching the gig from a hospitality box with a friend of hers and one of Noel or Liam's kids. Bez then went and opened some door or fire escape that he shouldn't have, in order to let all his mates into hospitality who didn't have VIP passes, and the next thing there's a load of lads in Peggy's box. Oasis's management were going to throw us off the tour after that, because Liam and Noel weren't best pleased. We had to go and have a meeting with their management and at first they said, 'That's it – you're off the gig.' But it got smoothed over eventually.

Quite early on in Oasis's career their management got rid of most of the hangers-on from Manchester around the band, which a lot of people in Manchester had a problem with – 'Noel and Liam have turned into fucking arseholes, man.' But I knew that, although Noel might have had a bit of a say in it, it was the management who did it really, and I can see why. I hate saying it, because I feel like a bit of a twat, but there can be a real lack of professionalism in the music game in Manchester, among the people who work in it. I'm not saying everyone is like that, but there is a bit of an attitude and a lack of professionalism at times. Everyone in the music game in

Manchester thinks they're Charlie big potatas. Everyone thinks they're fucking fantastic and should be treated like VIPs, whereas in London, even if you don't like them personally, people know what their job is, and exactly what they've got to do, and they get it done. I'm not in the business to make mates, never have been. I'd prefer to work with people who can get their job done.

The Mondays' reunion tour was only supposed to last six months or so, but we kept saying yes to more gigs, and the longer it went on, I inevitably started drinking too much and taking cocaine, as well as the gear, just to get through it. I'd really had enough by the time we got to Australia at the start of 2001 to do the Big Day Out festival. I was thirty-eight and I felt about fifty-eight. I was fucked. After the Australia gigs I just decided to stay on at Our Pete's, Our Matt and Pat's oldest brother, who lives in Perth. He's been out in Australia for years and all his family have grown up there. He used to be one of the heads of Sony Music out there.

I really wanted to try and come off heroin, and Perth is quite a small town, and quite quiet, so it seemed like as good a place as any to try and go cold turkey. I had no plans to do any music. I remember thinking to myself while I was there, 'I'm never going near a microphone again.' But Our Pete mocked up a make-do studio in his garage and thought it would be a good idea if I did some music to keep myself busy. It was a sound idea, but because I was going cold turkey I was coming down and sweating all the time, and just not very well generally and not in a great place mentally. I was quite dry artistically as well. I wasn't writing songs at the time, so what came out were more streams of consciousness than fully realized songs. A kid called Shane Norton and Stephen Mallinder of Cabaret Voltaire, who had an Australian band called Ku-ling Bros and knew Our

Pete, came up with these electronic backing tracks, and I just told stories over the top.

I wasn't in a good state at the time but, if anything, I saw it as a side project or collaboration – I didn't mean it to be viewed as my first solo album. I was possibly a little naïve in that respect; I perhaps should have realized that it would be perceived that way, but that wasn't supposed to be me launching a solo career. One of the streams of consciousness was about the Mondays' trip to Rio and what happened there. 'The Story' and '1987' are about the early Mondays days and 'Clowns' is about Wags' fear of clowns. He once told me that his worst nightmare was being beaten to death by clowns, with their big floppy shoes and big red noses. Not the sort of thing I would normally write a song about, but, as I say, I didn't really approach it as a normal album. Like I say, I was in a bit of a state at the time, and just wasn't thinking things through properly. I think I even thought the album might just come out in Australia, and nobody would even get to hear it back home.

I am now doing my first solo album, with Sunny Levine, which should come out in 2012, and I hope people aren't expecting a similar album to *Amateur Night in the Big Top*, as that Australian one was called, because it will be very different, much more fully realized.

The Haçienda had closed in 1997, but the building was knocked down in 2002, just after Michael Winterbottom had finished filming *24 Hour Party People*. I was on the other side of the world while a lot of the fuss about the Haçienda was going on, and not in a good state, so a lot of it passed me by, but I wouldn't have got as worked up as some people did about it.

I didn't think it was a travesty when the Haçienda closed. I hadn't been there for years anyway. I'd left it behind a long time ago. There was a bit of uproar when Crosby Homes bought the site to convert the Haçienda into apartments and put a sign up saying: 'Now the party's over you can come home', but it didn't bother me. It meant dick to me. It's over. Get over it. Move on. When you've lived it and done it, sometimes it's almost a relief when it's over.

I'm all for cultural tourism. If people want to come and see where the Haçienda was, that's fine with me. If people are into it, and it brings money into Manchester, then fair dos. If I went to Nashville or Memphis I'd be quite interested in finding out about the musical history there. I'm just not arsed about mourning the Haçienda. I was there. I don't need to relive it.

Hooky is now involved in the new 'Factory' club that has opened in what used to be the Factory offices, and then later became Paradise Factory nightclub, but I'm not one of those people who will slag him off for trading on a bit of nostalgia. I've even played the new Factory club myself. If the kids have an appetite for it, then he might as well be making some money out of it rather than anyone else. The next generations of kids are still discovering Factory and are interested in the story.

I even liked the film *24 Hour Party People*, when I eventually saw it on DVD, despite some of the comments I've made here and elsewhere. I thought Steve Coogan was great as Tony Wilson. The Mondays were portrayed as pure caricatures, which is fine, because it's just a film, but that's not what we were like in real life. I thought the kid that played me, Danny Cunningham, was a good actor, but if I was as stupid as I was made out to be in that film I wouldn't bother getting out of bed in the morning. The only thing that really wound me up was they had me wearing a Joe Bloggs T-shirt. Listen, I know my memory of those heady days is slightly hazy, but if there's one thing in this book I am 100 per cent sure of, it's that I have never worn a Joe Bloggs T-shirt.

Me and Felicia had a baby boy on 24 April 2002, Joseph Peter Ryder, and we decided to move out of the flat off Plymouth Grove and out of Manchester. Bez and Debs were living up in Hadfield, near Glossop, and a couple of places came up near them, so we ended up renting a house that backed on to theirs. Debs and Joanne, who I'd first gone out with in 1988 and is now my wife, actually took me and Felicia to see a few houses around the area as a favour, because they lived nearby and knew the area. A few times when I went up to visit Bez and Debs, Joanne would be round at their house because she was still pally with them. We had always had the same circle of friends, so I never went out of Joanne's life, although I was that wasted sometimes I didn't recognize her. A couple of times I ran into her, skagged off my brain, and said to her, 'I know you, don't I?' and she'd sigh and say, 'Yes, Shaun, it's Joanne, you've known me for fifteen years.' Then I would start talking to her and just mong out halfway through a sentence; my head would just drop.

A lot of people think I still live next door to Bez, but I was only there for a year, about eight years ago. They have this romanticized idea of me and Bez being neighbours and popping round to borrow a packet of skins or something. Hadfield is also where they filmed *The League of Gentlemen*, so the idea of me and Bez living there obviously greatly amused some people.

At the same time we were moving up to Glossop, I agreed to make a TV documentary with a guy called Richard Macer. He had actually been pestering me for a year or so to do it. He had just spent six months following Jordan around for a documentary called *The Truth About Me*, and he was a big Mondays and Black Grape fan and wanted me to be his next project. Half the reason I agreed was I thought I could use the documentary to show the Nicholls that I was on my arse, financially, because at that time they were asking every fucking week what I was up to, and what my assets were. I'm like, 'I live in a rented cottage in Glossop with my girlfriend and little lad. What assets!? You mean my fucking helicopter and my power boat?'

I was off the gear, but I was on methadone, Valium, Temazepams and cocaine. I was seeing Dr Nick, who I'd originally met towards the end of Black Grape, and he was trying to help me straighten out, but it was a long process. I had also bought a blender and got into making vodka smoothies for a little bit – put some fresh fruit in, then top it up with vodka. I also used to get horrific heartburn and I didn't really know what was causing it, so I started eating a phenomenal number of Zantac or Rennies to try and ease it. I had to explain to Richard that if he saw any white gunk at the side of my mouth during filming, it was Rennies, not cocaine. I don't know what was causing the heartburn then, because I don't get it now, but it seemed to me that if I took a lot of Zantac, it would get rid of it temporarily, but then it would come back more often and it got more severe. It took quite a while, but as I slowly reduced my intake of methadone and Valium, and stopped drinking so much, it did eventually go away.

The documentary was called *The Agony and the Ecstasy*, but there wasn't much ecstasy in it. I don't have many fond memories of that time. Me and Felicia weren't getting on well, and had pretty much split up by the time the documentary came out. I had also ballooned in weight. I do believe you are what you eat and I was a pie for a long time. I've always been up and down with my weight. I was a bit podgy as a kid, from my mum's cooking, then when I left home I was either on the gear or skint, so I was skinny as a rake. But since the end of the Mondays as well as being on and off the gear I'd been on methadone, and I thought that was what had caused me to put on weight, because there's a lot of sugar in it, so you get that big pile on. Now I know it was probably the start of my thyroid problem, which wasn't diagnosed until a few years later.

Looking back over that period, I think I really lost myself around 2000. I wasn't sure who I was, what I was, or what I was about. I started the whole process of working everything out when I was up at Too Nice Tom's in Burnley, but then I'd gone back on the gear, which had anaesthetized me and stopped the pain of thinking about it, but obviously didn't change my situation. I didn't have anywhere to live most of that time; I was sofa-surfing or staying in hotels. I was still on the gear, and the methadone, plus Valium and Temazepams half the time, plus cocaine and whatever else. I was only doing the gigs for the dough really, and even then I wasn't allowed to keep any money. Everything I earned legally had to go to the Nicholls.

Felicia eventually left and went back to Barnsley, taking Joseph with her. I was living on my own and I was at a bit of a low ebb. I wasn't on heroin anymore but I was on a concoction of other drugs. I still wasn't able to earn money legally, and at that stage there didn't seem to be any light at the end of the tunnel in that particular situation.

As I said earlier, I had seen a bit more of Joanne after I'd moved to Glossop because she was really friendly with Bez and Debs, my neighbours. She'd never really gone out of my life because we had quite a few mutual mates from the Haçienda and generally from going out around town, and we'd always really got on. She was a hairdresser at the time, and would pop round and cut my hair, as well as Felicia's and Joseph's, and would sometimes babysit for Joseph to help us out. But there was nothing going on between me and Joanne at that stage. Joanne is not the type to do that to another woman. She's a big believer in monogamy and wouldn't cheat on anyone.

After Felicia left, Joanne would pop round now and then to see if I was alright and would often bring some home-cooked food up; comfort food, like homemade potato hash. She's a really good cook, like my mum. There wasn't even anything romantic between us at first, we were just really good friends who were getting to know each other a bit more. The older you get, the more you appreciate friends who have known you a long time. But then I asked her out on what I suppose was a date, although I'm not sure either of us would have called it that. I took her out to the Palantine Pub in Hadfield and we had a nice meal and a laugh. We just got on really well and enjoyed each other's company, which is something I realized I'd not experienced for quite a while.

I think Joanne was quite apprehensive about getting involved with me at first. In fact I know she was, because she told me. Joanne had known me for a long time and had seen me when I was a bit out of control, and she didn't really want any of that madness in her life, particularly as she had a young nine-year-old son, Oliver, in the house as well. Joanne had done her fair share of partying when she was younger – that's how we met originally – but she had pretty much retired from that scene when she become a mother. She was also a big believer in your home as your sanctuary; that your home should be a place that is sacred, where you can escape from the madness. Whatever you did when you went out partying, you made sure you didn't bring that home with you.

Basically, Joanne wanted to make sure that if we did get involved then what she was getting was Shaun Ryder the person and not Shaun Ryder the rock 'n' roll caricature.

But by this stage, I was more than ready to change myself.

The heroin had gone, but I was still taking other drugs and

drinking more than was healthy. I knew it wasn't going to be easy to completely separate myself from my old lifestyle and leave it behind, and I knew it wasn't going to happen overnight. Old drug habits die hard. But I really did feel ready for the challenge. I think it's fine to party hard through your twenties and thirties but when you get into your forties you can't be living that same *24 Hour Party People* lifestyle anymore, or you're in danger of looking a bit sad. No one wants to be the last person left at the party, no matter how fucking brilliant the party has been. I knew a change had to come.

CHAPTER THIRTEEN

'Kiss me for old times' sake, kiss me for making a big mistake, kiss me for always being late, kiss me for making you wait, kiss me . . . good night'

Time moves much slower when you're a kid. A year or even a summer seemed to go on for ever when I was younger. The 1970s felt like a century, whereas the noughties seemed like five minutes. As you get older time just seems to vanish.

A lot of people think the Mondays re-formed again in 2004, but the truth is we had never split up since the first re-formation; we'd just been away for a little while. We didn't have a manager for a time, so me and Gaz were handling things between us, and if we needed any advice, Gaz would phone Elliot Rashman, Simply Red's old manager. So eventually Elliot and his friend Stuart Worthington took over as joint managers. For personal reasons, Elliot had taken some time out from the music business in the nineties, and I'm not sure how good a decision it was to come back from that to managing the Mondays. I'm not actually that difficult to work with on a day-to-day basis but Gaz and Bez were harder for him and he almost gave himself a breakdown working with us.

After we got together me and Joanne did a lot of talking, her more than me at first, probably. She tried to get me to talk about why I felt the compulsion to do various things; tried to get me to see that, if you're still partying hard when you get to a certain age, you're missing out on a lot in life.

I remember her saying to me, 'You know that kind of float-ing fluffy cloud feeling that makes you feel like you're on top of the world, Shaun? You know you can get that from *real life* as well as drugs?' But when you've been taking drugs for as long as I had, it can be hard to envisage that normal life can offer a natural high to match them.

She also used a bit of reverse psychology on me, saying stuff like, 'Look, if you want to just drink and take drugs all your life then you go for it, mate. Do that. It's your life, but aren't you getting bored of it? There're so many other things to do in life, rather than just getting stoned and having the same conversa-tions over and over into the small hours.'

She also laid down the law a bit in her house. There was no drinking, smoking or swearing, and certainly no drugs, although there was a little lean-to at the back of the house, and she stuck a TV in there for me and slightly relaxed the rules in there at first. So I would chill out there and watch films and have some time out. They say every man needs a shed. If Joanne's house was her sanctuary, then that was my own little retreat after I first moved in.

I stopped taking cocaine, I stopped taking methadone, I stopped smoking weed, and I stopped drinking for a while. I was completely straight, and I started doing a lot of thinking. A *lot* of thinking. Me and Joanne would stay up talking into the early hours. Everything started to hit me, and I just became overwhelmed. My nana had died in 1988, but it was only now that I started to grieve for her. But Nana's death was just a small part of it. All sorts of things that had happened to me since the late 60s hit me: all the things that I never let touch me when I was a kid, down to all the things I'd seen and done in Happy Mondays and Black Grape, but hadn't really felt because I was anaesthetized by heroin. That was a lot of catching up to do. I basically had to start playing catch-up on twenty years of feelings. I didn't really have many deep emotions for two decades, so when I finally came off the gear I felt like a ball in a pinball machine, being bounced all over the place.

I'm not saying I sat there crying to myself or to Joanne, sobbing my heart out. But you have to process this stuff eventually, mentally. If you don't process it at the time, then you have to process it all later when it catches up with you. I'm not naïve about the way these things affect you. I've read about people blocking things out, and I've been in rehab where they talk about how to process these things. I'd had various counsellors and professionals try and talk to me when I'd been in rehab before, but I clearly wasn't ready to go through the process, and was usually pretty dismissive with them. There's nothing any professional can say to you if you haven't got the motivation yourself. And when you do find that motivation, I think you need someone who you trust and can rely on to help you through it, and talk it through with you. Or I did, anyway. I needed someone close to me, who really knew me, to actually help me make the breakthrough, and I knew Joanne was the right person to help me pull through all that. I had so many layers of baggage from the past twenty years, and I knew Joanne could help me strip back those layers to get back to the real me. I knew it wasn't going to be easy and I knew I was going to be hit with twenty years of emotions fast-forwarding and hitting me all at once. Splat. But there's no way round it, because it's all in there. If it's been blocked out it will catch up with you one day.

I started exercising to help me come off the methadone, which I also hoped would shift the weight I'd put on. So I started spending up to eight hours a day on my mountain bike. Seriously. Eight hours a day, pedalling round Derbyshire through my cold turkey. But every time I stopped the exercise, the weight just piled back on, even though I wasn't really eating much, and I couldn't work out why. I had no energy at all, and I thought it might just be me getting older and nearing fifty.

It wasn't until a few years later, when I had to have a medical to get a visa for the States, that I finally discovered it was a problem with my thyroid and testosterone levels, which are all linked in. The doctors told me my thyroid had completely disappeared and I also had pneumonia. I'm now on Thyroxine and regular testosterone injections. But within a couple of months of starting the treatment, it had sorted me right out. I felt brilliant. Better than I had for years. I felt like a spring chicken. Born again. All those clichés. I felt like a normal human being instead of being bloated and tired the whole time. I'd been tired for years, but because I was taking methadone it had disguised what was wrong with me. Even when I was feeling like death warmed up, I would just take meth and get on with it. Which is how I wound up walking round with pneumonia, no testosterone and a thyroid problem.

In the meantime I had met a guy called Kav Sandhu, through bits of DJ-ing I was doing, and he had a club night called Get Loaded at Turnmills with a guy there called Danny Newman. I DJ'd at the club and in 2004 they decided to do Get Loaded in the Park on Clapham Common and asked Happy Mondays to headline. Kav was a DJ and club promoter and he introduced me to Mikey and Johnny who are with me in the band. Kav joined the band for a while, then left after we released *Uncle Dysfunktional* in 2007 to start his own band. Good luck Kav.

I was asked to do *Celebrity Big Brother* at the start of 2005, but I've never liked the programme, so I passed it on to Bez. I watched a bit of it when he was on, but I don't like the way they treat the housemates. They seem to pick people who have slight mental issues, lock them together in a little house, then just chuck booze at them and stir things up to get a reaction.

Damon Albarn then asked me to do vocals on a track on the second Gorillaz album. I'd always got on with Damon, even since his early Blur days, so I went down to the studio in London and did the track 'D.A.R.E.' He offered me points on the track, but I was still in the fucking situation with the Nicholls, so I just told him to keep it. I'd rather he had the dough than them. The video shoot was a bit of a nightmare. I'd put back on the weight that I'd lost, and in the video I was supposed to be this giant disembodied head, kept alive by a machine. Which meant I had to stay in this box, with just my head peeking out the top, for hours on end. It was a long day. 'D.A.R.E.' was a great success, it's Gorillaz' only No. 1 single in this country to date.

I also received an offer of a new set of teeth in 2005. Years ago I used to spend a lot of money in the Armani shop in Manchester, and I met this kid called Lance, who was working in there while he was a student, training to be a dentist. Lance used to make a hell of a lot of money off me in commission, because I was spending so much in the shop. In 2005, when he had all his qualifications, he got back in touch. He told me he now had his own practice in St Ann's Square and he offered to give me a new set of teeth. I actually had really good teeth as a kid; they were perfect and white and everything. But because of certain drugs I've done, particularly smoking crack cocaine, my teeth had started going. Lance offered to replace them with a new set, which cost a good £20,000, in exchange for a bit of publicity. The only downside was, the whole world was going to see how bad my Newtons actually were – Newtons is Manchester slang for teeth, after Newton Heath – because Lance wanted to take some before and after shots. *Granada Reports* also came down and did a little item on my teeth.

Normally, if you were having a complete new set, you would have it done in a series of one- or two-hour sessions, but I just had it done in two stints, one of eight hours and one of four hours. I hate going to dentists more than most people, and have done since I was a kid; it's almost a phobia with me. I remember seeing the school dentist once, when I was ten, and the anaesthetic didn't take at first, so I had to have a few injections and it freaked me out a bit. So when I was older I didn't go to the dentist for a long time, which is probably why my teeth got into the state that they did. I only went when I got really bad toothache and even then I would just say to the dentist, 'Here's £50. Can you just pull this tooth out?' Nobody in their right mind sits in the dentist's chair for eight hours, but Lance said he could do it in two stints if I could handle it, so I agreed. I just wanted to get it over with. I only had a local anaesthetic, but it didn't hurt as much as I thought it might do. I thought I would need loads of Valium to get me through it, but Lance made me as comfortable as possible and it wasn't as bad as I thought. The smell was actually the worst thing about it; when they were sawing and grinding down my old teeth, there was this horrible smell of burning flesh and bone.

By 2006 I was in a much better space, mentally, and I began to de-clutter my life by cutting out a few of the bad influences, and by that I mean people as well as substances. Elliot and Stuart suggested doing a new Happy Mondays album, the first studio album since *Yes Please!*, and Elliot suggested we work with Sunny Levine, because he knew him. Sunny is the grandson of Quincy Jones, which means he's pretty much royalty when it comes to production. He has worked in studios since he was about five years old. He started as a tea boy and worked his way up. Elliot had known Sunny since he was a little kid, because his dad, Stewart Levine, had produced some albums for Simply Red, Dr John and loads more big musicians, as well as The Rumble in The Jungle concert and movie. Sunny had grown up in that great production family, and Elliot knew that the two of us would be able to work well together.

So Sunny then came over and we worked at Moulah Rouge studios in Stockport. I probably only spent a day on each track, writing the lyrics. Sunny was almost working on two different versions of the album, because he would work during the day, with Kav and Gaz chipping in their twopenn'orth. Gaz would be arguing with Sunny over production techniques, telling him he was doing it wrong. This is Sunny Levine, Quincy fucking Jones's grandson, and Gaz Whelan from Swinton is telling him he's doing it wrong. Thankfully, Sunny is very easygoing. We get on really well; we're on the same wavelength and make a good team. I pretty much like everything he does, and he pretty much likes all the lyrics I come up with, and if we don't we can tell each other.

I would come in at night to lay down my vocals, and invariably it was Sunny's version of the track that we ended up using. It was quite similar to working with Danny Saber, in that Sunny just had a really good idea of the sort of beats I liked to write with. There were a couple of song ideas that didn't work out, but if we spent a bit of time on something and it wasn't working, we'd just drop it and move on to the next track. It was a really good way of working for me. We did a track called 'Deviants' with Mickey Avalon, an American rapper who had just released his debut album, and there are also a few other guests on there that we didn't advertise. Ry Cooder is one of them, and his son Joachim, who is a drummer and best mates with Sunny. We didn't exploit the fact at the time, because they were simply mates of Sunny's who did it as a favour to him. Because he came from this family of production royalty, he had a wealth of talent that he could pull from. I don't think the record company even knew Ry Cooder was on the album. Because we nailed it really quickly, I was keen to work with him again after that, and I've been working with him recently on my solo album.

After we finished the album *Uncle Dysfunctional* we played Coachella festival in Palm Springs. Elliot organized for Tony Wilson, who was quite ill at that stage, to introduce us and he gave a typically Wilsonesque speech about the Mondays pulling together 'the house music of Chicago and Detroit with punk rock' and how 'they changed the world'. Very Tony.

By the time Tony became ill, I'd become quite close to him again. I'd been round to his place a couple of times, and we'd also done some TV and radio together, and had a couple of meetings, because Elliot was really close to him. I'll always be grateful to him.

After the Mondays disintegrated, Tony was made up for me when I came back with Black Grape and it was such a huge success. I think he felt the success of Black Grape, after the Mondays, had vindicated anything he'd originally said about me when he used to big me up in the early days. He was also really apologetic that he'd fallen into the trap of blaming me for the Mondays' split up and the demise of Factory. Although he'd taken enough flak himself for the way Factory went under.

I always got on with Tony and I always respected him. I first knew him as the guy on *Granada Reports* who then got his own music show, *So It Goes*, and even back then he was Mr Manchester. If you wanted to be taken seriously in the music game in Manchester you had to have Tony's stamp of approval, even before Factory. I was never an inverse snob either. It never bothered me that Wilson went to Cambridge and I left school without knowing my alphabet. If someone is cool, it doesn't matter what background they're from.

I always appreciated having someone like Tony bigging up me and the Mondays, because I certainly wasn't going to do it. The Mondays were never going to go round proclaiming we were the greatest band in the world, like the Stone Roses did, so it was good to have someone to do it for us. Especially Tony. But when he would say I was the greatest poet since Yeats or whatever, I just took that with a pinch of salt. He even had a public argument about me in the press with Our Paul, not long before he died, when they were both writing in to the *Evening News*, Our Paul slagging me off and Tony defending me. That was all a bit weird and unnecessary.

I never expected Tony to get ill. He was a person who had come through so much, you just presumed he was always going to be there. I went to see him in hospital just before he died, and I felt like I let him down then, really. I felt like I should have stayed strong, you know what I mean? But my eyes just went. I looked at him lying there and you could tell he was dying. He was thin and he was shaking. Tears just started flooding out of my eyes, and I had to get out of there for a minute and sort myself out before I could go back in. I still feel like shit for that. Maybe he was touched by it, but I think he might have wanted me to be strong, because even though he was frightened to death himself, he was being really brave. I was the one that crumbled.

I went to his funeral at St Mary's Roman Catholic Church in town, which is known as the Hidden Gem. Like I mentioned before, they played the Happy Mondays song 'Bob's Yer Uncle' at the end of the service, which is not the obvious choice for a funeral, but typical Wilson. He always loved that song.

Death is a weird one. I've found recently that certain members of my family have become closer to me after they've died. People that I would only see once a week or once a fortnight, but after they died they've been with me all the time. I'll be like, 'How are you, Mary?', talking to them in my head when I'm thinking about them. It's as if they've come into my space more now than when they were alive.

Joanne was pregnant when we went to Tony Wilson's funeral, and then, on 10 February 2008, we had a little girl, Pearl Emma Elizabeth Ryder. I asked Joanne if she would have Pearl in St Mary's Hospital because all my other kids had been born there so it was important to me, and she was happy to have her there. Joanne's really good friend Big Jo was there, which was great as she's a big part of our life. We had Pearl christened at St Edmund's Church which was where I was christened, and that also meant a lot to me.

Your family and your roots mean more as you get older and, not long after Pearl was born, I saw a really nice house for sale. Finding out that Joanne was pregnant again with Lulu, we needed more bedrooms so we moved out of Glossop and back to Salford.

I was still trying to resolve the Nicholls scenario and went to see solicitor Bryan Fugler at Elliot and Stuart, and Fugler explained he could actually get me out of the Nicholls situation, but it wouldn't be cheap. Elliot and Stuart said, 'Nah, we're not paying that amount of money to get it resolved.' So it then dragged on another couple of years. Stuart was arrogant and naïve enough to think he could resolve it himself without a solicitor or lawyer. Eventually, he and Elliot fell out and Elliot walked away from the Mondays and left Stuart managing us on his own for a while. Then they hired lawyers to sue each other, which meant I was dragged into yet another managerial legal battle, which was the last thing I needed. They were supposed to be getting me out of my court case, and they actually got me embroiled in another one. For fuck's sake. I parted company with Stuart, and eventually decided I had to resolve the issue myself once and for all. So I went back to Bryan Fugler on my own and said, 'Let's get this sorted.' It wasn't cheap, and it took nearly two years, because it was a huge mess, but it's finally done.

Over recent years I've been offered lots of different weird reality and celebrity-type shows. It's a bit like that Alan Partridge sketch where he's coming up with random ideas for TV shows like 'Youth Hostelling with Chris Eubank' and 'Monkey Tennis'. One particular show I was offered involved me and Richard E. Grant swimming with crocodiles and sharks. God knows who comes up with these ideas. I turned it down but he went and did it with Ruby Wax and Colin Jackson. *Celebrity Shark Bait*, it was called. We did do *Ghosthunting with Happy Mondays,* with Yvette Fielding, in 2009, just for a laugh, for a bit of a nobble. I think Bez was a bit freaked out, though. It reminded me of when I was living with Suzy in Boothstown, twenty-five years before, and Bez would come round and we'd take acid and watch a vampire film or some Peter Cushing Hammer film, and then he wouldn't want to go home on his own.

After we filmed *Ghosthunting with Happy Mondays*, but before it was broadcast, we did V Festival, after which Bez left the Mondays again. He left over an issue about the guest list or something and he's been doing his own thing since then. I've not fallen out with Bez at all; I just haven't really seen him since. We've lived in each other's pockets for twenty-five years, so we probably needed a bit of a break from each other. You know that feeling you get after a massive great Sunday lunch, when you feel like you can never eat again? That's how I feel about our relationship at the moment, but you always end up eating again, don't you?

Bez is still living that *24 Hour Party People* lifestyle we had in our twenties. He still lives every day like that, and he's happy with it, but that's not what I want to be doing every day now. Bez is a force of a nature; he creates this whirlwind of chaos and mither around him, and it must be exhausting just being him. But throw Bez out of a plane and he will land somewhere soft. He always manages to land on his feet in some way, and I hope he keeps managing it.

On 1 May 2009, me and Joanne had our second daughter, Lulu Margaret Annie Ryder, born in Hope Hospital. Good old Big Jo was there with us again as support. So now there're five of us at home in Salford, and Joseph also comes and stays with us regularly.

Towards the end of 2009 I met my current manager, Warren Askew, who agreed to take over and help me finally make sense of the chaos. He was also instrumental in finally resolving the Nicholls situation, which I can't thank him for enough. I think he was a little bit wary about taking me on at first, because he didn't want to have to deal with the old wild Shaun Ryder that he'd read about, so I had to stress to him that I wasn't really like that anymore.

For the last couple of years I've gigged as either Happy Mondays or Black Grape, with the same band – my band – but

I'm finally ready to be Shaun William Ryder. Kurfirst wanted to sign me as a solo artist nearly twenty years ago, after the Mondays split, but I wasn't ready to just be me at that stage. I needed to be in a band, so I created Black Grape. When Warren took over, he finally made me see that I was ready to be Shaun William Ryder. We put together a new 'best of' compilation called *XXX: Thirty Years of Bellyaching*, and there will be the new solo album next year.

Working with Warren for the first time in quite a while, I felt like I was back in control of my career. It felt like there was a plan for the next couple of years, rather than just playing a few gigs here and there. He's a former footballer, he doesn't drink or smoke, and he gets on with me and Joanne really well. She helps me stay on the right track at home, and he helps me stay on the right track professionally.

Me and Joanne, we decided to get Lulu christened at St Charles's Church. Joanne was looking at alternative venues online one night and showed me the website of the nearby Court House and said, 'What about here?'

'It looks like a wedding venue,' I said. Joanne already knew that I really wanted her to be my wife, to be Mrs Ryder, so on a bit of a spur of the moment, I added, 'Shall we just get married the same day?'

'What? Just surprise everyone?' Joanne laughed. 'How funny would that be!'

Thankfully she said yes, so that's what we did. No one had a clue. The only people we told beforehand were Oliver, Amelia and Warren, because we wanted to make sure he and his family came up for it. Both our families just thought they were coming for Lulu's christening, then, when we went to what they thought was the do afterwards, we sprang it on them that we were getting married. Even my mam didn't believe me at first, and was telling people, 'No, no, Shaun's just joking.' We just wanted a low-key affair: we'd both been married and divorced before, and we didn't need to make a big song and dance about it. We knew how much it meant to us, and that's all that really mattered. I even made a speech, which I don't think I did when I first got married, although my memory of that is quite hazy.

After he took over managing me, Warren was keen to take me back to doing more television. Most of the TV offers I'd received over the years I'd turned down, not least because the Nicholls situation meant whatever big money they were offering, I could never keep it, but now that was finally resolved. The music business has completely changed since I came into it nearly thirty years ago, and nowadays you need to be doing daytime TV to sell records.

When Warren started negotiations for me to do *I'm A Celebrity . . . Get Me Out of Here!* I wasn't keen at all at first. I've never really embraced that celebrity culture, so I was really uncomfortable about doing it, but both my record company, Warners, and Warren thought I should do it because it would be good for my profile with a new compilation and solo album on the way. When I first started, *Top of the Pops* was the important breakthrough show; now you need to do the celeb-type shows if you want to get your albums into places like Tesco. The reality shows count, that's the reality. Joanne and the kids all watched *I'm A Celebrity* at home, so they helped persuade me to do it. Warren had also been in talks for me to do *Strictly Come Dancing*, but they were slightly more wary about having me as a contestant, because they thought I would swear on prime-time television. I didn't want to do *Strictly* either, and with hindsight it's a good job I ended up in the jungle, because at least that gave people time to see what

I'm really like these days. People got to see my personality and a bit of the real Shaun Ryder, whereas on *Strictly* they would have just seen an old man who's not a great dancer. So I'm really glad I did the jungle in the end, because it worked out great.

Ant and Dec are old Mondays and Black Grape fans, so they were made up when I agreed to go on the show. I didn't really know what to expect when I went in there, and they don't overly prepare you for it, because they want to see your reaction when things happen. Me and Warren had a couple of meetings with the producers, and Daisy Moore, who was the boss at ITV when it came to celebrity shows, said to me, 'You're going to hate me by the time you come out of the jungle.' But I didn't. It was nowhere near as bad as I thought it would be. The thing I was least looking forward to was being on camera twenty-four hours a day. That was my biggest nightmare. I just thought I wouldn't be able to switch off at all, particularly as I was going to be sat with a load of people I didn't know.

They don't give you any idea of who the other celebrities are going to be, but I think we did all right, really, with the mix of people we ended up with. I got on reasonably okay with everyone. I'd watched it a couple of times in previous years and they had some right idiots in there – like Paul Burrell, Princess Diana's former butler. What a knob. I was watching it one night and he was giving it, 'You'll never guess who rang me one night? Tom!' and one of the others said, 'Who's Tom?' and Paul said, 'Tom Hanks!' I just thought, 'You prick!'

Thankfully we didn't have too many luvvies in there, no name-droppers. I probably got on best with Nigel Havers and Dom Joly, but I thought everyone was okay. Lembit Opik was great and came up to Manchester for one of my gigs a few months after we got out. Jenny Eclair was great. I'd seen Stacey

Solomon on *The X Factor* and thought she was good, but I wouldn't have imagined we would particularly get on and become good friends, because she just seemed like a giggly young girl, but she was great. I did keep myself to myself a bit for the first week or so, before I came out of my shell. I think it took me about a week to say hello to Alison Hammond.

When you're forced to spend time with people, most of them usually turn out to be okay. It did give me a kick up the arse to be a bit more sociable. I'd got to the stage where I thought to myself, 'I'll be as unsociable as I want.' When you first get in the music game, you have to speak to everyone, but I'd got to the stage where I'd done all that and was happy being a bit of a grumpy old sod.

They didn't give us any idea of the tasks we might have to perform, but we did have to have a medical, and also tests where they asked you lots of questions to make sure you were capable of doing whatever they asked you to. My only real problem, as I mentioned at the start of the book, was that I can't breathe through my nose, only through my mouth, which was a problem when I had to jump out of the helicopter. We went to twelve thousand feet, which is the highest you can go without an oxygen mask.

I wasn't bothered about any of the other tasks, like having to eat things. That didn't bother me one bit. The one task I did that everyone remembers is the one where I was bitten by a snake. That really did hurt. It just sank its teeth right into my hand and the fucker wouldn't let go. I just gritted my teeth and said, '*You little . . .*', but managed not to swear. I could see the snake-handlers panicking, because obviously they didn't expect it to do that, and it wasn't letting go. It had big old teeth and it could have had my finger if I'd panicked, but my instinct told me to just keep calm, until they eventually got it off me, which took about forty minutes. The doctors gave me valium to calm me down.

They didn't warn me about swearing in the jungle, because they just bleeped it out, but the one time they did have a word with me was after I had to do a task with Gillian McKeith in the freezing water and she was being a bit of an idiot. I did trip out on her and swore quite a bit. Later that night, when you have to go and speak to camera, they did say to me, 'Shaun, this is a warning: you went a *little* bit over the top with Gillian today.'

That was the only regular contact we had with the production team, and obviously Ant and Dec came in to speak to us during the live show, when they announced who was up for nomination. I didn't hate Gillian or anything – she just had a bit of an attitude that she was unaware of, and was a little lacking in manners. If I ask someone to do something I'll say please and thanks, but Gillian didn't. She bollocked Stacey and made her cry, but when I did the same thing to her, she complained. The time when she fainted was ridiculous. Bloody hell, what a fanny. Some of the others also took things a little too personally, like Lembit getting the hump when Dom Joly took the piss out of him. He couldn't see that that's what Dom was in there to do. It's a game, it's a TV show. Dom was only doing that because it made good television.

I didn't arrive in Australia until shortly before I went in the jungle, so my body clock was still out of sync, and I was still awake at the crack of dawn at first, which is why it must have seemed like I was sleeping a lot during the day on the show. But once I settled into a routine, I was the first up. I'd be up at 5am when it was first light, then I'd go back and have another hour in bed at about 8am, before the live TV cameras came in.

I never thought I would last as long as I did in there, especially when I first got the whole 'Shaun . . . it *might* be you' treatment from Ant and Dec, when they were announcing who's up for eviction. That made me think I was making a bit of an idiot of myself. I think I was the first to get 'It *might* be you . . .' and I thought that meant you had almost been voted out, so I thought, 'Oh fuck. I'm embarrassing the missus and the kids here. Am I swearing too much? Fucking hell.' The last thing I wanted to do was embarrass my family, so I told them I was going to leave. I decided to do one day longer than John Lydon had done and then leave. But when I was asked to go to the doctor's hut for a check-up, he hinted I was doing okay and people were behind me outside, which helped change my mind. Me and the other celebs also worked out, after a few nominations, that the whole 'it might be you' thing was purely random, a red herring; it doesn't mean you were almost nominated.

I did get quite bored in there when I didn't have a task to do, so they started sending me on little walks, just to get me out of camp. If I did have to come out of camp for some reason, they would send me on a long circuitous route to where I needed to go, anything up to an hour and a half long, just to give me some exercise and stop me being bored. That's one of the reasons I lost a bit of weight making the show, because of all the walking.

I did actually find it hard in the jungle. When I said I was going to quit, they asked me if they could do anything to make me stay. I asked them to give me more fags as I was smoking more than I usually smoked at home, so they upped my fags for me.

Like I said, I didn't think I was going to last that long in there, so I was as shocked as anyone when I came runner-up to Stacey. When I came out of the jungle, my feet didn't hit the floor. I think I was given an hour to go and get a shower and get changed, and then it was straight into doing press, television, photo shoots, you name it. That night there was a party, with lots more press, and then we flew back to the UK and it was straight into doing more press and television. It was relentless. Even when Christmas came, I only had two days off – Christmas Day and Boxing Day – and then it was back on the publicity treadmill.

I hadn't really done much daytime telly before, particularly because I had a Channel 4 ban. There's no way they would have had me on a show like *This Morning* before I went into the jungle. When I came out, I felt all eyes were on me to see if I could handle daytime telly, and behave myself and not swear. It's not that difficult to not swear, really, is it? It's not the hardest thing in the world. My language is usually pretty fucking colourful, but I don't swear in front of my kids, so I can easily not swear on daytime telly. Me and Warren have a bit of an in-joke about this new alter-ego of mine, 'Showbiz Shaun'. If I'm doing some big high-profile TV show he helps me prepare for it, to get in the zone as Showbiz Shaun: 'Come on mate, we need Showbiz Shaun for this one'. After I'd done the *BBC Breakfast* and *This Morning*, which were both live, with no problems, then TV producers seemed to relax and realize Showbiz Shaun wasn't going to get them into trouble, and I was asked to do all manner of shows.

If I'm down in London to do a TV show or a day of press, I'll usually stay at Warren's house the night before. He's got a young family like me – his wife Hayley and their three lovely kids Harvey, Darcey and Winter.

Because Bez had already done that celebrity TV interview circuit when he won *Big Brother*, most interviewers and producers assumed I was exactly like him. But I'm not exactly like Bez. I never have been. That's why I brought him into the Mondays in the first place, because I thought we needed someone who was different from me. We were never the same person, never two peas in a pod. They also expected the Shaun Ryder of twenty years ago to turn up, off his nut, drink whatever was around and smoke heroin in the toilets.

When you get on that celebrity treadmill you do have to deal with some right goons. I generally find it's the ones who are C-list or Z-list but are deluded and think they're A-list who are the worst. You get some geezer from some shitty soap opera behaving like Robert De Niro.

The jungle did make a big difference to my profile and I get recognized on the street more than I did before, especially with the younger and older generations, because that's the demographic of the show. Before the jungle, I wouldn't necessarily get recognized walking past a bunch of schoolgirls in the street, but I do now. I get little lads running up saying, 'Did it hurt when the snake bit you, Shaun?' I also get stopped by grans and grandads, respectable old couples, to tell me they thought I was great on the show.

I'm still doing more TV, but I'm wary about keeping a balance with the music. I'm a musician first and foremost, not a generic celebrity. So me and Warren, spend half our time turning down offers of TV shows and appearances. He's pretty good at sifting through all the requests we get, so I probably don't even hear about some of the weirder ones.

Back in the day the Mondays and Black Grape tours were pretty messy affairs, as you can imagine, but we've got a really tight operation when we go on the road now. I've had the same band for a few years – Johnny on guitar, Mikey on bass, Dan on keyboards and Our Paul's son Jake on drums. They're all quite young lads, but they're good musicians rather than just garbageheads who are in it for the partying. Julie sings backing vocals and Tonn Piper comes in to sing Kermit's parts if we do any Black Grape numbers. Warren has installed Anthony Tang as tour manager, and they make sure it remains a tight operation. It's the only way I could do it now. I couldn't go on tour for weeks on end with a bus full of hangers on.

You've got to have a tough skin in this game, when all sorts are written about you in the papers and everyone has made their own mind up about you, from what they've perceived from some caricature of who you really are. I'm in a much stronger, more secure place emotionally now. I'm with someone I'm absolutely in love with, my wife Joanne, who will be there no matter what. I live a different, more relaxed life now. I get up with my two little girls in the morning and throw them in the swimming pool and have a bit of a splash about with them. If I'm not working, I'm happy just staying in and chilling out with the family most nights. I watch a lot of films and documentaries on things like the Discovery Channel.

Hopefully me and Our Paul are moving in the right direction, too. He lives in Los Angeles now and I saw him recently at my Uncle Tom's funeral and, though we didn't sit down and chat, we nodded at each other and said, 'Y'all right?', which is progress for us.

I wish I could see more of Jael and Coco, but it's difficult as one lives in New York and the other lives in Majorca.

I'm not ashamed of anything that's happened in my past, but there are parts of it I'd rather not celebrate. I don't have any real regrets, though. I wanted to be in a band, make good music, see the world and avoid getting a proper job. I did all four and had a fucking ball doing it. It was a rollercoaster ride, but that's what life has always been like for me – a few years of pure double-good times, followed by a few years of pure hard times. A cycle of ecstasy and desperation. Hopefully I've broken that cycle now. I'm not my own worst enemy any more. I'm not running from anything or using heroin to mask any pain. I know who I am, and I'm still pretty much the same kid I was at fifteen; I've just chilled out and grown up. I don't have a chip on my shoulder, and I don't really bear grudges.

And remember that the Shaun Ryder in the public eye is a caricature. He always was. I just played up to that image for a long time. When it came to sex, drugs and rock 'n' roll, the drugs came first a lot of the time. But the sex and rock 'n' roll were right up there. I did take all those drugs, and had a lot of sex, but we also made some great records. I've never been shy of acting up, especially in my twenties and thirties. But once you get into your forties, you need to grow up. There's nothing wrong with having a pint and getting off your shed now and again when you're younger. But if you're acting the same as you were when you were twenty when you're reaching fifty, there's something a bit sad about you. I still get people coming up to me in Asda or TK Maxx offering me a line. Sometimes I'll just laugh, sometimes it winds me up – it just depends what mood I'm in. If people can't see more to me than that caricature, then the joke's on them. I might be poorly educated in an academic sense, but I'm sharper and more astute than most people I meet, and if I was half as thick as some journalists or *24 Hour Party People* made me appear, I wouldn't get out of bed in the morning.

Like I said at the beginning of the book, people still come up to me and say, 'Do you feel lucky that you're still alive?' No, I don't. I'm glad I came out the other side, but I never saw it as life-threatening. If you think you're going to die, you will, and if you think you're going to live, you'll live. I just realized that breaking out of that lifestyle and the cycle I was in was going to be the difference between having a shit life and a good life. I've had the best times of my life on drugs and I've had the worst times of my life on drugs. When the band was starting to take off, the Haçienda was at its peak and we were running it from our little corner, there was nowhere I would rather have been in the world. When I was living in an unfurnished house in Burnley, on my arse, doing smack, I would rather have been anywhere else in the world.

But I never thought I was going to die, and I certainly don't now.

I've always lived for the moment, not the memories. I'm not sure exactly how I got out the other side. It took me a while, and I don't remember half of it. But I knew I would get here eventually.

I feel pretty lucky. I feel all right. In fact, I feel better than I have for years.

I feel alive.

INDEX